"For many reasons, schools don't sp[e]  development for all children, even tho[u] skill. Dr. Ann Kaganoff's *There's a Writer i[n]* for any parent, guardian, or teacher who is committed to helping a child develop writing and reading skills. With Dr. Kaganoff's instruction and explanations, a parent or a teacher can become an 'Informed Guide,' learning not just what to do, but how and why each recommended activity is important. The book's At-Home Model supports literacy development using personalized prompts that will engage your child in the process. Writing and reading don't just happen. These skills need to be taught, practiced, nurtured, and celebrated!"

Lori K. Dver, *MA, BCET, President of the Association of Educational Therapists*

"Would you like to help your child build comfort and confidence in their writing and reading skills? Dr. Ann Kaganoff, an acclaimed educational therapist, provides well-thought-out and easy-to-use strategies that parents can use to encourage their children in the development of writing and reading skills. These easy, yet effective ways to customize and personalize writing instruction are based upon your child's strengths and interests. These strategies are fundamental to all effective instructional practices. Parents and educators need this inspirational book!"

Daniel Franklin, *PhD, BCET, author of Helping Your Child with Language-Base Learning Disabilities*

"Readers will benefit from Dr. Kaganoff's extensive knowledge as a classroom teacher, teacher educator, staff developer, and educational therapist. With six decades of experience, she is a member of a rare class of educational professionals who have much to share, and we are lucky enough to have access to her wealth of knowledge in this book."

Dr. Diana Arya, *Associate Professor in Education and Faculty Director, McEnroe Reading and Language Arts Clinic, University of California, Santa Barbara*

"*There's a Writer in Our House!* is a gift not only to parents, but to teachers and clinicians as well. Dr. Ann Kaganoff, a master teacher and clinician, has written a comprehensive, clear, well organized, and easy to follow guide to helping children find joy in developing the writer within them. It is a valuable resource that belongs on the bookshelf of every parent and teacher of an elementary school child."

Nan Freund, *MEd, BCET, FAET, Board Certified Educational Therapist, Past President of the Association of Educational Therapists*

There's a Writer in Our House! Strategies for Supporting and Encouraging Young Writers and Readers at Home

There's a Writer in Our House! is an invitation to parents of children in first grade through fifth grade interested in actively participating in their children's early literacy learning from the very first steps.

Founded upon well-researched literacy instructional methods that have been informed by the author's clinical perspective as well as her years of experience with many kinds of learners, this book provides a valuable understanding of how both writing and reading contribute to child development in multiple areas. Chapters provide background concepts regarding grammar and specific critical thinking skills in both writing and reading as well as customizable, child-centered activities used to practice and build writing and reading comprehension skills.

You will learn how to advance and encourage your child's learning and communication skills by highlighting important literacy areas such as vocabulary development, background knowledge, and critical thinking. You will also learn to recognize and track the significant developmental achievements of your child as you proceed from the early to the more complex *At-Home* activities, as well as receive strategies for how to respond and give feedback in specific situations, such as when a child writes something that makes sense to the child but not to the parent, how to offer feedback that identifies and labels a child's strengths, and how to collaborate effectively with a child who is just developing new interests or a new willingness to try something that previously seemed "hard."

Practical, accessible, and most importantly, fun, this book is a must-read for all parents, regardless of background, seeking to support their children's ongoing literacy development confidently and effectively.

Ann P. Kaganoff, PhD and Board Certified Educational Therapist, has been active in the field of education for over six decades, at every level from pre-school to graduate school. She is a Past President of the Association of Educational Therapists (AET). She has been a frequent presenter at conferences on topics related to literacy and the practice of educational therapy. She also serves as a mentor and trainer for new and veteran educational therapists. She is the author of *Best Practices in Educational Therapy* (Routledge 2019), a book dedicated to furthering the practice of educational therapy.

There's a Writer in Our House! Strategies for Supporting and Encouraging Young Writers and Readers at Home

Ann P. Kaganoff, PhD

Routledge
Taylor & Francis Group

NEW YORK AND LONDON

Designed cover image: © Getty Images

First published 2024
by Routledge
605 Third Avenue, New York, NY 10158

and by Routledge
4 Park Square, Milton Park, Abingdon, Oxon, OX14 4RN

Routledge is an imprint of the Taylor & Francis Group, an informa business

© 2024 Ann P. Kaganoff

ISBN: 978-1-032-58823-0 (pbk)
ISBN: 978-1-003-45268-3 (ebk)

DOI: 10.4324/9781003452683

Typeset in Palatino
by Deanta Global Publishing Services, Chennai, India

Access the Support Material: www.routledge.com/9781032588230

To My Teachers and To All Teachers

*My mother was my first teacher. She taught me the love of books and reading.
I can still hear her voice reading to me and my little sister Alice. In a way,
Alice was my second teacher. She was blind from birth, and as I grew up with
her, I learned first-hand what it means to have a "handicapping condition."
She too loved books, and she read constantly from the time she learned braille.
She used to joke that her room could be an annex to the Library of Congress,
from whence came the shipping cartons with her next shipment of braille
volumes. I learned from my second little sister Elizabeth, who became a
teacher of deaf children and taught the little ones how to use the language of
signs. I learned from my two daughters Rachel and Tessa about the readers
who learned to read as easily as they learned to breathe, and who, once
started, have never stopped. I learned from wise mentors in graduate school,
from colleagues who practice educational therapy, and from teachers and
therapists I have trained. And most of all, I have learned from my students.
I have learned from their examples of courage, curiosity, persistence, and
determination. I have learned from their resilience in the face of difficulties
and struggles. Equally important, my students have taught me much even
when they are challenging and resistant, because I have had to work harder
than I knew I could to overcome their reluctance with my own ingenuity, my
own resilience, and my hopes for them. Needless to say, they have taught me
the ever-present value, to themselves and myself, of a sense of humor. As you
will see in this book, they have taught me the joy that can come from teaching
others. And so, To All Teachers, the ones near to us in time and space and the
ones far from us. Let us celebrate the joy they bring.*

Contents

Foreword

All parents want their children to succeed in life, and one of the keys to success is having a strong foundation of reading and writing abilities. As a former classroom teacher and reading specialist, I have observed the difference it makes when children have had ample opportunities to practice authentic, purposeful engagement in reading and writing. Such experiences can be found in schools, but other curricular goals can get in the way of providing more practice time and flexibility for children to grow into the literate beings that they are ever becoming. For parents advocating for educational support on behalf of their children, such opportunities can be even more elusive. And there are ways to garner support for children who demonstrate a particular disability that prevents them from expressing their true potential in school. However, the set criteria for eligibility are so stringent that most children who are tested for special education support do not qualify for such services – only 15% qualified for such services in 2022.[1] So, what happens to the rest of the student population in need of additional educational support? Schools have been overwhelmed by the number of students in need of support beyond what classroom teachers can provide. National authorities have reported negative impacts from the recent pandemic on the intellectual[2] and socioemotional[3] development of the vast majority (more than 75%) of our young developing readers and writers. The needs are real, and traditional school-based resources are unavailable to most families.

We collectively face the challenge of raising future generations of critical consumers, voters, professionals, leaders, and caretakers within a world that is changing at an increasingly rapid pace. But what many parents may not know is that there are resources available, which is why I am so pleased and honored to introduce Dr. Ann Kaganoff, a long-time literacy educator and educational therapist who is a leading member of the largely hidden national network called the Association of Educational Therapists. Most parents are unaware of the growing number of professionals in this network and what they can offer schools and families in need of research-based instructional and assessment support. I had the pleasure of meeting Dr. Kaganoff in my role as Faculty Director of the McEnroe Reading and Language Arts Clinic housed within the University of California, Santa Barbara. This clinic, or rather the original version of it, served as one of the training spaces for Dr. Kaganoff decades before my leadership appointment in the fall of 2015.

It was clear from our first meeting that not only do we share concerns about the state of needed support for our young students, we also share a philosophy about the ways to provide such support. Children who experience academic and socioemotional hardship in school contexts are immersed in language and instruction from those who emphasize skill building and test performance over research-based practices that foster authentic engagement in learning and literacy development. Words like *deficient*, *poor*, *lacking*, and *at-risk* surround them during teacher-parent meetings and related consultations with school leaders and evaluators. To date, traditional school-based remedial instruction reflects practices developed in the early 1960s; repetitive call-and-response flashcard drills and timed read-aloud tasks from prescribed reading programs have shown no to even negative effects on reading development.[4] Not all parents who read this book are seeking support for children who are showing learning loss or resistance to school instructional practices. Many families may be looking for ideas to support and encourage the continued development of their children's critical literacy skills. Such parents understand the lifelong value of competence in writing, reading, and critical thinking, and will value an approach that goes beyond the prescriptive programs ill-designed to engage the interests of the child.

This book offers something completely different for parents who are ready to make a difference and become informed guides for their children. Dr. Kaganoff's book provides all readers with the foundational background needed for understanding children's language and cognitive development. Her book also offers creative ideas and strategies for maximizing home-centered opportunities for learning and practice that are tailored to the strengths and interests of each individual child. These activities are not simply recipes or prescriptions. Parents will learn the underlying purposes for various literacy activities and how to engage their children in such activities through stimulating prompts. Parents are likely to especially appreciate how well the activities are tailored to fit into family life, which never stops. They will also appreciate the many ways that activities contribute to the development of a child's background knowledge and vocabulary. The extended family is a central topic of this home-based program, guiding children to become archeologists of stories and events that have been written and told. The high value placed upon what the child thinks about and observes, as recorded in what they write and what they tell, extends beyond not just the fondness of the doting parent. These activities serve to record stages of growth and development over time that are of value to the family and also of value for their child's further education.

Readers will benefit from Dr. Kaganoff's extensive knowledge as a classroom teacher, teacher educator, staff developer, and educational therapist. With six decades of experience, she is a member of a rare class of educational professionals who have much to share, and we are lucky enough to have access to her wealth of knowledge in this book. The reader should be aware that this is neither a program nor a workbook, but a thorough account of the theories and practices that guide caregivers or other family members in the phases of fostering the knowledge and skills of young emerging writers and readers. And not to worry, Dr. Kaganoff will be there with the reader the whole way through, providing notes to clarify and support each step of the process.

Diana J. Arya, PhD,
Associate Professor in Education Faculty Director, McEnroe Reading
and Language Arts Clinic, Gevirtz Graduate School of Education,
University of California, Santa Barbara, CA, USA

Notes

1 National Center for Education Statistics (2023). Students with disabilities. *Condition of Education*. U.S. Department of Education, Institute of
   Education Sciences. Retrieved from https://nces.ed.gov/programs/
   coe/indicator/cgg.
2 Lake, R., & Pillow, T. (2022). The alarming state of the American student
   in 2022. Brookings Institute. Retrieved from https://policycommons
   .net/artifacts/4140372/the-alarming-state-of-the-american-student
   -in-2022/4948916/.
3 National Center for Education Statistics (2023). Press release. Retrieved
   from https://nces.ed.gov/whatsnew/press_releases/07_06_2022.asp.
4 Butrymowicz, S., & Mader, J. (2018). The US education system is failing
   special needs students. *The Education Digest*, *83*(8), 26–35.

Acknowledgments

People who make contributions to our lives often do so with intention and purpose, so they are not necessarily surprised when we thank them and tell them why their actions meant so much to us. In my life, on the other hand, there have been parents of students who I cannot name here, and who, if I were to thank them in person, would be very surprised to learn that I think of them with so much appreciation for what they taught me. I am glad for the opportunity to thank some of them now.

Most parents of my students brought their children to me because they were highly involved in their child's progress. Their involvement was most often shown in our regular debriefing sessions or parent conferences by the kinds of questions they asked and by the concerns they cited. There were times, however, when parent involvement reached a higher level, as it once did with a mom who I had invited to sit in on a session. I needed her to observe her son's frequently rude and uncooperative (and unexpected) behavior that was interfering with our work in spite of my gentle reminders. None of this fit with what I knew of the family.

Mom came and sat silently throughout the lesson, but "Teddy" seemed to forget she was there and was his usual uncooperative self the entire time. She and I exchanged glances at the end of the lesson, but I was unclear about what action she might take. Something happened after that session because when Teddy showed up the next time, he was a transformed person, polite, attentive, and hardworking. No words needed to be exchanged between the two of us about the cause of his transformation. However, when he and I ran into each other at the local grocery some years later after we had finished our work together, he greeted me with this: "Remember that time when my mom came to my lesson and I was so rude to you like she wasn't even sitting there!" We both had a good laugh about that, both of us knowing that Mom had had a role in his transformation. He shared with me that he was now an award-winning sports newscaster (his dream job)! And I silently thanked his mom one more time.

Sometimes parent involvement showed a touching humility. This was the case with a mom who confessed to me that she had never understood the rules of grammar and could not help her eighth grader with his grammar lessons. She asked permission to sit in on a few sessions so that she could listen and observe the instruction. She became so completely engaged in the project that the "few sessions" turned into three months of regular attendance until she felt confident in her own mastery of the grammar material, at which point she and her son could manage the lessons on their own! I thanked this mom repeatedly (to myself) for the exceptional model she was providing. She was showing her son that even grown-ups have to deal with uncertainty and the humiliation of not knowing. She modeled a willingness to learn even when the work was very hard indeed. She was learning at the same pace as her child and kept showing up until the work was done.

And then there was the mom of a very impacted autistic seventh grader, who had been so obviously a trial to her parents because of her uncontrolled behaviors. I could tell when Mom turned her over to me at the door at the start of our lesson, just by the way she looked at her watch, that she was glad to no longer be the one in charge, even for just that hour. Her daughter was an ongoing challenge to me, even with her marginally modified behavior during our sessions. At one point, however, I did have to make it clear to "Lisa" in the tone of voice I used (that I had never used before and that I did not know I even possessed) that if she EVER AGAIN tried to climb over the upstairs banister on the second floor to see if she could jump down and land on the stairs, she would see consequences that even she had never seen before. With the support of her dedicated parents, Lisa went on to a special high school for autistic children, and in her senior year at that school, her mom called to tell me that her daughter was now working as a peer counselor to *younger autistic girls*. Mom and I were both proud, and I thanked Mom for being such a good model for me.

My educational therapist colleagues, who are parents themselves, are also professionals who understand very well the family dynamics that provide the context for the learners we work with. They get it about the challenges that confront not just the children who struggle, but all children who are growing up and participating in learning, each in their own individual way. I have been indebted to many of them over time, and to three in particular whom I would like to thank here (and not in order of importance).

Risa Graff of Chicago is a Past President of the Association of Educational Therapists (AET) and my friend of many years, who has been my Zoom companion through much of my writing and reviewing process for the chapters here. She has read drafts of chapters and has been a resource for insights both practical and theoretical. She has counseled me regarding the accessibility of my language and my message, thanks to her own professional writing skills and her background with learners.

Nan Freund, also a Past President of AET and my friend of many years, has shared her great wisdom about procedures and cases in our practices over the years and has always enriched my understanding of family dynamics and all kinds of learning issues that students encounter. Nan has contributed much to my professional growth not only on a personal basis but also through her dedication to the present and future training of educational therapists.

Marion Marshall, author of two timely books on assessment and intervention for learning disabilities, gave me valuable feedback early on when I decided to undertake this book for parents by making suggestions that have strengthened my writing throughout, thanks to her observations and powerful intellect.

I have acknowledged the work of Maryanne Wolf elsewhere (in my book on *Best Practices in Educational Therapy*) because she continues to inspire my thinking and my writing. I always mention her work on reading and the brain to my students, to inspire them to take reading seriously. Her latest book, *Reader Come Home: The Reading Brain in a Digital World*, makes an enormous contribution to our understanding of the impact on the children of today's digital world, and I here recommend it to all parents who are responsible for these very children.

My commitment to the *Language Experience Approach* began early on in my training in the Reading Clinic Program at the University of California, Santa Barbara in the 1970s. There I learned about it from one of its strongest advocates, Carol Dixon, who taught me, mentored me, and inspired me. I hope this book will show her how deeply and continuously such programs and mentorships continue to live on with positive impacts on learners old and young.

While the Reading Clinic Program at UCSB has grown and changed in the years since I benefited from the program, the Clinic continues to make a significant contribution to the entire Gevirtz Graduate School of Education and the graduate students who train there. It is a key conduit through which UCSB students gain the knowledge and expertise that will prepare them for certification programs in general education and special education. The Clinic, under the direction of Dr. Arya, serves the children of the surrounding community who are fortunate to participate in the Summer Reading Camp and other year-round programs, all hands-on, interest-based programs that go well beyond learning to become better readers. I readily acknowledge that such research-based and forward-looking programs are not available to families in every community in the land but if your community is served by such a program, you may find it worth your time to investigate it as a resource for your own family, or at the very least, worthy of your support in the community.

The team at Routledge and Prufrock Press deserve special mention. I thank Daniel Schwartz, Education Editor at Routledge, who enabled my contact at Prufrock Press with my new Commissioning Editor in Education, Rebecca Collazo. Rebecca has been available through the miracle of Zoom conferencing, to confer, answer my questions, and give insightful guidance in all matters relating to the preparation of chapters for submission and making the final manuscript as ready as it needed to be. She has been very supportive and understanding of my goals for the book and its ultimate outreach to potential readers, the parents that we both care about. And special thanks to Shelley Strelluf and the production team at Prufrock Press for their care in ensuring a professional and appealing final product.

Introduction

The Invitation

EASY ACCESS NOTES FOR THE INTRODUCTION:
WHAT YOU WILL LEARN

- The Early Literacy Skills: An Invitation to Parents to Become Informed Guides for Their Children.
- Addressing Children's Individual Differences in a Time of Challenges: A Clinician's Point of View.
- The Important Role of Writing in a Child's Overall Development.
- Introducing the *At-Home Model*: The Special Contribution Parents Can Make with Both Writing and Reading in the Home Environment.
- How to Get the Most Benefit from Reading This Book.
- The Wider Audience for this Book: Classroom and Special Education Teachers, Educational Therapists and Learning Specialists, Home-Schooling Families, and Teachers in Adult Literacy Programs.
- A Tribute to Those I Have Learned From.

There's a Writer in Our House! is an invitation to parents of children in first grade through fifth grade interested in actively participating in their children's early literacy learning from the very first steps. Parents can be a powerful influence in promoting positive beginnings to help their children become comfortable and confident as writers and readers, even as they must navigate

DOI: 10.4324/9781003452683-1

the changing demands of today's schooling to support their children. In light of these challenges, this invitation begins with a message of encouragement. You are a unique source of support and guidance as your children build the basics of writing and reading and as they come to understand the value of these skills in their lives. You can best support your children when you gain the confidence of being an *Informed Guide* to help your children start off on a solid footing as they learn to write and read.

This invitation comes from an author who is a parent, a grandparent, a life-long educator, and an educational therapist with many years of experience helping all kinds of learners to become writers and readers, at all levels. We will use these perspectives of both the educator and the clinician to help you develop a firm basis for guiding your child and to help you explore the learning processes involved when children are first introduced to writing and reading. In addition, our emphasis will include learning strategies combined with *enrichment opportunities* that help children expand their individual talents, interests, and strengths. You will find suggestions for how to make each learning activity meaningful to your child as an individual. This personalized approach helps ensure that the learning is relevant and more likely to last until tomorrow, next week, and even next year.

Given the high value of literacy skills, many parents of young learners are already committed to participating with their children as they are introduced to the joys of how to read and write. You might have already checked out the resources for how to engage in this important task, to have the necessary information about best practices to use when encouraging your children. You might have found the various types of programs, methods, and materials that are available for parents. Many of these approaches are founded on research and classroom applications, and many are indeed effective. However, in **There's a Writer in Our House!** the author adds a new way of looking at this process, with a clinical perspective. This perspective enables you *to tailor learning activities to the interests and strengths of each individual child* because it shows you how the learning activities can take advantage of the familiar environment of your home.

Addressing Individual Differences in a Time of Challenge

As a parent, you know that children respond in many different ways to what and how we teach them because children come with their own distinctive personalities, talents, and interests. We know that when they are truly engaged, they can be successful at learning even the skills that at first seem complicated. The goal of this book is to give you well-designed activities that present writing and reading skills in ways that you will be able to customize and personalize to build your child's confidence and competence. Here you will learn strategies that help your child write and read within the familiar context of your home, with activities that take advantage of learning opportunities that already exist at home. More importantly, we will go beyond the WHAT of the learning activities, to establish the HOW and the WHY so you will clearly understand how these writing and reading experiences contribute to child development in the areas of language, cognition, vocabulary, background knowledge, and critical thinking, and why they are important. And let's not forget promoting a love of learning and the growth of curiosity and inquiry!

The strategies and activities in this book have been developed in the firm belief that parents will willingly engage in the very best practices for helping their children with the process of acquiring the literacy skills. My work as a clinician has always shown me that parents can respond well to learning alongside their children. They can become confident *partners in learning* when they feel prepared, equipped, and confident themselves, particularly in areas where they may feel a bit "rusty" from a lack of recent exposure to certain skills and concepts. Parents can be especially motivated to engage with literacy skill learning because as adults, we recognize how important these skills are for success in all of education and life.

Parenting has always been serious work, no matter what decade or culture we find ourselves in. The years 2020–2023 have brought new and unexpected challenges for families as they have had to adjust to restrictions and restructuring for all family activities because of the COVID pandemic, especially in the area of schooling. This global pandemic has transformed many of the basic relationships between parents and children and their educational environments. Parents are being called upon to engage with their children's schooling in ways that no one expected and that no one could have prepared us for.

Researchers, educators, and sociologists are not yet able to determine the full impact of these changes on children's learning. But we can already see differences in the ways we deliver school instruction, and certainly in the ways children experience that instruction. This has placed unprecedented demands on the roles of parenting, as families have had to reallocate their resources of time and attention to refocus on the educational needs of their children. Parents have had to take responsibility for helping multiple children, at different age levels and in different subject areas. They have often had to discern, to the best of their abilities, what skills and objectives are most important, while having to make decisions with limited time and resources.

Helping Parents Meet the Challenges

There's a Writer in Our House! is well-timed to meet the needs of parents in a decade of unparalleled social and educational demands. If you are holding this book, chances are that you are searching for guidance and support as you navigate rapidly changing situations in which school resources may be limited for periods of time, causing interruptions to your children's education. This book seeks to answer your immediate questions about how best to help your children after the pandemic crisis of 2020 has forever altered our models of schooling and parenting. The ideas contained here for writing and reading are both current and timeless, and they draw upon one constant idea that endures. *Parents can provide a unique and special contribution to their children's literacy acquisition when called upon and when shown what to do and how to do it.*

The power of parents has been made clear to me in my many years of experience with young learners and their parents, giving me a deep respect for the role parents can take in this important enterprise. As an educator, in the broadest sense of the word, I have worked with learners at every level from pre-school to graduate school, and have been privileged to teach other teachers, colleagues, educational therapists, and of course, parents. I had always had a special interest in the children who struggled to learn to read, because of the impact on learning. Difficulties with reading are nearly always accompanied by lags in writing, but for many reasons, reading improvement has tended to receive greater instructional priority than writing. This may be because remedial reading programs appear more easily packaged than remedial writing programs. Over time, we have seen a wide array of programs developed for reading skills, with structured kits, learning centers, computer-based packages, and online applications. For the consumer of these programs, reading achievement has seemed to be easier to assess, with testing that is thought to measure progress.

As a clinician, I have had abundant opportunities to observe and teach a wide range of students who are just learning or are already struggling to read and write. This work has involved parents who have been especially attentive to their children's progress in learning to read and who want to help their children in this process. Parents have often shared with me the memories of their own early experiences with reading, ranging from the magic of getting lost in a favorite book to the terror of having to read aloud in front of the class. Whether they regard themselves as avid readers or not, parents generally identify themselves as "readers," and eagerly seek out suggestions for how to support their child with reading.

Why Is Writing So Important?

As you can see from its title, this book highlights the significant role that writing occupies in learning and thinking. Writing is far more than just a subject that is taught as part of the school's Language Arts curriculum. However, when we examine the resources that are available *to parents*, it seems clear that supporting early writing is different from supporting reading. There may be online programs for writing and summer camps for writing, but compared with the resources available to support reading, there are fewer to choose from. As a result, parents may begin to feel that the teaching of writing belongs only to teachers in the school setting. That's where we find the procedures and the curriculum for teaching writing: the books, the lessons, and the practice exercises. This is true even for home-schooling families, where parents are provided with the home-schooling curriculum for both reading and writing.

The *At-Home Model* for Early Writing

Activity books for early writing are most often presented in a workbook format, with "recipes" for what to do. My work as an educational therapist, however, has taught me how important it is for learning activities to be *individualized and customized* for each child. This tailored approach, which I have called the *At-Home Model*, has the benefits of being "child-centered" as opposed to being program-centered or method-centered. The At-Home Model for the writing and reading activities presented here capitalizes on the learning opportunities that can be found in the familiar environment of the home. This model recognizes that the available resources of the parent, in terms of time and money, are rarely unlimited, because it is important that the recommended activities should not be a burden for an already busy parent.

In Chapters 1 and 2, we discuss aspects of child language development as background for our work with the learning activities. We will note the differing demands that are placed on the young learner's language skills by both reading and writing. When a child "reads," he or she is responding to language that has been written by someone else. The reader's main task is to process the writer's message and incorporate that message in the form of *reading comprehension*. Reading is in the realm of "receptive" language. The task demands of writing are of a different order. Writing belongs in the "expressive" realm of language.

Here the writer must command the many different elements of creating and expressing the message. The writer must then orchestrate these elements so that the written output can be processed successfully (or not) by the intended reader. These two sides of language, receptive and expressive, account for the substantial differences between the types of materials that are available for instruction, at all levels of learning.

How This Book Began

I first realized the need for **There's a Writer in Our House!** a number of years ago. It began with a specific family I was working with as an educational therapist. The parents had been told by the school that their eight-year-old would need a great deal of *extra support at home* for writing. They seemed willing to step in, but really had no idea where to begin. I had searched for books that might contain the ideas that I already had in mind but found none. So, I set about to write out some simple directions for what I then called *Home Writing Activities*. I drew upon my teaching experiences over the years, both in the classroom and in teacher training. I used what I remembered doing with my own children. I drew from observing other teachers teach from my years of supervising student teachers in the schools. I drew upon my work as a clinician, where I developed a customized treatment plan for each child based on that child's interests, strengths, and needs. I drew upon a firm belief in the important role of writing as children begin their journey to literacy. And I thought about the powerful impact that writing has had on my own development as a teacher, clinician, and author.

My challenge was to make the *At-Home Writing Activities* seem doable and attractive, and hopefully even fun. I knew there might be parents whose only memory of school writing was of having their papers handed back, sprinkled with red marks to show where they had "failed" at writing. I expected there might be parents who feel uncertain about their own writing skills and so do not feel prepared to help a child "become" a writer. At the time I did not expect the level of urgency that parents might feel about teaching their children in the pandemic years that began in 2020, but I knew that if parents felt confident and committed, their children would know they were in good hands. While many of the chapters here focus on guiding the young writer, I am hopeful that you too will find joy in the experiences of writing together, At-Home

Applying the At-Home Model to Both Writing and Reading

The At-Home Model has clear benefits for early writing, which had been the original focus of the book. As you read on, you will see that the idea of a personalized and customized approach applies equally well to early reading. As the instructor for Reading Methods courses in teacher training programs, I made sure that my lectures on Beginning Reading had always presented an approach called the *Language Experience Approach* (*LEA*) because of its importance in early reading instruction. It is now included here for your children because it fits the At-Home Model so well, and because reading and writing belong together.

As you will learn in Chapters 8 and 9, in the *Language Experience Approach*, children dictate a "story" or an account of their activities and experiences. The dictations are often preceded by an activity or experience that gets the language flowing, or they may feature an experience that has been planned for just that purpose. The dictations take whatever shape or form seems important to the child at the time. They are recorded by the parent or a teacher, exactly as dictated. Because of their high value to the child, these stories can be transformed into instructional materials that can be used to support the reading skills. Dictated stories have been important in the instruction of many of my own clients. The approach has been relevant to parents as well as teachers, as I have found in parent workshops on *LEA*. And as this book will demonstrate, *LEA* is a perfect fit with the At-Home Model.

In the At-Home reading and the At-Home writing activities, I have emphasized how to engage the interests, the strengths, the curiosity, and certainly the humor of children. While many of their educational experiences are rightly *curriculum-centered*, at home you can make the learning *child-centered*. This kind of learning is personalized and validating for your children. When parents and children collaborate with each other, the journey may begin at home and then you may find yourselves taken to amazing and unexpected places. The reading/writing journey can be like that.

In addition to the activities in each chapter, you will find strategies such as

- ♦ How to respond and give positive feedback about a child's written efforts, even when the writing may not make sense to the parent.
- ♦ How to help children develop confidence as writers, even when they may not take to writing naturally.
- ♦ How to shape children's expectations and keep progress and projects going.
- ♦ How to help children self-evaluate their own progress and move from external praise to self-evaluation and intrinsic motivation.

For added inspiration and clarity, ***There's a Writer in Our House!*** includes real-life children's writing samples and dictated story samples. These are a good way to show parents what can happen with At-Home writing and reading.

How to Get the Most Benefit from This Book

Easy Access Notes. Easy Access Notes are found at the beginning of each chapter. Their purpose is to allow a preview of the chapter so that you can think ahead to what you already know and what specific questions you may have about the topics. You will be given a good idea of what to expect while reading and you will see how each chapter fits into the other parts of the book. You will be able to easily revisit any parts of the chapter or the book to check on ideas or activities that you want to reread.

Activity Levels. Activity Levels are provided wherever activities are introduced and described so that you can judge how well the activity might match the age and interests of your child. These levels are broad and are based on the kinds of instructional activities that are typically conducted in school instruction in the literacy skills. We take into account the wide variation that occurs across school programs, as well as the variation we see in the interests and achievement levels of individual children in all families who might use this book. If there is any doubt about whether the activity is appropriate for your child, you can make the decision based on their interests and prior experiences, while not underestimating the power of the new and the unexpected. Children who are engaged can maximize the benefits of any learning situation they experience. It is our job as parents to provide a rich and nutritious diet for them to choose from.

Downloads. Following selected activities that involve both writing and reading, you will find some charts on which you can record achievements over multiple periods of time. They are intended for repeated use to track markers of progress in specific areas, but also as a way to guide your own observations for what to watch for. The Downloads are marked as online resources that can be downloaded, printed, used to copy/paste text, and manipulated to suit your individualized use.

Who Else Can Use This Book? A Wider Audience for *There's a Writer in Our House!*

Classroom Teachers. Credentialed teachers are trained to teach the full range of literacy skills. They understand the relationships between reading, writing, study skills, and critical thinking. Classroom instruction, as we resume in-person learning, is generally conducted with children in groups, and teachers may have limited time for the individualized interactions that are possible for parents and children, at home. That said, there are always times when the classroom teacher finds opportunities to address children's individual needs. There will be pairs of students who can engage in the *Written Conversation*, or the *Paired/ Shared* writing activity (Chapter 3). There may be times when a classroom aide or a visiting parent can work with a second or third grader on writing activities. There are suggestions for ways to transfer from school to home in the use of these activities. A teacher might try different versions of journal writing activities that shift the focus from academic applications such as tracking the progress of the science project to the At-Home setting where students track the progress of learning to make jam or cookies or training the puppy.

Parents who read this book will find multiple references to ways in which the activities suggested for use at home can promote and develop skills that transfer easily to the school setting. Specific links to school writing and reading are detailed throughout when the discussion references *Planned Writing*.

Special Education Teachers. By training, special education teachers address the needs of children at a more individualized level. These special needs often cover a wide range of learning issues, including language processing difficulties, memory and cognition difficulties, executive function and attention disorders, and dyslexia and other reading disorders, along with the emotional by-products of learning disorders, such as anxiety and feelings of helplessness. Special education teachers are trained to take a diagnostic approach and tailor the instruction based on the individual needs that are identified through focused assessments. Their use of individualized interventions is highly compatible with the emphasis of the At-Home Model, on personalized and customized activities based on the strengths, interests, and needs of the child.

Educational Therapists, Learning Specialists, and Reading Tutors. Many of the insights discussed in this book are the result of my observations of the impact of writing achievement on struggling learners. In fact, struggling learners often benefit especially from being able to write with confidence. Practice in targeted writing activities can result in more effective organization of the student's thoughts and ideas. Practice in writing highlights the importance of background knowledge and vocabulary and may motivate a student to systematically try to expand both. Planned Writing is referenced wherever it applies to reinforce links to the school setting.

As will be further discussed in the *Questions and Answers* section of Chapter 2, writing has profound benefits to the individual child in all areas of language and cognition. The ability to write provides benefits to the young writer's self-confidence and self-worth. Writing promotes a special kind of personal identity and pride of ownership, often described as the *writer's voice*. Additionally, writing can leave a valuable footprint in the form of dated writing samples that document growth.

We can see a predictable impact when students can use the computer for writing. There is greater ease in editing when the young writer is not hampered by the laborious application of pencil to paper. Assistive technology applications may include voice-to-text software. We are able to witness the pride when a painfully constructed paragraph, produced from a printer, is legible and can be read with ease by both the writer and the teacher. When struggling learners make a strong connection between their own writing and the type of communication with another person that writing enables, children can be empowered and transformed by the act of writing.

Many learning specialists and educational therapists include the *Language Experience Approach* in their repertoire of strategies for struggling readers. Those who have yet to try *LEA* may want to consult the works of Sylvia Ashton Warner, who wrote of her work with the Māori children in New Zealand in *Spinster* (1958) and *Teacher* (1963). Also, see "When Parents are Co-Teachers: The Language Experience Approach (LEA) for Young Readers" (Kaganoff, 2013) for step-by-step directions for *LEA* with both parents and educational therapists in mind. The bibliography of that article (also contained here in Chapter 9) provides other references and sources for the use of *LEA* in teaching young readers. Chapter 9 in this book focuses on the use of *LEA* to expand reading development.

Home-Schooling Families. At-Home Writing and At-Home Reading are both particularly relevant to home-schooling families. Writing experiences and writing activities that are designed for the context of the familiar environment can be integrated into the home-schooling curriculum to promote confidence and competence with writing. When school instruction is conducted in the home, there are a wealth of connections to be made between family activities and the topics of formal instruction. The inventive parent and the curious student can collaborate to explore the many ways to link writing with learning, all At-Home.

The home-schooling curriculum for beginning reading will include well-specified steps for presenting skills and materials for home-schooling parents to follow. And there is always room for tailoring approaches to the individual strengths and interests of the home-schooled student, once you see how easily the adaptations can be made. Parents may find that the dictated stories and the follow-up activities allow for innovation and creativity, and all children benefit from an approach that engages their individual interests.

Parents who read this book will find multiple links to school-related skills in both writing and reading. These links are intended to reinforce both the At-Home opportunities and the home-school curriculum for literacy skill development.

Teachers in Adult Literacy Programs. As part of my training as a Reading Specialist (University of California, Santa Barbara), I participated in a summer program for a group of young adults who were identified with intellectual disabilities or cognitive impairments. The labels we used at the time have changed since those years, but some of the approaches we used then still endure. The program instructor recommended that we start off with *LEA*, in which our individual young adults would dictate a "story" that we would record exactly as it was dictated. The stories would then become the reading materials we would use to teach the skills of word decoding, sight words, and eventually, comprehension, vocabulary, and writing.

As I sat with an 18-year-old girl, who had been sent to our clinic with no reading skills, I tried to think of how to elicit some language that we could turn into a dictated story. Between the two of us, we decided she would dictate a letter to her friend and then learn to read the words in her letter. After about the third sentence, she looked up from watching me write her words carefully and clearly, and said to me, *"Nobody ever thought that what I had to say was important enough to write down."* Once she had practiced reading her own words, we then ventured into writing. In retrospect, much of my work on writing stems from that experience and has evolved into the goal of helping all learners, whether they are very young, struggling, or just unsure of what to say, to find their own voice. This book is my contribution to helping learners find their voice through writing and reading.

Parents Who Might Discover Their "Inner Writer." Sometimes the joys of writing are contagious. It is completely possible that as a result of joining in with your child to do At-Home writing, you might just begin to see the possibilities for yourself of finding your voice through writing. You may try out journal writing, write a letter to the editor, or send a really long and thoughtful email to an old friend. Lots of successful and productive writers got their start from small beginnings. It's a journey of discovery. Educators and writers frequently observe that *"We don't know what we know until we write it."*

Giving Thanks to All Those I Have Learned From

This book owes much to the many children, parents, and teachers I have worked with in clinics, in teacher training courses, in classrooms, and in my private practice. As Emerson observed, *"To teach is to learn twice."* Besides my own personal benefits from teaching, I continue to recognize that all children have much to teach us, including in the moments when they may struggle to learn. In fact, when children struggle to learn, they in turn become our teachers as we problem-solve together. We often learn the most from those who struggle the most. At these times, we remind ourselves that each child is successful *at something*. It is our job to identify that "something" and teach to that strength.

I have learned much from the parents I have helped. I have seen how they can be caring, resourceful, puzzled, and confused, often all at the same time. I have learned the importance of perspective, hope, and teamwork. And I have learned that seeds planted at a point in time may flower in the next week, the next year, or 25 years later. I plan to stick around for a while to see the flowers bloom.

Reference

Kaganoff, Ann. "When Parents are Co-Teachers: The Language Experience Approach (LEA) for Young Readers." *The Educational Therapist*, Vol. 34, No. 1, April/May 2013, pp. 6–11.

You can access Downloads by visiting this book's product page at www.routledge.com/9781032588230 (then follow the links indicating related resources, which you can then download directly to your computer).

PART I
The Emerging Writer

1

Setting the Stage for Success

Understanding the *WHY* and the *HOW*

EASY ACCESS NOTES FOR CHAPTER 1: WHAT YOU WILL LEARN

- ♦ The Role of Parents in Encouraging Writing: Understanding the Mind of the Young Writer.
- ♦ Getting Started: The Importance of the At-Home Environment and Looking Ahead to the At-Home Model.
- ♦ Providing Effective Feedback to Your Young Writer: Specific Examples.
- ♦ Two Levels of Feedback: Supportive Feedback and Informative Feedback.
- ♦ Markers of Progress.
- ♦ Using Informative Labels to Promote Specific Thinking Tools.
- ♦ Looking Ahead to Part 1 and Part 2.

Parents Are the First Teachers

Parents are the first teachers. From the moment a child is born or comes into the household, parents begin this important job. Some parents come to this teaching job with prior training. Some come with assistance and modeling from their own parents and other family members. Some have to adapt to the demands of "on-the-job" training. You teach your children in many different ways and for many purposes. You teach them how to cross the

DOI: 10.4324/9781003452683-3

street safely and how to ride a tricycle. You teach them how to behave with both family and strangers. You teach them how to manage daily life activities such as tying their shoes and brushing their teeth. At every stage of development, parents are called upon to anticipate the new challenges and to guide each child on the path.

Home and School

Often parents wonder whether they are up to this important task of being the first teachers, particularly when it comes to schooling. We know that parents have played an important role in promoting an interest in reading and a love of books when we see that there are literally hundreds of publications available to tell parents how and when to help children on the path to becoming **readers**. These parenting books have been written for all kinds of parents, from the confident ones to the less confident ones, to help them make the introduction to reading pleasurable and engaging. There are endless lists of recommended children's books and how to read them with your child. There are books that recommend reading aloud **to your baby** as soon as you can, to let that baby begin to hear the "language of books." As the little ones begin to understand **what a book is**, what could be more positive than sharing a beloved book by reading it aloud, especially when there are so many treasures of children's literature! Children seem programmed to love a good story that is supported by enchanting pictures.

But What about Writing?

Yes, what about **writing**? What should parents teach their young children about this important part of literacy? Does writing happen only when a child goes through the school door and begins school instruction? Do you wait for the schoolteacher to take over? Are there hundreds of publications out there to help you get your children started on *the path to becoming a writer*? No, there are not. But why not, you ask. Perhaps it is because *becoming a writer* can seem harder than becoming a reader. Written language is language that becomes *visible*, as soon as it is written down. You must form your letters correctly when you write them down. You must put your words in the right order in a sentence so that it all makes sense. There is the matter of good grammar and correct spelling! On top of all of that, there is the challenging process of deciding *what you want to say*. Writing can seem complicated.

You may be cautious about your role in encouraging writing, especially if you feel doubtful about how to approach writing. *Will I do it right*, you ask. Making a written sentence is different from reading a sentence that has already been written by someone else. Thus, you may have assumed that school is the proper place where children learn to be writers. Or you may have assumed that teaching about writing is best left to the professionals at school. We are grateful indeed for the teachers we remember who opened the doors to writing when we were fortunate to have had such a teacher. What can prepare a parent to assume such a role?

The Mind of the Young Writer

There is no single universal profile of "the young writer," even at the earliest stages. Early writers differ in every way imaginable because of individual differences in language development, cognitive development, and responses to the world around them. These early writers demonstrate different levels of curiosity, attention, and social awareness. In addition, young writers exist in multiple cultural and family contexts, where they have different levels of exposure to materials in print and to adults who engage with print. They may have different levels of sensory perception that affect how they look at their environments, and how they watch and listen with different levels of attention to what is going on around them.

All young writers have one thing in common. **They have to be taught about reading and writing.** Children come into the world with an innate ability to use language to communicate with others in their language community. Most are remarkably successful at becoming language users. On the other hand, everyone who is able to read and write had to be taught to read and write. Scholars who study the development of literacy sometimes call reading "an unnatural act," because **no child is born with the ability to read**. Some children take to it more rapidly than others, but the ability to read or write is not innate. We can say that each young reader and each young writer has to develop a model of reading and a model of writing. Once they get started with the process, children can then begin *to identify as readers and writers*.

For some young learners, the path to reading and writing can seem intuitive, and the trip can seem lightning-fast. For others, the instruction has to be painstakingly explicit and repetitive. For the adults who want to guide the children, their first task is to understand the nature of this important job. That is, the adults may have to try to shift back to a state of "not knowing" about reading and writing in order to understand the background that must now be built. So how can a busy parent make such a giant leap when you are already paying attention to so many things?

We begin with good news. You will find that the ideas in *There's a Writer in Our House!* will help you integrate writing into activities you are already doing with your child. Writing can become one of the many ways you communicate with each other at home. You will learn how to offer encouragement that is specific, genuine, and focused on strengths. You will find examples of activities you and your child can engage in together, and you will get guidance as to what age level is the best fit for a particular activity. You will also learn the many ways that writing proficiency is important to your child's development. And perhaps most rewarding of all, as you track and save the results of the activities in this book, you will have a record of what your child has accomplished, and you will be able to recognize the markers of progress.

What Is the Starting Point for At-Home Writing?

The parenting process occurs at many points in time as we raise our children. The process involves the events that came before, the events that are happening right now, and things that might happen tomorrow or at some time in the future. There will be many variations in the households that use this book, in the ages of the children and the amounts of formal and informal schooling they may have already received. In other words, it is unlikely this book will enter a home where a child has had no exposure to reading and writing. Thus, while there is structure as to how these activities are introduced and used, there is *no typical entry point*. The activities presented for you in Chapter 3 may be completely new to some children, while for other children they may offer opportunities to fine-tune skills they already have, allowing them to shine and to "be the expert." It is hoped that every family will build upon the activities. It is hoped that you will improvise and expand the opportunities that present themselves, with creativity, spontaneity, humor, and engagement, At-Home.

Introducing the At-Home Model

In Chapter 2, you are invited to capitalize upon the special knowledge you have of your children, thanks to your unique home setting and your unique family experiences. You will learn about the *At-Home Model* which offers a new way to think about how to use this special knowledge to promote important writing and reading skills through activities that are specially designed to fit well, At-Home. Using a *Question-and-Answer* format, we will present some questions you may be asking, along with answers to explain the purposes and benefits of the activities that are featured. The At-Home Model allows you to go beyond just the simple directions for **WHAT** to do with the writing and reading activities and helps you further understand **HOW** to do them and **WHY** they are important for your children.

The Order of the Activities Is Important

The order of the writing activities you will find in Chapter 3 has been carefully chosen to make the entry into writing as welcoming as possible so that participating in the activity is appealing to your child. The first activity you will meet, the *Writing Wall*, is deliberately chosen as an introductory activity because it involves writing that is temporary. What is written can be easily erased or changed. It is a very forgiving kind of exercise where your child can feel free to experiment with how to choose words and build sentences. As you proceed through the chapters, the activities involve writing that can become more permanent. While the *Writing Wall* was designed with beginning writers in mind, you might find unexpected benefits when your younger ones are joined by older brothers and sisters who want to add their comments, questions, and jokes to the writing on the wall. When more family members participate, everyone reinforces *the importance of At-Home writing*.

The order of the activities can easily be adapted to the different levels of experience that children have already had with writing. For example, some may have had school instruction on how to write directions for how to do something. Some may have done a similar activity to *Paired/Shared* writing, where two writers both write about the same topic and then share. As you look at the descriptions of the opening activities, you will probably spot some that will appeal to your own child's interests and sense of humor. You will note that when the activities switch from the *Writing Wall* to paper and the writing becomes more permanent, you have the opportunity to discuss, examine, and reflect upon what has been written. In addition, with the transition to more permanent writing, you are able to give feedback about the different strong points of the efforts. You will introduce the important processes of *revising and editing*, which are part of the eventual goals for proficient and confident writing.

Giving Feedback to Your Young Writer

Giving feedback to children is a natural part of parenting that begins early in their lives. It is an essential part of their development as social beings, and it is an important responsibility for every parent. Parents engage in many forms of feedback with their children, and it is called by various names, depending upon the situation: *praise, criticism, discipline, character building, instruction, scolding,* and *helpful suggestions.* Sometimes it is experienced by the child as a negative (criticism), and sometimes as a positive (praise), but the purposes are generally the same: to guide the young child toward confidence, maturity, and self-understanding. Parents must deliver these forms of feedback in all sorts of states of mind, from calm and thoughtful, to frustrated, annoyed, and worried. Most books on parenting strategies and parenting techniques offer advice on how to handle many types of situations with their children, which may include joy, sorrow, and even danger. These books are often written from a psychological or a child development point of view and are useful to both the inexperienced parent and the parent who has done this before.

When you get started writing with your child, you may wonder what kind of feedback or "correction" to give *about writing.* A letter might be unclear, such as a backward 's.' A sentence might seem a bit mixed up. Children might be stuck when they haven't yet learned how to spell a word or because they have never seen *what the word looks like in print.* Writing has a very visible outcome, and young writers can be very aware of how their writing efforts *look.* This is a sensitive area for both parent and child. Much depends on how you have handled situations such as these before, where guidance has been needed and has been given. We will talk about two levels of feedback that you might find useful in interacting with your children.

Two Levels of Feedback: How and When to Use Them

Giving feedback is necessary when we respond to children's efforts in both writing and reading *because it shows we are engaged and attentive.* It is also a complex operation. We may have to make a quick decision about what to say to maintain the enthusiasm for the activity and keep a child's involvement positive and productive. Feedback always requires a high level of focused attention, and the rewards can be significant. For the child, feedback that shows we are paying attention is a clear indicator that we

value the efforts being made. You will begin to notice that paying attention in this manner *helps you develop more highly skilled
habits of observation* that enable you to respond more effectively,
the very next time.

For our purposes, we will show how the two levels of feedback each make a different contribution to the way you guide
your children. Both levels are illustrated with examples, and
both are connected to the activities in ways that you can practice and experiment with in the different kinds of contexts for
writing. Their purposes are similar, but as you will see, the
second level will require a different form of parent attention
based on the reasons that feedback is being offered. Level One,
as you might expect, is *General Feedback*. Its purpose is to support the efforts of the child but also to offer specific guidance
about the writing or reading task. It is tailored to the relationship that already exists between you and your children. Level
Two is called *Informative Feedback* because it has a high component of information in addition to the support you are giving.
This information serves to help the child develop *specific learning tools*, as you will see in the following sections. Practicing
both levels of feedback contributes to the overall purpose of
helping *you* develop the tools to become *Informed Guides*.

Feedback Level One: General Feedback

There are no hard and fast rules that apply to every relationship,
but we will offer some general guidelines that will be in harmony
with the goals of the activities. We want every child to be engaged.
We will try to minimize discouragement and any anxiety kids
might feel about being "correct" about everything, especially
when the writer is just a beginner. The activities are designed to
keep both parent and child on an equal footing as much as possible because you are both joining together to write. When you
participate together, you can develop routines for feedback that
are agreeable to everyone. These General Feedback routines can
be tailored to each family, and they support the frameworks and
the purposes for the second level, Informative Feedback.

Example Comments to Show Interest and Approval

Children respond to positive encouragement. Here are some general comments of approval you can offer about what your child has written and the good effort you are seeing. These comments are tailored to the activities introduced in Chapters 3 through 7:

- ◆ *"Good sentence about the dog, Maggie."*
- ◆ *"Oh, that's funny. I love your sense of humor!"*
- ◆ *"You got my joke. Good for you!"*
- ◆ *"You are really catching on to writing."*
- ◆ *"I really look forward to reading what you wrote."*
- ◆ *"That's the longest sentence you have written so far!"*
- ◆ *"You spelled that right. Good for you. It's a tricky word to spell."*

Making Your Comments More Explicit:

- ◆ *"You remembered to capitalize* Andy *because that's a name. Good job."*
- ◆ *"I see you used that new word we found in your book yesterday."*
- ◆ *"You used a good action word there in that sentence about the dog park."*
- ◆ *"I see some good color words in your sentences."*
- ◆ *"Grandpa will think that part is really funny."*
- ◆ *"Your sentences today told about two good ideas."*
- ◆ *"I can really see in my mind what you are writing about the squirrel."*
- ◆ *"I can see that we have both been wondering what to do about the cat digging in the potted plant."*
- ◆ *"You used some good words to describe how bright the fireworks were."*

Encouraging Your Child to Write More:

- ◆ *"What else can you tell me about how the tree house looked?"*
- ◆ *"What would be another sentence to tell more about the broken skateboard?"*
- ◆ *"What happened next after the ball bounced off the roof?"*

- *"After that, did the dog do something else that was funny?"*
- *"Can you tell what else happened when you helped Grandma with the cookies?"*
- *"Tell what you spotted after the car window was opened."*
- *"Can you tell more about how you helped Rickie get the bike back on the path?"*

Four Feedback Tips for Starting Out

1. Tips for Forming the Letters

For the beginning writer, the physical act of forming letters can be a significant challenge. Most writing instruction in the early school years begins with how to handwrite the print form of letters before cursive writing. Cursive writing, if it is taught at all, is generally introduced at third-grade level. The beginning activities described in these chapters have assumed that the writer has some mastery of forming letters and some degree of confidence in the process.

Parents may want to verify which pattern of letter formation is in use at their child's school so that you can make or purchase printed models to have on hand for the child to look at and copy. Suppliers of educational materials are a good source of such models, often in the form of a wall-mounted chart, for easy reference. There are a number of well-regarded programs for acquiring handwriting skills, such as *Handwriting Without Tears*, that are available in both printed workbooks and video instruction. See Section 5, Chapter 11, for what you can do if you are concerned about a possible delay in acquiring this skill.

2. Tips about Spelling

When parents and children write together, spelling is bound to come up. The first word they learn to spell is often their name because parents are eager to focus on such a meaningful application of spelling. Children are introduced as early as pre-kindergarten to the beginning concepts about letters and sounds as part of school reading instruction when teachers introduce the rules about how letters and sounds go together. Some children will be very curious about how spelling works while others will want to get on with writing their ideas, with a little help from you. Some have already heard about the *spelling tests* in school. It is very important to keep discussions about spelling positive but still maintain the focus on *expressing their good ideas*. This is the way to keep spelling anxiety from becoming an obstacle to written expression.

Children's first attempts at spelling are known as "invented spelling." What may seem like *errors* to parents can actually offer a window into the child's progress in figuring out how letters match to sounds. Spelling is a developmental skill and invented spelling offers interesting and useful insights. Spelling mastery varies widely across individual children, age groups, and school programs. When children begin kindergarten and first grade, they soon learn that spelling is part of schoolwork. If you are able to keep a few examples of invented spelling, you can provide important data for the teacher who is teaching these beginning skills, such as how well a child is actually *hearing some of the sounds* in the spoken words. For example, if a child writes *'wet'* in a sentence where she meant to write *'went,'* she may not be distinguishing the sound of *'n'* just before the final letter, *'t.'* With exposure to printed words, your child will begin to link these minor variations in sounds to the letters we use to represent the sounds.

When we customize At-Home writing, we can keep the experience positive by identifying and praising the correct matches of sounds to letters. We can point out which of the letters have been correctly chosen before we provide the rest of the letters that spell the word in question. In my work as a clinician, I have learned it is important to stay with the purpose of the activity, especially when the focus is on written expression. Thus, I may *return to the spelling later*, after we have finished with the writing. However, when spelling becomes an item of interest in At-Home writing, there are a number of constructive ways to talk about it.

If your child asks how to spell a word, tell him or show him the correct spelling. If he attempts an unfamiliar or unknown word, first check out and verify what word he *wants to write*, then underline or point to all the letters he used that are actually correct (to validate the attempt). Then write the word in conventional spelling above his attempt. It is important to not turn the writing activity *into a spelling lesson at that moment*. Unless, of course, you have one of those truly curious kids who really wants to know how to spell those words, in which case spelling can be combined with writing! With time, children will learn to depend upon visual memory of the spelling patterns, that is, how the word *looks* as well as how it *sounds*.

3. What to Do When a Sentence Doesn't Make Sense

Children in the early grades, that is, first through third grades, are still in the formative stages of understanding how written language is different from spoken language. When they are in the midst of writing, they can "hear" the thoughts they have in their minds but are gradually learning how to transfer the ideas they *meant* to the words they wrote down. As adults, we often find that something similar happens with our own writing!

When your child's written sentence doesn't make sense (to you), it is a perfect opportunity for discussion and collaboration. You can wait for your child to finish her thought, then read the sentence aloud to her or have her read it to you. She will often self-correct when she "hears" what she has written. For example, if a word (or two) is missing, she is likely to spot the omission and provide the word. You might rephrase the written sentence and ask: *"Did I get the right idea about what you meant?"* You could suggest possible meanings of what was written: *"I think you are telling me that Flora was mixed up about how to play the game. Is that the right idea?"*

You can set the stage here for your role as a good listener and for your willingness to just experiment with the different words and word combinations that can be chosen to share a thought. If there are any signs of reluctance or frustration, be ready to say: *"Shall we just use the eraser and write something else, or shall we talk it over some more?"* Or you might suggest leaving the sentence in question on the *Writing Wall* or the paper for further consideration the next day, or at the next time. This way you are introducing the ideas of *editing and revising*. Each experience like this can add to your child's growing awareness of how written language is created. In addition, you are modeling *the processes of collaboration and positive feedback.*

4. What to Do If Your Child Is Willing to Write Only "A Little Bit"?

When parents and children begin to explore the writing activities together, there will naturally be an imbalance. The simple fact is that parents already know how to write, regardless of how much or how little they use writing in their lives and work. Parents will tend to write more than their child will, both *because they can* and because they are very motivated for the writing activity to work! They might feel that they are providing a good model by writing a lot. Children can be sensitive and possibly insecure about their early writing skills when they are seeing a comparison between themselves and their parents, or possibly to an older sibling who might be watching to see what's going on.

If you push too hard for more sentences or more words, you risk the possibility that your child will feel resistant or inadequate. And you risk the likelihood that your child might feel right from the start that writing with Mom or Dad is an impossible task because the big people are always better at it. So the question becomes, how much should you push (or encourage)? If your first impulse is to keep the activity positive and appreciate whatever writing output you are able to get from your child then you are on the right track. Above all, remember that you are planting seeds here, and some of them will take their time to sprout and grow! Be encouraging and generous with praise. Reassure your child that you are really excited to be able to write together like this, and you can't wait to see what will happen next time.

Markers of Progress

In the early stages of their educations, children often show rapid spurts of growth, particularly when they consistently practice a skill. Because writing is so visible, parents can watch for a number of signs of growth.

Well-formed sentences. A child's first sentences might consist of a few words that seem a bit mixed up or scrambled, even though the words appear to center on one topic. In other words, the sentence seems more like a *spoken sentence*, with fragments of meaning linked loosely together. Think about how we adults often scramble sentences when we are not quite sure how to say what we mean. You will learn to watch for the appearance of more organized sentences in which both the subject and the verb are easily understood. *"His the ball its gone"* will eventually be replaced with *"Our puppy lost his ball."*

Longer sentences. As your child becomes more skilled at writing, he will start adding descriptive words such as adjectives that show color, size, and so on. You might see connecting words such as *"When…"* or *"After…"* that signal more complex sentences. You might want to casually note the number of words: *"Oh, look, your sentence has nine words in it!"* This observation is not meant to start a competition for sentences with the largest number of words. Instead, you can help him become aware of the many options we have for *adding information* to what we want to say, and thus plant the seeds for the more advanced skill of *elaboration.*

More sentences. As your child writes more sentences to express her thoughts or to answer a question, she is showing that her confidence as a writer is growing. She may also be showing you that she has lots of ideas to share! You might see sentences that introduce a topic and then add detail. This indicates a growing ability to elaborate her ideas, and ultimately to arrange written sentences into whole paragraphs.

New words. As children begin to write, they develop a greater awareness of words and how words work. Chapter 4 discusses vocabulary development in more detail because of its great importance to learning. School-age children encounter dozens of new words on a daily basis, both at home and at school. Their At-Home writing provides an excellent window into the new words that are entering your child's permanent and functional vocabulary. As a parent, you start to see how well your child is picking up on various shades of meaning, an important aspect of effective communication. You can see when they are deliberately being *silly* or are trying to *persuade* you about something, and you can use these words in your feedback comments to point out how words and sentences can have different functions. You also can often detect the source of the word they are using. Did the new word come from family conversations, from the books they are reading, or from things kids said on the playground at school?

As you can see, when you are paying attention to these aspects of beginning writing, as you engage in purposeful writing with your children, you yourself are also taking the opportunity *to practice a higher level of observation*. You are becoming more aware of different components of your child's writing and noting why they are important. You are laying the foundation of Level Two Feedback, *Informative Feedback*.

Level Two: *Informative Feedback* – What Is It and How Does It Work?

The parents who engage in the activities promoted here for both writing and reading have a unique opportunity to practice another form of feedback that is not always addressed in books on parenting. This feedback involves some special skills that parents can practice as they explore the literacy activities. These skills may be different from what we typically expect from parents because they require a higher level of observation and attention. This form of feedback is called *informative feedback* because it involves both observing the child and guiding the child. And as the name indicates, this feedback offers the child a special level of information. The purpose of this section is to detail the strategies and practices that parents can use to engage in *informative feedback*. These practices are especially relevant in the kinds of activities that are possible with the At-Home focus on writing and reading.

It is very likely that you have given your children positive comments that included teaching them some useful truths about dealing with the challenges of daily family life, which is a big part of feedback. However, we will look at feedback from a different perspective when we look through the lens of *informative feedback*. The informative feedback process involves giving specific kinds of information in the form of *labeling*, each with a different purpose and a different focus. We will discuss its uses in the activities in both reading and writing, and you will be given examples of the kind of comments and labeling that go with the specific activities.

Begin with Messages of Support

First priority is given to showing your children how much you value their efforts, depending on the specific activities you are doing. In other words, you tailor the message to the activity, but you always start with the positive. There are common characteristics to all feedback associated with the activities that are recommended here because they all involve communication in some form. You always begin with an interest in what the child is trying to communicate. You want to *be sure you understand what they intend* when they are either writing or sharing ideas through talking. When you ask for clarification with positive and supportive questions, you give them the opportunity to examine their ideas more closely as they begin to share what they are thinking as writers and readers. In the act of asking for clarification, you show that you value what they think and say.

Feedback for Clarification

Informative feedback offers a powerful way to guide how children think about writing and how they can think about their own learning tools. As you read the discussions about the activities, you will find examples of the kinds of comments you can make that are not only encouraging but that also point out and identify specific aspects of the writing that are worthy of paying attention to. When you note that a word is a *descriptive* word or an *action* word, your child is learning an early lesson about *how words **function** in communication*. Later on in school when they learn about nouns, verbs, and adjectives, they will already have a sense of how those words function, as a result of their At-Home writing activities.

Always Say/Never Say

You can ALWAYS SAY, *"You used a really good word to name the place the puppy likes to sleep."* You can ALWAYS SAY, *"When you wrote the words 'sticky as a marshmallow,' I could tell exactly how the plant felt to you!"* You can ALWAYS SAY, *"When you wrote the words 'beautiful yellowish butterfly,' I could tell what colors you were seeing in your mind."* You can ALWAYS SAY, *"When you wrote the word 'tumbled,' I thought that was a really good action word for the trampoline."*

On the other hand, it would be very discouraging to the child if you said, *"I really don't get what you are talking about!"* This would be an example of NEVER SAY. It is true that from time to time you might not be able to make sense of what your child has written. Your child is in the process of selecting the right words and forming clear sentences, and it takes time and attention. A better response would be, *"Read it to me and we will figure out what word we could change."* When the writing becomes a collaborative partnership, your child can then join in *the ownership of the improved product.*

These reactions to the writing activities are examples of *support and clarification feedback* because we use our comments to help children focus on specific aspects of what they have written. We make comments about word choices or sentences that we think are especially effective, and in doing so, we can go well beyond just a general remark. In other words, when we say, *"Nice job,"* your child may not know *what part of the writing* is deserving of the positive comment. When we label the "good" word *by naming the part of speech and connecting the word back to the rest of the sentence*, they may understand exactly what makes it "good." They may be better able to collaborate to make it a good sentence when we focus on some part of the writing that is unclear by saying, *"Read it to me and we will figure out what we need to add or change to make a good sentence."*

Using Labels to Promote Specific Thinking Tools

Throughout this book, and particularly in Chapters 5 through 10, we emphasize how parents can play an important role in their children's development through the process of *labeling*. Labeling is a critical element of *informative feedback* for many reasons. We use labeling when we give names to things like parts of speech, kinds of paragraphs, or different kinds of thinking operations like categorizing and questioning. You will find many examples of specific useful labels as you proceed through the suggested activities.

You will note that all these examples have something to do with how we *use language to talk about language and think about language, and the role of language in thinking*. For young children, spoken language and written language are both a part of how they connect with others in the home, in activities, in relationships, and in situations of all sorts. Language awareness grows as they listen, observe, test, and learn. For example, when a grown-up first reads to them, they may get an initial notion of a "word" as something that has some sort of independent identity that we can talk about or point to. When children begin school instruction, this is generally the time when they learn about the various functions of words, word boundaries, and different forms of word meaning. Other examples will include how we talk about different thinking processes, such as making comparisons, understanding sequences, or explaining an idea to different readers and listeners (intended audience). However, they don't need to wait for formal schooling to learn how words work together when we read, write, and think, At-Home.

You may argue that this is a form of instruction, and it is really the work of the trained teacher in the school classroom. And indeed, a great deal of attention is given to the way children acquire these understandings because of the importance of how we communicate using language. But parents play a role as well. The activities proposed in these chapters have all been based upon the underlying idea of the important role of parents in these processes. As you engage with the activities, you will also engage in a form of observation that will not only give you good data on your child's development, it will also give you opportunities to contribute to that development in very specific ways.

Chapter 10 focuses on *questioning, making comparisons, and categorizing*, with activities that show parents how to provide labels so that children can use these processes as *tools for thinking and learning.* As you go through the steps of the activities that are suggested, you may observe your child make a comment about a category by using the category name, or notice the use of a comparison, thanks to your help with labeling, and thanks to their growing awareness. These processes are becoming *consciously labeled thinking tools.*

The use of informative feedback is a never-ending process. It has no fixed beginning point and no fixed ending point. It can serve to build trust because it focuses on strengths instead of shortcomings. It can build objectivity because *the labels are meant to be nonjudgmental in nature.* It can serve to indicate that Mom or Dad is really paying attention to what is said or written in a way that is thoughtful and respectful. It can indicate, in real time, that what your child thinks and says really matters to you as a parent. And even better, it can indicate that their output can be identified with labels that point the way to more purposeful forms of written expression. Everybody wins.

The Journey So Far

The purpose of Chapter 1 has been to set the stage so that you can become an *informed guide* with background about the WHY and the HOW of the activities that you may find worthwhile engaging in. Along the way, you will see suggestions for the countless opportunities to be creative and to actively tailor the topics and approaches of the activities to your own particular home environment. My hope is that it will be a journey of discovery for all the family members involved. Don't forget to follow the tips about how to document the writing as it is happening, particularly the dates when it is happening.

A final quick note about how you might view the activities assembled here in the following chapters. An informed guide does need specific suggestions for *what to do*, but not necessarily a recipe book that a parent just dips into for something to do on a Saturday afternoon. Rather, the informed guide needs *an operating manual* that is clear about the purposes of the activities and their benefits, particularly in the developmental areas that are important for every child's literacy education. Much depends on parents' engagement, their contributions of their own ideas, and their openness to the creative possibilities of the journey. The good news is that when you see the flowers that grow from the seeds you are planting, you can freely take some of the credit and share that credit with your children! Travel with joy!

Looking Ahead

In the Introduction you found an invitation to parents to participate in a key part of their children's education, acquiring literacy skills. In the chapters of Part 1, **The Emerging Writer**, we focus our attention on writing at home. You will find ideas in this book to help you make writing an integrated part of things you are *already doing together*. Writing can become another of the many ways *we communicate with each other at home*. You will learn how to do this with encouraging words, with examples of activities, and with hints about what age levels fit best with each activity. In addition to showing you how to begin, this book will reinforce the many reasons *why writing is so important to your child's development*. And perhaps most rewarding of all, as you track and save these activities, you will have a record of what your child has accomplished. If you have read this far, you can tell you are in the hands of an author who believes passionately in writing: in the benefits of writing, the power of writing, and the joys of writing. You can help bring your child into the community of writers, and maybe bring in yourselves in the process. Who can tell where the path might lead!

In Part 2, **The Emerging Reader**, we turn our attention to reading at home, because reading and writing belong together. We will show how parents can play an important role *at home* in the development of reading skills. We will show how At-Home reading activities can easily be woven into every family's regular home schedule. The benefits of reading are universally recognized, and we will link them to the At-Home Model in ways that highlight specific thinking processes that can be especially cultivated at home, particularly for early readers. If your children are already on the path to being readers, you will find reinforcement for what you are already doing to encourage the reading habit, and you also will find ways to expand some of the foundational reading skills, such as background knowledge and critical thinking. Beyond reinforcing beliefs you have about the importance of helping your children to become proficient readers, we will point out the ways you can help them become committed participants **in the community of readers**.

2

The At-Home Model for Young Writers and Readers

Questions and Answers

EASY ACCESS NOTES FOR CHAPTER 2: WHAT YOU WILL LEARN

- Introducing the At-Home Model for Writing: Questions and Answers.
- Using the At-Home Model to Support Writing Development.
- Linking At-Home Writing to School Writing.
- Customizing and Personalizing Activities Based on Your Child's Strengths and Interests.
- How Writing Impacts Specific Areas of Child Development.
- The At-Home Model for Reading: How It Complements At-Home Writing and Expands Reading Development.
- Getting Off to a Good Start in Reading: The *Language Experience Approach (LEA)*.
- How *LEA* Impacts Language and Reading Development.
- Signs of Growth to Watch for in the Dictated Stories.
- Benefits to Parents from At-Home Writing and Reading.

DOI: 10.4324/9781003452683-4

How This Book Might Enter Your Home

As a parent, you know that parenting does not happen only at single points in time. It happens along a continuum of events as we care for and raise our children. For this reason, books such as this one must take note of the events that came before, the events that are happening right now, and what might happen tomorrow or at any time in the future. In a similar way, book authors recognize that the education of our children is an ongoing operation with no single starting point, and certainly with no ending point.

The messages contained in this book are based on two assumptions. The first is that the readers (parents, about-to-be parents, grandparents) are interested enough in what they can do to help their children, that they are reading the book in the first place. Interested parents may be focused on one child in particular if writing or reading skills seem to be an issue. Or they may be parents with a grand plan to get all the children off to a good start in this important area of literacy. They may already endorse the idea of using writing and reading activities that are incorporated into the ongoing life of the family.

The second assumption is that there will be many variations in each household, in the ages of the children and the amounts of formal and informal schooling they may have already received. In other words, it is unlikely this book will enter a home where a child has had no exposure to reading and writing. Thus, while there is structure as to how these activities are introduced and used, there is no rigid entry point. The activities presented in the following chapters may be completely new to some children, while for other children they may offer opportunities to fine-tune skills they already have, allowing them to shine and to "be the expert." It is hoped that every family will build upon the activities. It is hoped that you will improvise and expand all the opportunities that present themselves, for creativity, spontaneity, humor, and engagement, At-Home.

In the Introduction, you found an invitation to parents to participate in a key part of their children's education, the literacy skills. Chapter 1 offered background information to enable

parents to become Informed Guides when they choose to participate with their children on the journey to acquiring these important skills that are foundational to all of education.

In Chapter 2, you are invited to build upon the special knowledge you have of your children, thanks to your unique home
setting and your unique family experiences. This chapter introduces the *At-Home Model*, a new way to think about how to use
this special knowledge to promote important writing and reading skills through activities that are specially designed to fit
comfortably, "at home." We will first look at some questions you
may be asking, along with answers to explain the purposes and
benefits of the activities that are featured. The At-Home Model
allows you to go beyond just the simple directions for **what** to
do with the writing and reading activities and helps you understand **how** and **why** they are important for your children.

The Q&A format was chosen because it is a useful way to introduce ideas that can provide important background in a concise
manner. Every topic included here is relevant to your interest
in the literacy skills for your child and why they are important.
We will emphasize a conviction that your contributions matter a
great deal, and we will explain how. You are encouraged to use
these ideas to reinforce your reasons for reading the book in the
first place, and to reinforce your intentions to keep on reading!

The *At-Home* Model for Writing: Questions and Answers

**Question: What is "At-Home" writing? How is it different
from *school writing*?**
Answer: *At-Home* writing activities are intended for parents who
want to help their children with writing, but who may feel that
writing is a particularly challenging skill to tackle. The goal of
At-Home writing is to build comfort and confidence with writing,
in order to promote competent writers. We purposefully begin
with family-shared experiences and family-shared communication, and then we show how parents can introduce activities
that are designed to expand their children's individual interests
and their experiences of the world around them through writing.

At-Home writing activities invite children to comment and reflect upon their experiences by writing about them in a way that often makes the experience more meaningful. As you will see, one of the many benefits of the activities is that your child can discover his or her "voice" through writing. **Pride of ownership can be a powerful motivator and a source of competence**.

School writing has a different goal. School writing generally is connected to the instruction that students receive about new ideas and new information based on the school curriculum. It requires them to explain what they have learned, to expand what they know, and to combine new knowledge with new vocabulary. Sometimes this comes easily, but sometimes it seems very challenging because at first the materials and new ideas may be unfamiliar and may seem complicated. However, school writing and the *At-Home* activities have much in common. The *At-Home* activities are designed so that when children acquire writing skills at home, those same skills will apply when and where they are needed at school.

Family writing activities tend to be more spontaneous since they are based on a family's shared experiences. However, parents may want to strengthen the link to formal school-required writing that is curriculum-centered and topic-based. Skills that are being developed in the more informal family activities can transfer to formal writing, to build the skills that are covered and expected in the school setting. Links to school writing are noted throughout Part 1, and particularly in Chapter 5 when we introduce *The Writer's Toolbox*.

Question: Is this a curriculum for writing?
Answer: There are programs for child writing that include published guides, workbooks, online programs, and writing camps. Most are designed to teach the mechanics of writing, along with different modes of writing, from creative writing to expository writing. *At-Home* writing, on the other hand, is completely individualized. It is tailored to the interests and experiences of your child. Feedback and structure are provided within the activities so that children can learn both the mechanics of writing and different techniques of writing. In

addition, they are encouraged to experiment with different topics to write about. For you as a parent, these activities provide a useful window where you can observe critical aspects of your child's growth and development.

You will be shown how to build upon the skills that are introduced in the informal start-up activities in Chapter 3, while new skills are gradually added through the structured writing activities found in Chapters 4, 5, and 6. For example, in Chapter 5, you will find a reference section for parents and young writers who are ready for the basic grammar tools that all writers depend on when it is time to reread, evaluate, and edit their own writing. With these tools, you will be better able to support your child with school-related writing assignments, especially when it comes to the important process of editing. Writers agree that good writing is all about *editing and rewriting*. There is much that young writers can learn from editing their own work. It's an important school skill and an important life skill. Chapter 7 celebrates the creative aspects of writing, with descriptive writing, poems and songs, and an assortment of word games.

Question: How can I add *At-Home* writing activities to my busy family schedule?
Answer: Even before the pandemic years, when parents took on additional schooling responsibilities, moms and dads were often involved in promoting **book reading** at home. Many materials were available to show parents how to do this, such as reading workbook activities and lists of recommended children's books. Then, when schooling had to change to virtual and online learning, many parents recognized the need for similar guidance to help children with writing. ***There's a Writer in Our House!*** will show you ways to bring *At-Home* writing into family activities and experiences that are already happening. You will be encouraged to look at these activities through the *lens of the writer*. What goes on around the house provides an ongoing supply of writing opportunities that you might not have noticed before! You will find many reasons here to feel motivated and engaged. Read on to learn these reasons.

Question: Why is writing important for my child?
Answer: Writing is a key element in all literacy learning. In school, writing holds a top spot in the language arts curriculum, beginning as early as pre-school and continuing through all levels of higher education. With all this attention to writing in the schools, why might we need a book that promotes activities for practicing writing at home? Parents have been faced with daunting responsibilities, helping children navigate a complex and busy world, with many changes in the structure and delivery of school learning. It is the purpose of this book to persuade you that you can play an important role in guiding your child on the path to becoming a young writer, and further, to show how this can be done, *At-Home*. Every chapter will explain and emphasize *the importance of writing* in a child's overall development as a learner and thinker.

Many great writers got their start at a young age. As you engage with your young writers at home, you may indeed foster some great writers or even some very good writers. But the greatest goal of all, in guiding and encouraging your child to write, is to show that writing is desirable, worthwhile, and doable. *At-Home* **writing activities let children know that what they have to say is important. Through** *At-Home* **writing, you can be witness to the unique person that is within each child, as expressed in their writing. Just as important, it is a way for children to document their thoughts and ideas as they grow and develop**.

Writing can be a magical way for children to discover what they think about things. In the act of writing, they make decisions about how to frame their thoughts so that another person can understand their words and ideas. They think about which words to choose so that someone else will understand the idea in their mind. They have to think about the order of the ideas: what to write first, then next, and then at the end. These decision elements are often invisible when we read the writings of others, but as parents and teachers, we can do much to foster these powerful benefits that come when a child learns to think like a writer.

When children first learn to read, they gradually realize that SOMEBODY wrote the words on those pages. It is only a short step to thinking, "*I can be a **writer** too.*" When children are first learning to be writers, there is often great emphasis on what they produce: the complete sentence, or the five-sentence paragraph. And both of these are important, especially for school writing. However, ***There's a Writer in Our House!*** is designed to highlight one of the greatest benefits of writing: *learning to think like a writer.*

Question: How does At-Home writing contribute to a child's development in thinking, expressive language, and vocabulary?

Answer: When you try *Activity One, the Writing Wall,* and the activities that follow, you may be quickly convinced that these At-Home writing activities are important. You will often see unexpected engagement or enthusiasm from your child which further convinces you that these activities are worthwhile. But the benefits of writing go far beyond engagement and enthusiasm. Writing can impact child development in at least three very significant ways.

Thinking Skills. Although you may connect writing mainly with a child's communication skills, perhaps the most important benefit of becoming a writer is the effect on a child's cognitive development, or in other words, on how a child is learning to think. When children write, they draw upon their knowledge of the world. They begin to organize this knowledge in a meaningful way. They have to think about the here and now, using written language to talk about the immediate and the concrete when they write about things we can touch and feel. They can also think and talk about ideas that are abstract, such as *truth*, *hope*, *memory*, and *fairness*, as well as ideas involving time and space in order to write about past events or far-away places. In many ways, writing helps children *know what they know*. They will experience setting priorities and making judgments, which are all thinking operations. When parents engage with their children's writing, they contribute directly to their development as effective thinkers.

Language Development. Writing activities have great benefits in the area of language development. We want our children to be fluent in using language to communicate their ideas or to share information. In the early stages of writing, children become aware that written language is a visible form of spoken language, but it is different from spoken language in several important ways.

They learn through writing that language has a structure that is consistent. They learn to make different kinds of sentences. They learn to use some kinds of sentences to ask questions and some to make requests. They learn how one sentence can lead to another, as we add details or as we write about a sequence of events or steps in order. Some kinds of sentences tell a story about a spider named Charlotte, while other sentences teach us facts about turtles. And some kinds of sentences can even be silly or tell jokes and riddles. It is true that they can learn all of the above through reading the language written by other writers, but they learn it very directly *through their own writing*.

When children are exposed to longer portions of text, they begin to see the shape of a story or an argument, with a beginning, a middle, and an end. They encounter the words that signal how the information is organized in patterns, such as time order, comparisons, or cause and effect. All these language-based understandings prepare children for the learning that is to come in middle school, high school, college, and beyond.

Vocabulary Development. As they write, children can practice choosing words and putting words together in different word combinations. They learn about parts of speech and how they function, such as the naming words (nouns), the action words (verbs), and the describing words (adjectives). They learn that some words have meanings that are similar to each other, such as *glad* and *happy* or *flat* and *level*. They learn that some words have opposites, such as *hot* and *cold*, *high* and *low*. They learn early on that *words matter* as they experiment in expressing their own ideas.

They can discover that there are differences in how they would explain an idea, depending on whether the explanation is for Grandma or for a younger brother. They can practice using the new vocabulary words that come from new events and new experiences. When new vocabulary words are used in writing, those words are much more likely to remain in a child's *permanent vocabulary*.

Question: How do we get the most benefit from the *At-Home* writing environment?

Answer: At-Home we can build confidence and comfort with writing. Informal kinds of writing, such as the *Writing Wall* and the *Written Conversation* (Activity 1 and Activity 3 in Chapter 3), are activities that have important benefits because this is writing about familiar topics that are here and now. When the topics are familiar, children are more able to convert their spoken language into written words. Children cannot write meaningfully about something they do not know or understand, though at times in their educational lives, they may be asked to do so. When writing is meaningful to children, they are more likely to discover that they have a voice which they can use.

At-Home activities are about shared experiences and shared backgrounds. Family members are well-known for being able to read each other's thoughts or for being able to finish each other's sentences. These family behaviors may not always lead to greater tolerance and greater understanding, but they are a bonus for *At-Home* writing, at least in the beginning stages. **The beginning writer wants, above all, to be understood**. Familiar topics and activities are the perfect starting points because there is comfort in the *known*. In addition, sentences that are written down can be reread and examined. As the activities are explored, there will be time to experiment with editing and practice different ways to evaluate what you wrote. In the context of the familiar, these steps will help your child along the path to becoming a writer.

You will be shown how to document and preserve your children's writing. If you have read this far, you will easily understand the fascination that parents often develop over children's early writing, especially when the things they write are embedded in the family experience. You are in a position to preserve your child's writing in a way that is unlikely to happen in a busy classroom or with online learning. This is not simply the obsession of the doting parent, because over time there is a broader benefit when you preserve kid writing. It is a bit akin to the geologist being able to read the geologic layers to analyze rock formations or periodic changes in the earth's surface and climate. You will be able to spot spurts of growth in vocabulary, fluctuations in your child's interests, and other valuable insights into cognitive, language, and social development. It's all there in the layers.

Question: What should I watch for as we begin *At-Home* writing?
Answer: The opening activities focus on children at the beginning stages of schooling, particularly from first grade through fifth grade. However, this age range can expand to accommodate the needs of specific children. The tools and devices we use for writing will shift and change as technology changes, but the benefits of writing continue on into higher education, as well as into vocational and professional life. As a teacher of students of all ages, and particularly as an educational therapist for students with special needs, I have seen first-hand the many ways in which children benefit from being able to write. This is often dramatically true, even when they had found it to be a great struggle at the time.

I have seen students whose most frequent experiences with writing have been experiences of failure. Both writing and spelling are very *visible* skills. You can view the output and tell a great deal about the skill level of the writer. Few among us love to do something that makes us feel inadequate. The early failure experiences can take a long time to reverse, and their toll is seen in the children who vocally *hate* writing. I well remember the little red-haired third grader who had met with me only two or three times when I brought out our first writing activity. She looked at the writing materials, immediately dove under the desk, and from the depths said clearly, "***You can't make me write!***" With patience, instruction, and family support, that little girl became a prize-winning high school writer and a capable college graduate.

There have been students who were not sure of their own ideas, or were not even sure if they had ideas, until they began to write. They of course had their own thoughts, as all children do, but the thoughts seemed scrambled and unclear. The act of writing enabled them to sort their thoughts and give them form and shape. With support and guidance, scrambled thoughts could become clear. Even more important, children could examine their thoughts once they were written down. This great step is called "metacognition" in psychological terms, literally thinking about thinking. Thus, through thinking about thinking, writing helps children *know what they know*.

Question: What are the *Task Demands* that will present a challenge?

Answer: Many children can find the act of putting pencil to paper quite exhausting. When you think about all the systems that are required for a child to be able to write a sentence or a paragraph, it can be both overwhelming and discouraging. The physical act of making the letters is difficult at first for many children, and all their energy has to be dedicated to making those shapes, some of which look a great deal like each other (think *b* and *d* or *m* and *n*). While the physical operation is being mastered, there is the business of matching letters to sounds to arrive at *spelling* the words you need. Then there is the decision of which words to choose, with so many to choose from. And finally, you have to know how to organize those words into groups that convey an idea so that someone else can understand what you mean.

As grown-ups, we might compare all this to the act of driving a car. We must master the physical control of the vehicle, knowing how to start, stop, and steer. We must be vigilant, not only about keeping the car in the right place on the road but also about knowing what is in front, behind, and beside the car. We must have some idea of where we want to go, and how to get there. We might have to make choices about different routes. Finally, we need to be able to recognize *when we have arrived*.

Today we have tools available to take some of the exhaustion out of writing. The computer has been a blessing for many young writers once they have mastered the keyboard. However, the computer, in spite of spell-check, auto-correct, and grammar-check features, cannot *think for the child*. The thinking aspects of writing have to be developed carefully and with patience, both at home and at school. When parents help a young child develop confidence and comfort with writing in the familiar environment of the home, they can guide that child on the path to becoming a competent young writer.

Question: Is there a specific age when a child "becomes" a writer? How will I know when it happens?
Answer: Like reading, writing is developmental. We often measure children's progress in reading by looking at the "difficulty level" of the books they choose or feel comfortable with. The difficulty level of writing output is harder to measure because very complex ideas can sometimes be expressed in a few words. Think about the famous "Six Word Story" attributed to Ernest Hemingway:

> *For sale.*
> *Baby shoes.*
> *Never worn.*

Your child's enthusiasm for writing may wax and wane as interests shift and change. The important message to give your emerging writer is that writing is important, writing is valuable, and writing is doable. The goal of *There's a Writer in Our House!* is to help you engage with your child with writing in a way that is encouraging and supportive, but also informed. You will know when your child "becomes" a writer whether it happens slowly, all at once, or several times!

Question: How do I keep the writing partnership going?
Answer: When children see that their writing is valued by their significant grown-ups, they will be motivated to keep going. When children gain perspective on their own progress and confidence, they will be motivated. When children see their parents write along with them, they will see writing activities as a partnership. Perhaps most of all, they will see the writing we do At-Home through a new lens, *the lens of the writer*. As a parent, through this lens, you will identify activities that you can easily integrate into family life as a way to promote writing. In fact, your attention will be drawn *to the potential writing value of simple tasks* that you might normally overlook for the sake of efficiency. These opportunities might prove to be undiscovered gold under your feet!

There may be moments when writing activities seem to be a struggle. When that happens, you will have the suggestions in Chapter 11 for how to analyze the reasons for the resistance or the struggle. You will have a plan for what resources to look for. Most of all, you will have the confidence that you can sort things out and find a way to get back on track.

The *At-Home* Model for Reading: Questions and Answers

Question: What is "At-Home" reading? How is it different from *school reading*?

Answer: Many children learn their first lessons about reading at home when they see reading happening around them. There is an abundance of enthusiastic books for parents that support reading from the very beginning. Books such as *How to Raise a Reader* (Workman Publishing, 2019) are full of suggestions about reading to our children, about introducing "little books," and about sharing the children's classics that have stood the test of time. Reading is a high-value activity in the minds of parents, and we send many signals to children that reading is desirable. In Chapters 8 and 9 you will see how *At-Home Reading* activities can share many of the characteristics and benefits of *At-Home Writing*. These activities are individualized and customized to make reading a personalized experience for your child. You will see how *At-Home* reading takes advantage of the familiar home environment to build comfort and confidence with reading.

School reading has a different goal. School reading introduces children to new ideas, new information, and new vocabulary. The school reading curriculum is designed to introduce skills in a sequenced manner so that each new skill builds upon previous learning. It is the job of the school to make sure that all aspects of reading instruction are included, based on current research in reading. School instructional materials are specifically written to fit the different developmental levels of achievement as children progress through their reading lessons. The school's job is to introduce children to multiple books that have come to be regarded as classics in the area of *children's literature*. These books expose children to many genres, including realistic fiction, historical fiction, biographies, myths and fables, fantasy, drama, and poetry. In many schools, the reading curriculum is linked to what the children are learning in science and social studies. The teacher will encourage children to practice reading at home in self-selected books for *independent reading*.

Question: There seem to be many methods to teach beginning readers. Is there an approach that fits well with the At-Home Model?

Answer: There are multiple programs for helping children become readers, including many types of workbooks and other materials to support the introduction of skills, and subsequent growth in reading. In Chapter 8, we introduce one approach that is particularly well suited to the At-Home Model. It is called the *Language Experience Approach* (*LEA*). In *LEA*, children dictate a "story" or an account about an individual interest or experience. Their stories are written down (or typed) as they are dictated, by the parent or a teacher. These stories are subsequently activated and used as instructional reading materials that support many aspects of reading instruction. Chapters 8 and 9 take you through the step-by-step procedures for recording children's stories and show you how to use those stories to practice important reading skills.

Question: How can I maximize the connection between the activities for *At-Home* writing and the activities for *At-Home* reading?

Answer: There are many intersections between the *At-Home* writing and *At-Home* reading activities. You will see opportunities to build on your child's existing interests and then expand those interests. Both approaches offer ideas for introducing new information and new vocabulary through new experiences and interests. For example, the *Writing Wall* can be used to highlight new words that have been introduced from available reading materials. The new vocabulary words are likely to show up in both the writing activities and the dictated stories. These new words could show up on a part of the *Word Wall* that features new word families such as sports words, action words, or scary words.

Strength in reading can easily be combined with strength in writing and vice versa. As a parent, you can be on the lookout for ways to connect writing and reading, and you can encourage your children to spot connections as well. For example, they can write a letter to a character in a book in the same way they might write a letter to a friend who has moved away to another town. They can write a book review for someone they know who might like that book, explaining why the person would find the book interesting and enjoyable.

Question: How does *At-Home* reading boost overall reading development for the New Reader?
Answer: Specific reading skills are promoted through follow-up activities with the dictated stories. Strength in sight vocabulary (the words a child recognizes on sight, from memory) promotes reading fluency. Children gain greater awareness of the *sound patterns* as they play rhyming games and other games with their Word Bank words. Some children will incorporate the patterns found in their storybooks into their own dictated stories. And finally, the *critical thinking skills* that are introduced in Chapter 10 connect well to reading comprehension, especially when we help children transition from their own dictated stories to the stories and articles they read in published children's books, magazines, and other print sources.

Question: How do we get off to a good start with *At-Home* reading?
Answer: Chapter 8 presents the steps for introducing the dictated stories and shows how the stories can be activated to promote reading development. These activities are intended for children at the beginning stages of reading, but the dictated stories can also be used with children who are not catching on to how reading "works." *LEA* stories help struggling readers make the *speech-to-print* connection with their own words and with sentences that have high value and a high level of meaning to the child who made those sentences. The dictated story activities

also work well for new readers who are learning to read in a second language. For some young readers, the dictated stories provide a way to "jump start" the reading process because of their focus on the familiar. Children can develop a special kind of confidence when they are reading their own words, as those words are recorded in the dictated stories. They can go on to practice their reading skills using these very same words from their stories. They can experience ownership of the words and ideas in multiple ways, not only by producing their stories but also by using their stories as learning activities.

Question: How do we get the most reading benefit from *At-Home* reading?

Answer: Just the way we did with At-Home writing: we build confidence, comfort, and then competence with reading. With a strong start using the children's dictated stories, we can transition to published materials like library books or children's magazines. These materials will include chapter books as well as beginning science and other non-fiction books. These forms of reading are similar to the books used in school for reading instruction, enabling *At-Home* reading to support school reading activities. When school and home share similar reading materials, children will encounter many of the same vocabulary words that are important to fluent reading and new learning. When children encounter words in multiple sources, those words are more likely to enter and remain in the child's permanent vocabulary, especially when the words are encountered *in meaningful contexts*.

Question: How does *At-Home* reading promote language development?

Answer: In addition to building a reading vocabulary, *At-Home* reading with the dictated stories makes children aware of how language conveys meaning. As your children reread their own stories, you will see that they often spontaneously edit sentences that are scrambled or that may need additional words to make the meaning clear. Each time they reorganize a sentence to make it better, they recognize how readers understand sentences in books. Each time they elaborate by adding additional words, they learn the technique of providing supporting details. They will become more able to recognize important details in the printed materials they read. They will also increasingly be able to recognize the "language of the writer."

Question: What signs of growth shall I watch for?
Answer: As with *At-Home* writing, the dictated stories and the follow-up activities are a way to document growth. We use many of the same markers as we did with writing. These markers include improved sentence structure, growth in vocabulary, longer and more coherent stories, use of imagination and humor, and stories with a wider variety of topics. The stories will reflect a child's emerging thinking skills. Stories offer a window into what your child is finding important enough or interesting enough to tell a story about. We may forget from day to day, or week to week, the amazing thoughts we hear from a child. With the dictated stories, they can be dated and preserved to be enjoyed next month or next year.

There is an important group of young readers and writers who may especially benefit from the dictating and recording of their stories. If your child is in this group, you will understand what I am talking about. You may be lucky enough to have a child who has an unusually imaginative or creative way of looking at things. She or he may have a tendency to go beyond the conventional and become fascinated by the "what if" or the "why not." Their stories may cause the grown-ups to roll their eyes and just say, *"But that can't happen!"* These children may grow used to giving up on trying to convince us, or they may grow up to write a new *Harry Potter*. In between they may have a parent who takes their stories seriously enough to write them down. And to use those same stories to teach both reading and writing skills. And to save the stories, to "Remember when…" It can happen.

Question: What are the benefits for parents?
Answer: You are in a unique position to observe your children in *the context of the familiar*. You can note emerging interests. You can note when your child adopts new words and shares the

perceptions that arise from new experiences. You can note how children respond to the events at school or after-school activities. You may not be able to closely observe a child's reaction to classroom instruction, as the teacher might, but your observations can focus on your child as an individual. In the busy classroom, one child's reaction to a story, a task, or a classroom event may go largely unremarked, and the child may even forget all about it and it will no longer be available as a timely topic for writing, reading, and discussing.

At home, on the other hand, much that happens in your young child's life (including the teen years) can serve as useful opportunities for writing. And while it is not always possible to give your child your undivided attention, the writing/sharing bargain provides opportunities for many forms of communication. These opportunities are precious in the short term and a good investment in the long term. Ideas that we write down tend to linger in the memory and can be revisited for further comment or further additions. Strengths developed in the home can go far to counter the limitations of the busy classroom or online instruction that may result in hesitant writing or reading skills.

As you read about the suggested activities in the chapters, think about which ideas you have already considered. Then think about how you might extend the activity in ways that will be just right for your own child. Think about new ways to look at family experiences in terms of *their writing potential or story potential*. For some parents, this book may be an answer to existing concerns. For many, it will be just the beginning of good things. There might be times of resistance and reluctance. But please don't get discouraged. Think about what you might expect to learn from your child. Children can be excellent teachers.

Every parent is a "first-time" parent at some point, even when you have multiple children. Parenting brings awesome challenges and awesome rewards. Parenting is both a responsibility and an investment in a future person, especially in a time of pandemic stresses, when the future itself may seem uncertain in ways we did not imagine. Even before COVID-19, we were living in a time when there was much that competed for our children's attention, and it was often difficult to set priorities for what to do with the moments we are given. What better gift can we give to our children than our own involvement as they acquire the skills of reading and writing? Our involvement sends a clear message that both reading and writing are important enough for us to spend time participating with them as they learn.

It may strengthen our commitment when we realize that we are not doing these activities as something "extra." *Our involvement is something essential, something each child truly needs.* We have seen many educational activities relegated to the computer and other depersonalized devices for online instruction and remote courses. We can change the balance for our children to highlight activities that enhance each child's sense of self and identity by incorporating opportunities that center upon the unique individuality found in every child. It becomes a two-way street when we realize there are benefits to ourselves as parents when we work with our children in these ways. We can benefit the entire world, one family at a time.

A Message of Hope

A well-known writer who was interviewed on National Public Radio (October 2016; https://www.npr.org/2016/10/04/496592323/gloria-naylor-the-women-of-brewster-place-author-dies-at-66) about her life as a writer was describing the personal importance of writing and how writing had shaped her life. I had missed the beginning of the interview so did not catch her name, but she made a comment that stuck with me. She said, *"People without hope do not write books."*

Writing is an act of hope. We hope someone will read what we wrote. We hope that what we wrote will make sense to someone. We hope that what we have to say is worthwhile to someone. We hope that when we read it again later, it will still be worthwhile to us. And if it is not, we hope to have the courage to try again.

When our children write, we hope they will learn that they have a voice. We hope they will value their own thoughts and ideas. We hope they will always have an appreciative reader like Mom or Dad or another family member or friend. We hope they will develop a love of language and an appreciation of the power of language. We hope they will read other writers with a new respect for what it takes to be a writer.

Parents make an enormous contribution to their children's well-being and education, particularly when Mom and Dad can feel confident in their own ability to be an Informed Guide to their children. Guiding the young writer and young reader is no exception, once you know what to do. This book has been written with the purpose of providing that guidance and inspiration. Having a writer in the house is good for everyone. And everyone can be proud knowing that every writer is a reader, too.

Writing Through the Ages

We can look to the past for inspiration about the many ways writing has changed history. This moving passage is taken from *The Invention of Wings* by Sue Monk Kidd, a story based upon the Grimke Sisters, Sarah and Nina, who were among the early abolitionist women with remarkable backgrounds. They were not only daughters of a Southern slave-owning family but also brave women who found their voices in the anti-slavery movement. They had left their home in Charleston and found refuge with Quaker families in the North. Uncertain about where to live or how to proceed in speaking out, they consider daunting options:

> *Then one morning while my sister used the last of our paints to capture the bare willow outside the window and I walked my trenchant path on the rug, I suddenly stopped and gazed at the pewter inkstand. I stared at it for whole minutes. Everything was in shambles, and there was the inkstand.*
>
> *"…Nina! Do you remember how Mother would make us sit for hours and write apologies? Well, I'm going to write one…a true apology for the anti-slavery cause. You could write, too… We both could."*
>
> *She stared at me, while everything I felt and knew offered itself up at once.*

They did write, and they did speak. And they did make history.

Bibliography

Kaganoff, Ann. "When Parents are Co-Teachers: The Language Experience Approach (LEA) for Young Readers." *The Educational Therapist*, Volume 34, Number 1, April/May 2013, 6–11.

Kaganoff, Ann. *Best Practices in Educational Therapy*. New York: Routledge, 2019.

Kidd, Sue Monk. *The Invention of Wings*. New York, New York. Penguin Books, 2014.

Paul, Pamela, and Russo, Maria. (Editors, *The New York Times Book Review*). *How to Raise a Reader*. New York: Workman Publishing, 2019.

Bibliography for Language Experience Approach, Beginning Reading and Writing

Coker, D. Jr., and Ritchey, Kristen. *Teaching Beginning Writers*. New York, London: Guilford Press, 2015.

Cullinan, Bernice. *Pen in Hand: Children Become Writers*. Newark, DE: International Reading Association, 1993. ISBN 0-87207-383-1.

Franklin, Daniel. *Helping Your Child with Language-Based Learning Disabilities*. Oakland, CA: New Harbinger Publications, 2018.

Goodman, Yetta M., Ed. *How Children Construct Literacy*. Newark, DE: International Reading Association, 1990. ISBN 0-87207-534-6.

Graham, S., MacArthur, C., and Fitzgerald, J., Eds. *Best Practices in Writing Instruction*. New York, London: Guilford Press, 2013.

Levy, N., Burke, A., and Wallace, R. *Not Just Schoolwork: Activities for Critical Thinking and Written Expression*. Nathan Levy Books, LLC, 2013.

Morrow, Lesley, Ed. *Family Literacy: Connections in Schools and Communities*. Newark, DE: International Reading Association, 1995. ISBN 0-87207-127-8.

Nessel, Denise D., and Jones, Margaret. *The Language Experience Approach to Reading*. New York: Teachers College Press, 1981. ISBN 0-8077-2596-x.

Strickland, Dorothy S. and Morrow, Lesley Mandel, Eds. *Emerging Literacy: Young Children Learn to Read and Write*. Newark, DE: International Reading Association, 1989. ISBN 0-87207-351-3.

3

At-Home Writing Activities

Getting Started and Keeping Going

Activity Level: 5–9+ years

EASY ACCESS NOTES FOR CHAPTER 3: WHAT YOU WILL LEARN

- ◆ Organization and Sequencing of the Activities.
- ◆ Format for How the Activities are Presented:
  - ○ Name and approximate age level of the activity.
  - ○ Purpose of the activity.
  - ○ Instructions.
  - ○ Prompts and ideas to lead with, building on your child's strengths and interests.
  - ○ What to watch for.
  - ○ Benefits for your child.
  - ○ Real-life examples.
- ◆ Activities to Try Out: *The Writing Wall, The Written Conversation, Writing Directions for Someone to Follow, The Family Response Journal, Paired/ Shared Writing* (prompts given in all cases).
- ◆ Adding New Features with Each New Activity and Building on Previous Activities.
- ◆ Making the Activities Reciprocal: Parent and Child Taking Turns.

DOI: 10.4324/9781003452683-5

Let's Get Started

Even before starting school, children have been introduced to writing at home when parents teach them how to write their names in this first, most personal form of writing. With this kind of introduction, children have been *shown* the process rather than being formally taught about it and they can immediately see that writing has a purpose. As we begin the At-Home activities, we will assume that your child has had some experience with how to hold a marker or pencil, and how to form the letters. As you will see, each activity recommended here involves some parent planning at the beginning. When you do the suggested advance preparation, you give the activities a greater chance of producing a confident writer, particularly if you have not already begun At-Home writing. Each activity has been designed to allow for family preferences and for multiple opportunities for creativity, collaboration, modification, and adaptation. Parents will typically start things off, but soon children are invited in to participate, at whatever level is most comfortable for them.

As you glance over the entire section, you will see that the activities start at a level that is easily managed by the youngest writers, starting with skills that have been introduced for some children in kindergarten and for most children by first grade. As you proceed, the activities increase in complexity and are further tailored to the individual child and the individual family setting. Therefore, the order of the activities is important. The recommended age level is given for each activity. Let the journey begin.

Activity 1

The Writing Wall: A Wall-Mounted Whiteboard or Chalkboard

Activity Level: 5–6 years to 9 years

Purpose
Activity 1 is designed to bring writing into your everyday lives to make writing a part of the flow of family communication (Figure 3.1). Many families already use message boards in the

FIGURE 3.1 Photo of the Writing Wall

house as a place to leave reminders or messages for other members of the family about school schedules, to-do lists, shopping lists, and so on. The *Writing Wall* takes this functional idea a step further by designating a wall space to share observations and thoughts at a more personal level. As part of preparing for the wall, let your child know this is more than a reminder list or a to-do list. It is a special kind of *family sharing*.

Instructions
Your home might have a hallway or passageway leading to a child's or parents' room. Your child's room might have a small amount of wall space that is not occupied by posters or windows. Any spaces where the family congregates are ideal places for the wall-mounted whiteboard or chalkboard that will serve as the *Writing Wall*. The vertical surface of the wall is ideal for promoting the use of the large muscles of the arm as children form the letters. However, if wall space is limited, find a small portable whiteboard (approximately two feet by two feet in size) that can be moved from one location to another. **Please note that the *Writing Wall* can be skipped if it is not appropriate for your home or your child**.

Installing the whiteboard can be a family project you do with your child. Children can help decide where the board should be mounted and what color markers or chalk to use. You might have one color for each parent and a different color for each child to choose. Be sure the whiteboard is positioned so that a young child can reach it to write comfortably. It might have a tray for storing markers or chalk, and your child could take responsibility for being sure the writing tools stay organized and in place.

Setting up the *Writing Wall* is an opportunity to generate some curiosity and interest by talking about how the family will use this new kind of writing. The goal is simple. You will write messages on the *Writing Wall* as a special way to communicate within the family. Your children can practice writing by responding to your messages, or by writing ones of their own. The suggested prompts that are included here will help you get started. You will note that the prompts focus initially on matters that are likely to be a part of a family's everyday life, though this might change as individual family members adapt the wall to their own purposes.

Some families may take advantage of the wall for written reminders. Some children may want to use the wall to state requests or to ask a question about something they have been wondering about (parents are allowed to do this too). Conversations may emerge between or among smaller subsets of family members. Some family members might enjoy word games and jokes. In all cases, it is important for the exchange to be a positive way to show the value of communicating by writing, especially for the little ones who are just learning how writing works.

What to Watch For
Since children are not usually allowed to write on walls, take the opportunity in the very beginning to emphasize the purpose of this surprising activity, especially for the new writers. You can tell them that we can use writing in many different ways and in different places. Even the beginners will understand the idea of practicing a new skill, and how practice helps us get better at it. They may be intrigued by the benefits of practicing writing in an unusual way, like on a wall (but *only* on the *Writing Wall*).

After you have talked about how the wall works, you can take the lead by leaving a message that might be especially interesting to your child using one of the suggested prompts that may inspire you. You can write about something that took place during their day, or about anything of family interest. Since you know your child well, you can probably come up with some ideas that will make her or him curious. A curious child is likely to be engaged enough to want to add a response. To make your message easy to read, use clear print letters, and words that you think they will recognize. **Be available to read any words aloud that might be unfamiliar**. Keep in mind that, as an added benefit, younger siblings at the pre-reading stage will also get some beginning reading experience from looking at these messages.

Remember to keep the notes spontaneous and casual, emphasizing ideas that your child can relate to. You can write a single sentence or a question, leaving room for a response. Even a single sentence about something familiar may be enough to get a young writer started with his or her own ideas. From the very beginning, let your child know how much you value the responses by reading them aloud together and commenting on them. You can gradually encourage longer notes from your child by asking, *"Can you tell me more about that?"* Or *"What other sentence could go with these words you wrote?"* Note how this kind of comment highlights *the language* we use to talk about writing: *words; sentence*.

Benefits for Your Child

- ◆ The *Writing Wall* clearly establishes the "speech-to-print" connection and teaches children that you can write down the very same words that you can *think and say*.
- ◆ Others can read your words and write something back to you.
- ◆ Written language is different from spoken language in ways that we can talk about when we look at the written words.
- ◆ You can practice writing about lots of your different ideas.
- ◆ Other people in the family can join in and write on the wall.
- ◆ The *Writing Wall* is a special place for writing, and it is the ONLY place where you can write on the wall!

Helpful Prompts for Parents to Start With

Do you need a little inspiration to start a project such as this? Here are some ideas to get you started. Note that prompts are often in the form of a question your child could answer, which might be an easy kind of prompt for some children. Other prompts are in the form of a comment or statement. Both forms are equally valuable, and you can tailor what you write to your child's interests.

♦ Write about something interesting from your day that had a connection to your child: *"The people down the street got a new puppy. Did you see them walking with the puppy?"*

♦ Write about something your child did that pleased you. Tell what and why: *"You sure did a good job helping Marty pick up the toys. That was a great idea for using the big cardboard box."*

♦ Write about something your child is looking forward to: *"We are going to have game night tonight. What game would you like to play?"*

♦ Write a question about a household dilemma: *"How are we going to keep the cat out of the laundry basket?"*

♦ Write a question about someone in the family: *"Your cousin wants a new picture book for her birthday. Shall we get her another book about cats?"*

♦ Write a question you had in your mind about the wider world such as the neighborhood, the weather, etc.: *"Where can we try to fly the kite if it's windy tomorrow?" "Where shall we go to walk the dog?"*

♦ Write about something that made you happy: *"I was so glad to see the beautiful peaches at the farmers' market. We can make peach jam. Do you remember when we did that last summer?"*

♦ Write about something that made you mad: *"I can't believe the ice cream melted so much before we got home!"* or *"The dog next door woke me up again this morning!"*

♦ Write about something you wondered about: *"I was wondering what was Grandma's favorite toy when she was little."*

♦ Write about something that surprised you: *"I did not expect the water in the sprinkler to be so cold!"*

◆ Write about something you would like to do soon: *"I was thinking we should make a pie together."*

The first prompts you use will vary from family to family, depending on family members, where you live, and activities you like to do. First prompts may stick to familiar household events such as birthdays, Mother's Day, or Dad's sprained wrist because they are relevant to your child. The *Writing Wall* also offers opportunities to promote curiosity about new questions and new topics. As parents, you will note how your own family's topics expand and/or change focus over time. This is family history in the making.

If you are writing on the wall after your child's bedtime, you may have time to write, erase, and write your message again. However, if your child is watching as you write, you can add commentary:

◆ *I'm writing down something that happened today that you will think is funny*
◆ *I saw someone today who knows you.*
◆ *I'm writing about a big surprise I had today.*
◆ *I'm writing about something I got mixed up at the store.*
◆ *I'm writing about something I forgot to get for you!*
◆ *I'm writing about something I forgot to tell you.*

Your Child's Turn

When you first introduce the *Writing Wall* project to your family, it has novelty value. If you are writing your message while your child is watching and reading along, you will usually have no problem with getting a response. Sometimes your child can hardly wait to snatch the chalk or marker from your hand, and you may find that the wall gets quickly filled with back-and-forth sentences. However, for some children, you might need to offer some ideas to write about when it is their turn. Remember you are prompting a child to write something that might follow what you wrote, but it could also be something that starts off a whole new idea. You will soon add new ideas to this list of prompts as you find out what kinds of messages are most likely to encourage a response.

Prompts That Encourage Writing

- *You can write about something that made you mad, or happy.*
- *You can write more about the dogs in the dog park.*
- *You can write about something you were wondering about when you read what I wrote. Did you agree or disagree?*
- *You can write a question for me to answer.*
- *You can write about how you think we should cook the chicken for dinner.*
- *You can write about a new topic.* (And you can have one ready to suggest).

Sentence Starters for Everyone

- *Today I remembered…* "that we are going to be sure to call Ryan to wish him a Happy Birthday."
- *Today I saw…* "that new girl from church. But I can't remember her name."
- *Today I wondered about…* "when we will be able to use the new hiking trail."
- *Today I hoped…* "there would be a birthday card in the mail for me."
- *Today I guessed…* "the rain would be over by noon and we could play outside."
- *Today I liked…* "the fruit you chose for morning snack."
- *Today I decided…* "to look for a longer book about marine mammals."
- *Today I wished…* "that we would have only one more week of cold weather."
- *Today I noticed…* "the finches are finding more seeds on the ground."

Activity 2

The Written Conversation

Activity Level: 7–11+ years

Making the Transition from Wall to Paper

When you write on the *Writing Wall*, it is easy to add to, change, or even erase what has been written. The wall is so visible that it can inspire conversations about when we choose to write, and what we choose to write about. It can lend itself to discussion of what we meant, in the moment of writing, especially when we might want to clarify something that was written. This kind of writing can be wonderfully experimental in nature. Your child may write sentences that are insightful, funny, and delightful, and you may have to immediately preserve them by taking photos of the *Writing Wall* to send to Grandma and Grandpa.

However, what's written on the wall is here today and gone tomorrow, even with dated photos. When you make the transition to paper, you can now preserve sentences in a more permanent way, both as a joy to see in the moment and as documents of progress. With the transition to paper, you will be able to put dates on what is written, and thus be able to keep a historical record of your child's development. Of course, the historical record can be kept by means of the photos on our smartphones but consider the message you are giving to your child about the value of his or her writing when you preserve these samples to show them off as "treasures" in later years.

Purpose

Children are often delighted when we surprise them by doing something that is "usual" in an unexpected way. *The Written Conversation* is a good example of using the unusual to demonstrate how we use writing to communicate. Though the mechanics of writing are still important, the focus here is on communicating immediately, in real time, through writing. The written conversation is a simple activity in which the parent and child take turns "talking" to each other in written form. First, you explain that this is a conversation with "no talking." Both partners get to "say" what they want, but you will take turns writing down what you have to say. With a big piece of paper in front of you, and two pencils (so that you can erase or cross out), you are ready to begin.

Instructions

Set aside time enough to be able to show interest and diminish interruptions. Be prepared with your own starter sentence. Surprise is good; so is humor. You might begin with a comment or a question written on the sheet of paper, and then indicate that your child can follow with a written response. The response may be another question or a comment related to the first item. This turn-taking can last for several responses, and ideally, for four to five turns. You can use talking if your child asks for help with spelling, or you can encourage the use of "best guess" spelling. There may be exchanges in which you do not understand your child's intended meaning. If so, you can write: *"I think you are telling me about Marco's party because I see a word that might be 'birthday.' Is this right?"* If your child finds it difficult to clarify by means of writing, then switch to talking for explanation and further clarification.

Be sure to date your conversations and save them in a book or folder. They often become family treasures. You can encourage your children to share these conversations with an attentive listener, such as a relative or friend (grandparents are ideal), by reading aloud what has been written. This activity can be repeated, set aside, or revisited, as the participants choose.

Keeping quiet while you are each writing can be a real test of your child's ability to concentrate. You might set a goal for the number of turns you will each take before you give up the game. Even if you get only four to five turns, remember that the more children are engaged in conversation (both spoken and written), the more practice they will gain in communicating. They will acquire words, information, and ideas. They are getting good practice in using sentences to respond to questions or ask questions. If the conversation loses momentum and stalls, you can offer a suggestion based on what you know your child is interested in or has been doing lately. Questions are usually helpful to get things going again because they reinforce and show your interest.

Good Ideas to Lead Off With

Look back at the *Writing Wall* activity for ideas to start the conversation. They also work well here. In the case of the *Written Conversation*, the child's response will be immediate, and a series of turns can then take place. You might try some comments that are likely to cause your child to ask a question:

- ♦ *I had a big surprise when I went to the grocery store today.*
- ♦ *Today I saw a lady that you know from school who asked about you.*
- ♦ *You won't believe what really made me mad today.*
- ♦ *I decided what to do about the broken wagon.*

Your child, in turn, might try to arouse your curiosity. Play along. Write down a leading question or two when it is your turn, questions that your child can answer easily.

An Example of Real-Time Comments, Questions, and Answers

This written conversation is about the first week of school, between a mom and her son who is just entering second grade. It took place in a pre-pandemic setting:

> *Mom: I barely remember my 2ⁿᵈ grade teacher but I loved my teacher. Every year I wished for my best friend to be in my class. Are you nervous about 2ⁿᵈ grade?*
>
> *Son: Yes I am nervous. How about you?*
>
> *Mom: No, because you have a great teacher and you know many kids in your class, including 1-2 great friends. Also more friends on the playground.*
>
> *Son: I mean when YOU were in 2ⁿᵈ grade.*
>
> *Mom: Oh, sorry I misunderstood. No, I don't remember being nervous about school. I enjoyed school. Only when I moved schools for 6ᵗʰ grade I was nervous. Starting a new school and in a new neighborhood was hard at first.*
>
> *Son: OMG! I forgot that you moved! Shoot. I don't know what to talk about now.*
>
> *Mom: That's fine. What do you want to talk or ask me?*
>
> *Son: I don't know. My life.*
>
> *Mom: What about your life? You're only 7!*
>
> *Son: I can only roll to my 6 year old memories but there's so much that we did.*
>
> *Mom: Like what? What was your best memory? Or favorite?*
>
> *Son: When we went to the Redwood trail*
>
> *Mom: Really? What about any other trips? But first what did you like about Redwood Trail?*
>
> *Son: The ziplining on a tire*

Benefits for Your Child

The written conversation promotes the following ideas about writing:

- Two-way written communication can take place in real time.
- It's important to think about what your partner in a conversation needs to know.
- Writing partners can use each other's words in their responses.
- Writing partners can use different ways to show that they understand each other's ideas.
- You can surprise your partner.
- You can change the topic if you want to.

Activity 3

Writing Directions for Someone to Follow: A Higher Level of Challenge

Activity Level: 7–11 years

Purpose

The *Writing Wall* and the *Written Conversation* have set the stage for an activity at the next level of challenge: *Writing Directions*. Giving and following directions are important, both in and out of school. When we give directions, we have to think about what the other person needs to know. Children after the age of six or seven are gradually learning how to take the point of view of someone else, and giving directions is a good activity to help them understand how to do that. There are also a number of important cognitive and language operations involved when we write directions:

- Planning and sequencing.
- Determining what the *steps* are, how many steps are required, and in what order.
- Identifying the intended outcome.
- Identifying whatever supplies are needed, if any.

- ◆ Labeling any items involved, as well as labeling the actions that are required.
- ◆ Evaluating the effectiveness of the directions when we review what we wrote.
- ◆ Understanding the perspective of the person who might follow our directions.

The Writing Directions activity involves *rereading* what you have written and editing it for clarity and accuracy. It provides the opportunity to observe how well the directions worked for the other person. Writers can learn as much from their mistakes as from their successes when the other person misunderstands, takes the directions too literally, or gets the point exactly as intended. There is an added benefit when you talk over what worked well, and what needed to be changed. Or when you can share a good laugh over how the directions were interpreted. This activity can be adapted to a wide range of reading, writing, and vocabulary levels for children at the first and second through fifth grade levels in school.

Instructions

Phase One: Parents Go First

The direction-writing activity takes some practice, but it's worth the time. You might need to show a younger child exactly how to do this. Begin with simple directions that include no more than three or four steps. Avoid trying to write directions for tasks that are physically complex. Think about how difficult it is *to tell* someone how to tie a shoe or how to eat with chopsticks when it is much more effective *to show them how*. If the task seems doable but the directions are too complicated at first, you can break the task down into parts, or you can set the task aside until later, or you can choose a different task. This should not be viewed as a failure by any means. There is a great benefit to your child here when you practice converting a task that may involve movement and action into a verbal form, but it is not always possible with all types of physical movements. Even if your child can convert only a small portion of the physical action to a verbal form, this skill has wide application in life, and will always come in handy.

To start off, you need to lead the way and help your child follow the directions at each step. If it turns out that your directions are not clear, this will become obvious immediately. The results can often be very funny. The humor is part of the fun and can lead to effective editing when you and your child work together to repair the directions. Repeat Phase One as many times as you need to get the benefit of repeated experiments in writing directions. Be sure to save a few samples of both the successful and the not-so-successful experiments.

Phase Two: Your Child's Turn, with Parent Helping
Now let your child select the activity. With your help, have them write out the directions that you, the parent, have to follow. If you do exactly as the directions literally tell you, more humor and more re-writing might result. If your child has picked a complicated task that will require many steps, it may help to focus on just one portion of the whole task. This process can show a child how every task has component parts, and you don't usually have to write down the whole thing all at once! This is a good time to introduce the common sequence words that signal steps in order: *first, next, then, finally.*

Phase Three: Everybody on Your Own
Both parents and children should practice the first two tasks at least three or four times. Say, *"Let's talk about what we each did that worked well for each other."* Find examples of the specific words that you each had to choose carefully. Talk about how you tried to imagine in your mind how another person would read your directions. Talk about your mistakes, especially the ones that made you laugh, and describe how you corrected them.

Now you are ready for each of you, parent and child, to select a directions task independently and write your directions on your own. Each partner then has to be able to figure out the intended meaning and outcome of the directions. This is probably the highest level of this particular activity, so focus on being not only patient but also generous with your encouragement.

Take care that the independent direction-giving activity does not lead to frustration on the part of your child, especially if those carefully crafted directions turn out to be unclear. The goal here is collaboration that leads to success, or at least to a mutually appreciated outcome. You might say, "*I think you want me to X. Is that right? What other words could we use to explain that?*" Feedback of this kind is a good way to practice the art of *paraphrase, that is, saying the same idea using different words.*

Example of Writing Directions: Mom and Son (Third Grader)

Son:

1. *Get the eggs from the refrigerator and push and roll them on a clean napkin.*
2. *Put the inside of the egg on a napkin and mash them.*
3. *Then, open the fridge and get mayonnaise and squirt it on the squished eggs.*
4. *Finally put the eggs and mayo in a bowl and mix it.*

Mom:

1. *Take a hard boiled egg which is cooked from the fridge.*
2. *Place it on the clean kitchen counter. Gently press and roll the egg until the shell begins to crack. Once the shell is cracking, roll the egg gently back and forth until the shell comes off. Remove shell completely and then rinse egg under cold water. Set aside to dry. Do the same for the remaining eggs.*
3. *Once the eggs are clean without shells, place in bowl and mash with a fork.*
4. *Put 1 tablespoon of mayo and pinch of salt and mix together.*

Ideas for Direction-Writing (not to exceed four to five steps)
A. In the Kitchen
  - ◆ How to set the table for lunch.
  - ◆ How to unload the glasses from the dishwasher.
  - ◆ How to get milk from the refrigerator and pour it into a glass.
  - ◆ How to make a peanut butter and jelly sandwich.
  - ◆ How to peel a banana or an orange and get it ready to serve up.
  - ◆ How to put the food in a pet's food dish.

B. In Your Child's Room
- ◆ How to put away the pieces of a game or puzzle.
- ◆ How to set up a game with a favorite toy.
- ◆ How to sort and put away the clean (and folded) laundry.
- ◆ How to make the bed.
- ◆ How to tidy a room and put away toys.
- ◆ How to get ready for reading time.
- ◆ How to choose a book to read tonight.

C. Friends and Family
- ◆ How to bring Grandma her coffee.
- ◆ How to get a puppy (or dog) ready for a walk.
- ◆ How to get the kitty into the cat carrier.
- ◆ How to help Dad unload the groceries from the car.
- ◆ How to help a friend choose a book to read.
- ◆ How to set up for a game of checkers (but not directions for *how to play*).

D. Getting from One Spot to Another
- ◆ How to get from the back door to the front door (or vice versa).
- ◆ How to get from the house to the car.
- ◆ How to go into the front part of your school and go to your classroom.
- ◆ How to cross a street safely.
- ◆ How to go into the front door of a familiar building and find a familiar room inside.

What to Watch for in the Writing Directions Activity

You can extend this activity in many ways to increase the benefits. When you follow the directions, exactly as stated, you are *validating your child's efforts* at giving accurate directions. When you note which parts of the directions worked well, and which parts did not work, your child receives a very useful lesson in *self-evaluation*. Finally, there is an important lesson for all writers here: *Keep in mind what your reader needs to know!* What can you assume the reader already knows? What must be stated explicitly in case the reader does not know? These benefits have a direct pay-off in subsequent school writing when your child is able to think about the writing task from the reader's perspective, especially when that **reader** is the teacher.

Benefits for Your Child from Writing Directions

- ◆ Promotes thinking about the reader's perspective and keeping in mind what the reader needs to know.
- ◆ Teaches important ideas about steps in order (sequencing), such as how to organize and prioritize the necessary steps.
- ◆ Gives practice in how to define *what is a step* in a series of steps.
- ◆ Promotes the skill of how to choose words carefully and precisely so that another person can understand what you mean.
- ◆ Builds an awareness of what we need to look for when we read other kinds of directions for other types of tasks.

Activity 4

The Treasure Hunt

Activity Level: 7–10+ years

Purpose

The Treasure Hunt is a variation on writing directions. In this activity, a "treasure" is selected, which can be an actual treasure, such as a new toy, or something that the child wants. Or it can be an item that belongs to the person who gets to be the treasure hunter. For younger children, it is a good idea for the parent to start the activity. Older children (ages eight years and up) who have heard of *scavenger hunts* might be very capable of writing the clues themselves using the model below.

Instructions

The directions for this activity are simple. As with many of our writing activities, the parent goes first to provide a model for how this works. You start by hiding the treasure in an obvious or not-so-obvious place and then write a series of clues for finding it. The clues are written on 3×5 or 4×6 index cards in language tailored to the reading or writing level of your child. You will need five to seven index cards to get started. Write directions that are simple and clear. Each direction should lead to a point where the child will find another index card that offers the next clue. The last index card gives directions to the spot where the treasure is hidden.

For example, you might write the following directions:

- Card 1. *Look under the red pillow on the sofa.*
- Card 2. *Look in the black pot on the shelf by the refrigerator.*
- Card 3. *Go to the upstairs bathroom. Look in the top left-hand drawer by the sink.*
- Card 4. *Look under the mat by the front door.*
- Card 5. *Go to Mom's closet. Look behind her running shoes.*

This activity is easily reversed, with the child taking the lead and writing the clues. You will want to observe what kinds of items your child might consider a "treasure" that **you** will find worth hunting for!

Benefits for Your Child

- You introduce the idea of taking another person's perspective. Most kinds of writing require the writer to adopt the perspective of the reader and to think about what the intended reader needs to know. Activities that involve a role reversal, where your child has to practice taking turns being both reader and writer, make this lesson clear in a very direct way.
- Writing directions offers many opportunities for creativity as well as precision of expression.
- Both direction writing and direction following offer many opportunities for having fun with writing, especially when the directions don't turn out exactly as planned. The clue could be humorous: *"Go to the place where Dad is supposed to put his keys."*
- The Treasure Hunt usually involves moving around in space, either within the house or outside. Planning where to place the clues and how to sequence the clues might cause your child to view your family's indoor and outdoor space in a new way when looking for the best places to hide the clues. The treasure hunt might allow for some fresh perspectives on familiar places.

Activity 5

Bringing in Brothers and Sisters

Activity Level: 6–7 years to 10+ years

Purpose

We have discussed the power of writing within the context of the familiar environment. The At-Home activities allow you to work with your young writer one-on-one to give that child the benefit of your undivided attention as much as possible, at least in the beginning. As you can see, all the recommended activities, such as the *Writing Wall*, are very visible and are meant to be engaging. They also can be expandable to allow for more than only a single writer. If you are just introducing the activities for a new writer in a family with siblings at multiple age levels, chances are there may be an older brother or sister who knows a good deal about writing and may want to offer a bit of advice or help. Or there may be an even *newer* new writer who tags along and would like to try out the activity to see what the fuss is all about. Encourage both older and younger siblings to join in the fun and highlight your family's common bond of shared topics.

Instructions for Mixed Ages

You can adapt the activities for other siblings depending on their ages and interests. Older siblings may enjoy being the experts here and showing off their own growing skills in writing by helping their younger brothers and sisters. The younger siblings may just want to enter the community of writers at whatever level is comfortable. For example, an older sister might feel quite at home sharing a written conversation, while a younger child may be quite happy just to watch the conversation unfold, turn by turn. With the Treasure Hunt, an older brother or sister could conspire with the young writer to select the treasure and see if they can outwit the parent who tries to find it. *The Family Response Journal* (Activity 6) and *Paired/Shared Writing* (Activity 7) are both well-geared to families with children of mixed ages.

What to Watch For

You might be fortunate to see some interesting dynamics here between siblings when you have them engage in the Treasure

Hunt. On the positive side, there may be some constructive cooperation as children of different ages join in an unexpected kind of communication, as they would in a written conversation, or as they engage with each other to carry out the tasks in the direction writing activities. Children can draw upon their own background with family members to come up with clues or solve them to find the treasure in the Treasure Hunt.

On the other hand, if the dynamic exposes any friction between children, especially if the older child becomes bossy or too critical, it's time to go back to the purpose of the activity and stress the communication aspects of the task. You can look for ways to make it easier for the younger child to solve the clues with well-placed hints, and you can acknowledge how much older children are benefiting from their added practice in writing with their intended reader in mind.

Benefits for Your Child

The benefits for all involved are similar to the benefits of both the *Written Conversation* and *Written Directions*:

- ◆ Development of the writer's understanding of the intended reader's perspective.
- ◆ Awareness of the developmental nature of writing, and appreciation for the skills that each partner is learning.
- ◆ Critical thinking in reading and writing with a focus on sequencing.
- ◆ Opportunities for creativity, humor, and fun with writing.
- ◆ Opportunities to appreciate the unique contributions of family members of all ages.

Activity 6

The Family Response Journal

Activity Level: 6–7 years to 10+ years

Purpose

Once your young writer becomes skilled at the *Written Conversation* activity, or the adaptations of the Treasure Hunt activity, you are ready to try the *Family Response Journal*. This is a writing activity that may last for three weeks, or it may last for three years, or longer. Keeping a journal has always been a way to document one's thoughts and experiences in a more permanent form, similar to a diary. Children are often asked to keep journals for school assignments, such as documenting the steps in a science project, or writing down their thoughts when reading an assigned book. The *Family Response Journal* is much more informal than a school journal, but the idea of it is just as important. As a family activity, it is a log in which ongoing family activities are recorded. Because all family members can record the events and experiences as they happen, your journal will document family history written by everyone in the family and it may become a much-treasured keepsake.

Families who keep response journals often have a favorite entry that they return to again and again. Journals that stick around for a while often remind children of what they thought and how they wrote when they were "little." One family has a journal in which their nine-year-old son recorded that he was being rushed to the hospital in an ambulance with a bacterial infection from swimming in the bay. He kept writing all the way to the hospital, where he finally turned the journal over to his mother with the comment: *"You do it, Mom. I am too sick to write!"* Even when there was a lot going on, it was important to this family to maintain the journal, and the mom continued to write down the hospital experience! Bradley frequently shared this dramatic event, well recorded in the journal, as it was part of his "life story."

This particular record is priceless. But perhaps most significant, this event showed that the journal was important to everyone in that family, adults and children alike. Through the journal, families often discover that being a writer is important to everyone, no matter what age. And parents can anticipate that children who feel comfortable with At-Home writing are more likely to feel comfortable with many forms of writing, both at home and at school.

Instructions

The *Family Response Journal* builds upon the *Written Conversation*, except that it involves all the family members, including those brothers and sisters who may have already been exploring the previously suggested activities. You will need a standard notebook or binder with a firm cover, lined paper, and plenty of pages. The lines on the pages should be wide-ruled or could even have a dotted line between the solid lines that show the younger child how to place the short and tall letters (this type of paper is referred to as "primary school paper" and is very helpful to the beginning writer). Your child can personalize the binder cover with art.

The journal is begun by the parent, who dates the first page and writes a thought or observation (for ideas, see also the suggestions for the *Writing Wall*). You can use the journal to write memories that may have been triggered by something that happened that day. Or you can write about something you "wondered" about. In a busy household, parents may think about a lot of things *that they don't get a chance to say*. Think about the times you felt proud of a child's achievement or all the examples of perseverance that went unremarked at the time but could now be written down. You can bring in a vocabulary word from a recent book or add a further response to a question that was asked and only hastily answered. Observations about figurative language expressions or common sayings can be fruitful.

Following the opening comment, any family member can respond, and when you do, be sure to date each entry. There are usually no rules as to how often the journal must be used or how long each entry should be. If there are to be rules, they should be agreed upon by the journal contributors. The most important rule is: **Don't lose the journal**. Designate a place for it and make it a requirement that it must be returned to its place where it can be removed again for writing.

Some parents enjoy coming up with little-known facts about themselves, especially when the distant past seems very distant to their children! The journal can be a place for parents to write down their own childhood memories that others in the family might not necessarily know about. Don't be hesitant about sharing memories. Those of us who have lost our parents and grandparents over time often comment that we wished we had asked them more questions about their lives when they were around to answer! Examples of starter thoughts can be in the form of questions, with the journal offering a place where you can answer those questions. Or you can offer comments that might prompt a question from a family member.

- *Have I ever told you about the stray dog that followed me home when I was seven?*
- *Have I ever told you about the time the teacher got mad at me in first grade because I couldn't tie my shoes?*
- *Do you want to know why I used to hate having my hair cut?*
- *Today I saw someone who reminded me of my seventh-grade science teacher. She was the one who got me started on collecting small shiny rocks with a suggestion that surprised me.*
- *When I first got my new glasses in sixth grade, there were so many things I had to get used to.*

If the *Family Response Journal* catches on, you can experiment with many forms of starter thoughts that are adapted to the interests of your own family. The joy of the journal is its flexibility and its adaptability. The journal may be much in demand when there is a lot going on, or it may be set aside from time to time. It can be a place to record special insights or experiences. It can be a record of both good times and bad. It is a place to share reflections, appreciations, and special requests. If there is an artist in the family, illustrations can be added. Even visiting guests and grandparents can be invited to contribute.

What to Watch For

Your family will develop your own journal topics. Here are some you might explore:

- Best/most interesting thing that happened this week.
- Surprise of the week.
- Person of the week.
- Biggest problem of the week, and how it was solved (or not).
- Funniest moment of the week.
- Word of the week.
- Achievement of the week.
- Funniest pet trick of the week.

Keeping It Going

Family trips or vacations can be good opportunities for the *Family Response Journal*. If there are multiple family members on a trip, everyone can take turns to be responsible for journaling the day's events. Some amount of encouragement may be needed, given that trips are often busy, and the number of details that can be recorded may seem overwhelming to a young writer. You can help by narrowing the focus of what could be selected from the many details and events of the trip. You could focus mainly on the food. You could describe the weather. You could record the moments of wonder when you all see something you have never seen before (Yellowstone National Park comes to mind!).

In addition to the kind of trip we connect with travel, a "trip" can include a visit to a particular playground or a visit to the dog park. For most young children, any new experience can become a topic for the journal. The journal can be an ongoing place for sharing creative ideas, such as what to plant in the garden or what to make for dinner. It can be a way to explore how we can use our imaginations in even the most "ordinary" family activities.

Another way to keep the journal going is simply to keep it lying around in plain sight. This is especially effective if there are visits from appreciative family members such as grandparents, aunts, and uncles. Children are often eager to spontaneously share the contents of the journal, and grandmas and grandpas are ideal readers and contributors. Younger children can get things moving if given a "word of the day" so that the family member can be challenged to use the word in a journal entry. Families who keep response journals often have a favorite entry that they return to again and again. As noted, journals that stick around for a while can remind children of what they thought and how they wrote when they were little.

Benefits for Your Child

Children using a *Family Response Journal* can:

- ♦ Learn the social benefits of written communication.
- ♦ Appreciate family experiences from multiple different perspectives.

- ♦ Record and preserve family history and memories.
- ♦ Learn to value different points of view and different ways in which family history is remembered.

Activity 7

Paired/Shared Writing

Activity Level: 7–10+ years

Purpose

Paired/shared writing is writing that can be done simultaneously, with you and your child sitting side by side, or the two of you can do it separately and then later exchange what you have written. Parent and child both agree upon a single topic, and each will write a few sentences about it. There is often a good deal of humor in comparing the two perspectives, and you are sure to gain some good insights into how your child views the world. From your viewpoint as a parent, here is an opportunity to share important aspects of your own history and life experiences that don't necessarily emerge in the course of daily conversations.

Instructions

For this activity, keep in mind the issue of the imbalance between what a parent can write, and what your child might write. You as the parent have more memories and background to draw upon, so you are likely to have a good deal more to write, especially if you really like the topic. This is not a competition to see who can write the most, but you will want to be sensitive to the fact that your child may feel you have the advantage in terms of amount, types of details, vocabulary, and so on. This is not to say you should shorten or censor what you write. *Being yourself is the best model you can provide.* Consider the examples in the list of possible topics, below.

Example Paired/Shared Topics

- ♦ Story of my day: best/worst things about my day.
- ♦ A valued possession or treasure: what it is and why it is valued.

- ◆ Best memory of Thanksgiving, July 4, or other family event.
- ◆ Best unusual pet I think we should have in our household.
- ◆ Things that are a waste of money.
- ◆ An experiment I'd like to try.
- ◆ Best rule I have ever heard.
- ◆ My favorite word and why I like it.
- ◆ If I could have a pet (iguana, squirrel, hawk), I would…
- ◆ If I could have my own (tractor, rocket, glider), I would…
- ◆ Would you rather eat breakfast, lunch, or dinner foods all day? Why?
- ◆ Write about the best gift you ever got. Explain what it is and the reasons why.
- ◆ Write about the best gift you ever gave. Explain what it is and the reasons why.
- ◆ What do you do when you feel sad?
- ◆ Pretend there is no school tomorrow. What could we do instead?
- ◆ Pretend you could teach the class at school. What would you teach and how would you teach it?
- ◆ If you could trade places with someone for a day, who would you trade with? What would you do?
- ◆ If you could be an animal, what animal would you be? Why?

What to Watch For

Writing activities that involve shared perspectives often reveal differing interpretations of the topic itself. Think of all the possible meanings of the word "gift" in the "best gift" topic. Gifts can be both concrete and abstract, things that we unwrap or things that we experience. This activity offers good possibilities for discussion following the writing and may prompt some "pre-writing" definitions of terms.

Benefits for Your Child

- ◆ Appreciating the different perspectives of people we know well.

- ◆ Seeing how people of different ages interpret questions or topics in different ways.
- ◆ Using post-writing opportunities to question and discuss.
- ◆ Answering unexpected questions that may emerge for either parent or child.

An Example of a Paired/Shared Topic: *Best Gift Ever*

Dad's paragraph.

The best gift ever from when I was a child was on my 9th birthday. At that time, one of the earliest versions of a video game player was the Atari. You would put a rectangular shaped tape into the player and had joysticks to play the game. The most favorite game was Pac-Man. I had wished for this game for so long that I was nervous about opening my present from my parents. While they sang the birthday song to me, I saw the wrapped present which was next to the couch and it was one big rectangular box with 2 small rectangular boxes on top. Even though I thought it was the game I still wasn't sure and it made me even more eager to open it (I couldn't wait for the song to be over so I could). Finally the song was done and I opened it. It was the Atari game with TWO cartridges...Pac-Man and basketball! I was so excited and happy and relieved. I couldn't wait to play it!

Daughter's paragraph (second grader).

Best Gift Ever!

The best gift ever I had was my cookbook from Santa Claus. It had 57 recipes in it and one of them was cinnimom sugar another was french toast, and one more was crepes. I really thanked Santa Claus. It was the BEST GIFT EVER!

Reflections on Chapter 3: How At-Home Writing Shapes an Understanding of the Writing Process

The primary goal of ***There's a Writer in Our House!*** is to introduce young learners to writing through activities that promote comfort and confidence with the writing process. These activities are designed to allow children to explore how writing works.

The explicit benefits to the child have been noted following each activity. There is an additional underlying outcome that may be less obvious but that has important educational and intellectual benefits. When young writers are first watching adults write during these shared activities, they may imagine that there is an inner "dictation machine" that produces the words that the adults simply write down. It may seem that their sentences are already fully formed in the mind, and only need to be copied on paper or on the computer as the mind dictates them. But gradually an important insight will emerge. *Writing is a thinking process* and writers don't always know what they know before they write about something. For both new writers and experienced writers, *writing can help you find out what you know.*

In the course of doing the activities, you may comment aloud about an insight or an idea that came to you as a parent while you were writing about one of the prompts. This kind of comment reveals how active your mind can be while you are writing, and it gives your child a good insight into *how we think **while** we write.* You are helping your child understand that writing is a thinking process that everyone can participate in, in different ways.

The value of writing extends to parents as well. When you interact with your child through the writing activities, you become conscious of the wealth of topics that can be explored through family writing. You may be amazed at the unexpected bounty of writing opportunities that exist in your home, as you view home life through the *lens of the writer.* You may find that you yourself increasingly view your own world through a writer's lens, as you listen to your own "inner writer." You may find yourself more willing to experiment, along with your child. Both parents and children enjoy multiple benefits from writing together.

4

The Young Writer's Assets

Background Knowledge, Vocabulary, and Thinking Skills

Activity Level: 6–7+ years

EASY ACCESS NOTES FOR CHAPTER 4: WHAT YOU WILL LEARN

- The Young Writer's Assets: Background Knowledge, Vocabulary, Thinking Skills.
- How We Can Build on the Foundation of Spoken Language.
- What is Background Knowledge and Why Is it Important?
- How Vocabulary Is an Important Asset.
- Vocabulary-Centered Activities to Expand Vocabulary.
- How We Connect Vocabulary Words to Background Knowledge in Long-term Memory.
- Thinking Like a Writer: Specific Thinking Skills That are Promoted by Writing.
- Ways to Reinforce the Young Writer's Assets: Functional Writing, the *Quick-Write*.
- Experimenting with Different Forms of Writing: Wordless Picture Books.

DOI: 10.4324/9781003452683-6

Developing Learning Assets

Parents are used to thinking about assets, whether they are material assets such as a house or a car, a skill set that allows you to have a job and care for your family, or a talent that gives you pleasure and helps you make a contribution to others. Young children are continually developing important *learning assets*, both as a result of being in school and as a result of your efforts at home. The home-centered writing activities introduced in Chapter 3 have emphasized writing in a familiar context based on the experiences and ideas that your child already understands and can share by writing about them. We know that children can engage better when there is a solid link between the writing activity and *what they know*. We also know that parents can help avoid any anxiety that might develop when tackling something that *looks* as complicated as writing. The activities have all been designed to *build and expand* the essential assets your child needs to become a writer. Chapter 4 will focus on how *you* can help build and expand these assets most effectively.

The Foundation of Spoken Language

Spoken language comes before written language. To best understand the foundation for written language, we briefly review how young children first learn spoken language. When parents talk to their young child, the context is rich in body language and the surroundings are usually familiar. The words you use refer to things that are "right there," such as the person speaking or the child listening. Parents seem programmed to make utterances to the baby that contain the actual words we use, along with the sounds of comforting, cooing, and even mimicking the sounds that the baby is making.

As you expand upon the communication function of language, you automatically include many of the signals that highlight your intended meaning. You hand your child a cup of milk or juice. At the same time, you are looking at the cup, moving the cup toward her hands, and speaking simple words: *"Here's your milk, Janie. Hold on to it so it doesn't spill."* As she gets older, you may be in the market, with Janie pushing the "little kid" shopping cart, right behind yours. You stop at the bin of potatoes, and you say, *"Let's pick out some potatoes to cook for dinner."* She participates in choosing the potatoes and putting them in the little cart. The object is clear, the gesture is clear, and the meaning of what you said is clear. Your child is on the way to becoming a successful language user, and you are there to witness and smile at how well she is catching on.

Background Knowledge, Vocabulary, and Thinking Skills

With spoken language as the foundation, children are ready to draw upon a set of specific assets when they begin to write. These assets include *background knowledge, general vocabulary, school vocabulary*, and *thinking skills*. We will discuss each of these assets in turn. Using the framework of knowledge, vocabulary, and thinking, parents will see many ways to foster and promote these asset areas systematically, at home. We do this through activities that are designed to help children begin to *see themselves as writers*. You will find ideas here that you have already thought about. Now, as you think about these ideas as *a writer's assets,* you will promote them more purposefully when you supply the *labels* that are easily understood by children. As these assets grow, children learn to talk like writers and think like writers, which is in itself a remarkable step of growth.

When you transition to writing in a more formal way, you will see similarities to what your child may be doing in school, but you will be able to take advantage of the language you can use at home. Because it is familiar, it may be more easily understood by your child. When language is written down, you now have words and sentences you can look at, point to, and talk about. You can consider the options and the possibilities of word choice and sentences. For example, you might ask, *"What would be a good word to describe the wagon?"* or *"What is another sentence you could use here to tell about the rainstorm?"* You can think about what words might make us laugh or might create a picture in the mind. You can discuss whether a specific sentence should go at the beginning, in the middle, or at the end. You can think about what details to add to make the sentences clearer and more interesting.

Every writer needs these resources. The opening activities in Chapter 3 have shown that writing is always *about something*. Children are discovering that all writers depend upon what they already know, and they are also learning that *their background knowledge can be increased in many ways*. Parents can help children add to their background through experiences that form a foundation for the topics they might write about. Background knowledge always involves the vocabulary words that we use for sharing ideas and information about topics. In the same way, school vocabulary is used to label the many ways in which we organize and store knowledge. And finally, writing promotes thinking skills in important ways. Writers have to consider which ideas to write about, and then decide how best to organize and express those ideas. These writing assets don't just happen accidentally. *They can be identified and systematically promoted over time.* They are resources that can be updated and added to, as children encounter new tasks, new topics, and new purposes for writing.

The Young Writer's Assets

Background Knowledge: What It Is and Why It Is Important

So far, we have emphasized that writing activities located in the familiar context of the home can promote confidence and comfort with writing because children are writing about what they already know. We have used their At-Home knowledge as a good starting point for many of the activities. As children begin formal schooling, background knowledge increases. They are systematically exposed to enormous amounts of new information and new ideas on a daily basis. School learning involves the places, persons, and events that they will be expected to know about as educated students. They learn by listening, reading, and discussing, and by participating in a variety of school instructional activities, including homework. They learn from activities such as sports, field trips, and interest groups. They learn from each other.

Learning at home can have similar advantages. Children can learn much from family events and outings. They can learn from child-oriented TV programs, videos, and other electronic media. They may be able to travel to places that are new to them. And they can learn from books. When they are introduced to books as new readers, they find that books are always *about something*. They may attach to a favorite book about a curious monkey, a pet dog, a very hungry caterpillar, or an adventure into the forest. And while they are experiencing the joy of a good story, they are also acquiring new information that *builds background knowledge*.

The foundation of information that children are building on a daily basis plays a major role in all of learning. Because of its critical importance, parents will want to promote its development. Young learners are storing data that helps them understand how the world works. They are beginning to make important *connections across areas of knowledge* and to see relationships. In this way, for example, they can think about both whales and prairie dogs, and understand how they are alike and how they are different: both are mammals and both feed their young with milk. Baby whales can even drink their milk underwater! Do you know how they do that? (See **Bibliography** at the end of this chapter.)

Young writers use background knowledge to explain, describe, connect, examine, question, and support. For this reason, we expose children, as much as we are able, to the kinds of experiences that build background to make the child's resources as strong as possible. Programs for children such as those at museums and libraries are designed to promote curiosity and knowledge through hands-on and direct learning. Other options include online programs and videos that can expose children to new learning in many ways. With these experiences, they can have a lot to say when they write and many connections to make.

Vocabulary: What It Is and Why It Is Important

With new background knowledge comes new vocabulary. Vocabulary development is a critical part of every child's education, both formal and informal. A well-rounded vocabulary promotes the ability to think clearly, to learn effectively, and to communicate well. Parents can take advantage of the vocabulary opportunities that are already available at home to make significant contributions to vocabulary development. The ongoing daily activities of the family can easily become naturally occurring opportunities for focusing on words. For example, experiences at home often include listening to Mom or Dad read aloud from a good book and then discussing what it was about, a good way to add to a child's growing vocabulary. Words can be discussed in the car, at the table during meals, or at any moment during family events. Parents can take the lead in a discussion of the "good words" that come up, which may be words that are new to your child, or words that are already connected to the activities you are doing.

In fact, you have been doing vocabulary development all along, from the first moments children are learning to talk and listen. You have provided labels for familiar items, events, and operations in the child's environment: *juice*; *milk*; *doggie*; *slide down here*; *come to Mommy*; *let's get in the car now*; *it's raining*. As they become more fluent with language and are exposed to new experiences, you continue to label things and activities in their environment. Parents do this labeling almost without thinking about it because it makes communication flow more easily and clearly. It helps everyone understand what we are all talking about.

Word Labels and Word Boundaries

The process of labeling has another important function that we may not even notice right away: the name (label) of an object has boundaries that are more specific than the boundaries of some other kinds of words. Think about how a child will hear it when we give a label to a food such as an apple: /apple/. They can hear that word as a stand-alone item and can understand what it is referring to. Whereas when we refer to actions or events, the child may hear such sounds as *gonna*, *hafto*, *c'mon*, or *will'ya*. These forms of words generally occur in conversation and are heard as part of the flow of the sentence. The individual words get sorted out later when the child sees them in print or learns how to read and spell the words one at a time, but the early labeling provides the child's first exposure to the idea of word boundaries. This is a key understanding for the young writer.

This important labeling process continues as your child enters pre-school and elementary school, or as new events happen to the family. When you label the parts of shared experiences, you help your child understand what to pay attention to in the busy surroundings. You are adding to the tools that your child needs in order to think about the experiences and store them in memory. Unlabeled experiences fade quickly from memory, but *well-labeled experiences are more likely to endure.*

Vocabulary-Centered Activities

There are many benefits to this focus on vocabulary-centered activities. First, you are teaching your child that words are both interesting and important. When you show an interest in words of all sorts, your child will learn that words are worthy of attention. The At-Home writing activities have set the stage to model the idea that words are important, with such comments as *"That's a really good word that Dad just used about the baseball bat." "I am thinking of a really good word for what happened to your shoe." "I am thinking of the words we could use to tell about how the rainbow looked."*

When you highlight words in this way, it is a good idea to follow with a question about the word's meaning: *"Do you know what that word means?"* It is best not to assume that children know the meanings of all the words *they can say.* As you listen to the response, you have the opportunity to correct any misconceptions about how to use the word in question. You can give examples of where that word will or won't fit. This can be especially true for words that have multiple meanings. You can talk about how the pitcher had a *lucky break* when the batter dropped the bat, but that's a different *break* than when that pitcher had to be careful so he would not fall and *break his arm.* You can also throw in the idea that the baseball *pitcher* (a person who *pitches*) is not the same *pitcher* (a *container*) we use to serve the lemonade!

Vocabulary activities give your child many opportunities to practice the important skill of expressing word meaning. Your child might say, *"I know what it means but I just can't explain it."* This is a good chance for you to provide a synonym or to model how and when to use the word. It is also an opportunity to consult the dictionary or computer for an accurate and well-worded definition. In addition, these activities give you a chance to practice how we think about context and how it determines a word's meaning since the words we choose to use often depend upon the context. This is particularly true for figurative language. When we describe something as *cool*, the meaning of the word "cool" is different depending on whether we are in the swimming pool or the toy store.

Finally, vocabulary development is a critical skill in school learning. Children are exposed to hundreds of new words each year as a part of school learning. Many of these words are important terms for the operations they are learning in math and science, such as *process*, *amount*, or *comparison*. Other words apply to how we think about books, such as *character*, *plot*, or *conflict*. As they learn these words, each new word becomes yet another tool they can use for thinking right now, and for connecting to additional words in the future.

Highlighting Specific Words

Signs All Around. Here are some ways to show children how to focus on specific words in specific places. If you are driving somewhere in the car on the freeway, and you pass a sign marked EXIT, you can point to other places where you might see that word, such as in a theater or airplane. You can talk about the opposite of *Exit: Enter.* You can discuss why exits are important, and why we should know where they are. You could ask your child about other words connected with *Exit*, such as freeway names and numbers, or important location names.

If the *Exit/Enter* activity catches on, you can focus on the familiar STOP signs along the roads and streets. Ask what is the opposite of STOP, and you will get START or GO. You might then discuss whether there are signs that say START, and if there were, what would that mean? Road signs are among the many examples of specific words in the familiar environment that might prompt word games while you are driving, riding a bus, or out for a walk and begin a long family tradition of playing with words.

Making Lists. Most families are likely to have grocery lists, to-do lists, or wishlists. Listing can emphasize how we organize the world into *categories* and the way lists help us remember words. If there is a musician in the family, it will be easy to make a list of musical instruments, which can be subdivided into string, percussion, and wind instruments. Depending on where you live, you can make lists of different kinds of toys you would take to the beach, or items to take on a hike. You could list toys for big kids and toys for little kids and see where there is overlap.

Lists for Listing. Here are some starting ideas for listing, and you will add more as you and your children think of them. Children's lists can be personal, or something to share with your family as a collaborative activity. Children can exercise their good thinking skills when they have to defend why something does, or does not, belong on a specific list.

- Items around the house, such as tools, toys, or snack foods.
- Words about something that is scary.
- Words that tell something is big (or small).
- Words that tell something is very negative, or very positive.
- Words just for pets and what they do.
- An unusual word I learned and how to use it.
- Things I can do alone.
- Things we can do together.
- Items of clothing that have a special function, such as wetsuits for the ocean, ski jackets, or running shoes.

Using At-Home Activities to Expand Vocabulary

Family activities serve to enlarge children's general vocabularies by adding new words and examining the many words that have more than one meaning. As you might well imagine, the kitchen is a wonderful place for paying attention to words. Think of all the specialized vocabulary for cooking: verbs such as *chop*, *peel*, *boil*, *sift*, *stir*, and *mix*, or nouns such as *ingredients*, *plate*, *pan*, and *sauce*. Many common words have multiple meanings, and children can experiment with the different contexts the word might be found in. When baking cookies, you might *sift* the flour, or if you were a detective, you might *sift* through clues to find out who kidnapped the neighbor's dog. To *chop* an onion suggests an entirely different meaning for the word than when the recipe calls for baking a *lamb chop*. The possibilities are endless, and children can be easily encouraged to add to the collections.

Paying attention to words in this way is likely to inspire your child to be curious about word meaning, and to feel comfortable in asking questions about words. You promote vocabulary development when you encourage your children to try out the new words and give them positive recognition for the new words they have added. Everyone can celebrate when the new words show up on the *Writing Wall* or in the *Written Conversations* (Chapter 3).

Vocabulary Lists for Specific Interest Areas, Such as Sports

Most activities that people engage in require specific words that name the objects or processes for that activity. A good example is sports. Children who follow sports or who play sports can be encouraged to make lists of terms that are specific to their favorite sport. They can develop various ways to categorize these lists:

- ◆ Sports equipment.
- ◆ Team names.
- ◆ Positions on the team.
- ◆ Specific "plays" or "moves" that lead to a good outcome.
- ◆ All the ways to say that your team won.
- ◆ All the ways to say that your team lost.
- ◆ Special sports places.

Using these lists, your child can think of words that are used only in a single sport versus words that are common to many sports. For example, lots of sports require a *ball*, but only ice hockey uses a *puck*. These word lists also provide a good opportunity to explore sports words that can have more than one meaning. Examples might include *quarter* (a period in a football game, a fraction, a coin worth 25 cents); *ball* (a round object hit with a paddle over a ping pong net; a baseball thrown but not hit by the batter, unless it's a fly ball; a fancy dance); and *net* (the meshed fabric that is stretched across the tennis court, pickle ball court, or ping pong table; a device to catch fish; a three-sided structure used to trap the ball in soccer).

If your family still has the *Writing Wall* around, it is a great place to display the family's favorite (or longest) lists. Many *Writing Walls* transition to becoming *Word Walls*. Good writers are famous for keeping lists of useful words as well as lists of promising ideas. Your child might just develop a list habit that will come in handy for later schooling when the teacher has the students make "brainstorming" lists before writing about a topic.

Words for School: How to Reinforce School Vocabulary

Once your child is in school, you will receive abundant examples of school words on the worksheets and homework instructions that are part of schoolwork. Many school words are necessary for following directions and getting assignments done. These words are often the labels for school-related concepts and academic operations. Additionally, school words are used to signal important logical relationships, such as cause/effect, time order, sequences and processes, comparisons, and categorizing. You can discuss these words with your child, as appropriate, and incorporate the words into ongoing conversations at home. For example, you can note ways we use comparisons to understand something: *"The tree was as tall as our house." "The hiker was panting like a dog on a hot day." "Ricardo can jump way higher than Jose because he has longer legs than Jose."*

You can watch for the key words for following directions or for sequential order, such as *first*, *next*, *then*, and *finally*. You can also note when these words occur in non-school contexts so that your child develops an understanding of how word meaning can be flexible and dependent on the context where it is used. Thus, we would say: "*Neil Armstrong was the **first** man to set foot on the moon. Sally Ride was the **first** woman to go into space.*" We would also say: "*When you want to make an omelet, **first** you have to break the eggs.*"

Parents can actively reinforce word meaning when they bring these school words into home discussions and conversations. In doing so, you can enhance your child's ability to effectively use these words in school learning and school writing. Words that are well understood are more likely to show up in your child's written language. Words that are incompletely understood can be monitored for further clarification. All these home-based processes allow parents to support and collaborate with the learning that is happening at school.

Connecting Vocabulary Words and Background Knowledge

You will begin to notice how many of these "vocabulary words" are the names of important ideas, concepts, and processes that are the foundation of general knowledge and school learning. As children are exposed to the information in their science, history, math, and literature classes, they will need increasingly complex words for complex ideas. While not all parents may feel equipped to *teach* these concepts (this is, after all, why we value well-trained teachers), you as parents can be *active partners in learning*. You have now seen many ways to encourage your child to share new information from school. When this sharing takes place in a non-critical and accepting environment, *it makes learning more permanent.*

School-age children are constantly in the process of consolidating knowledge. Often, they may not feel competent to discuss what they have learned in school, especially if they do not yet completely understand it themselves. Kid-friendly prompts, such as *"Word of the Day"* might lead to the kind of sharing that helps your child monitor how well he or she understood the message at school. As a reminder to parents, in our busy family interactions, we may find that we *assume* that children understand the meanings of words that are commonly used, even words they themselves are using. It is best to not take that understanding for granted, given the number of new words that they are encountering. It is always appropriate, in a kind and interested way, to inquire: *"Tell me what you think that word means."*

Helpful Scripts for Parents. It is rarely effective to greet your child with that time-honored question about the school day: *"What did you learn in school today?"* We all know too well that the answer is often, *"Nothing."* The *Writing Wall* can serve a new purpose here. It can become a *Word Wall* where you can record new school vocabulary items. Children can write something they have learned using the new words. The word lists are a way to remind children about how much they are learning. Then when a new topic comes up in school learning, it is easy to say,

- ◆ *"Let's see how we can connect this new word to what you already have learned about our community (or animal behavior or unusual insects)."*
- ◆ *"What words do you already know that can connect to this new information about the space flight (or famous historical landmarks, or endangered sea turtles)?"*
- ◆ *"Remember when you learned about how plants grow from seeds? What new words did we learn then?"*
- ◆ *"Where should we look to find more information about **that**?"*

When parents help focus the whole family's attention on vocabulary, there are benefits to reading as well as to writing. Each new word in a child's vocabulary offers a potential connection to other words, to experiences, and to new ideas. Children can gain new power and confidence from the ability to express their unique ideas and thoughts with well-chosen and well-understood words. The better you know a word, and the more you know about it, the faster you read it. Thus, writing benefits reading, and reading benefits writing. Everybody wins!

The Young Writer's Assets

Thinking Like a Writer: Skills to Watch For

No matter what topic you write about, writing is a *decision-making* process. It begins with the first decision: *deciding what to write about*. After you decide on your topic, you have to think about what you already know about the topic. Then you have to decide what you want to say and how you might say it. These decisions might be made before you start when you are just planning, but many decisions also emerge *as you begin to think about* your topic. Many writing experts argue that *you don't know what you think about something until you write about it*.

We engage many important thinking skills when we write, and parents can use their own observational skills to watch for and label these skills when they are observed:

- ◆ *Order*: What do we tell first, next, and then after that?
- ◆ *Priority*: What idea is so important that we must tell it first, and how do we circle back to it for emphasis in our conclusion?
- ◆ *Perspective*: How will we communicate to the reader how we view the topic?
- ◆ *Intended audience*: What does our reader need to know that we must be sure to explain?
- ◆ *Details*: How many supporting details are needed to make our topic clear?
- ◆ Could we make a *comparison* between our topic (or event or action) and something else to help our reader understand it even better?
- ◆ Where could we include some good *examples* to help explain our idea?
- ◆ What *synonyms* or *definitions* do we need for an important term?
- ◆ Where could we use *humor or exaggeration*?
- ◆ If it is a complicated idea or topic, will we need to state it in more than one way by using *paraphrase*?
- ◆ How do we bring all the ideas together at the end in a *conclusion*, so that our reader will understand *what we think and why it matters*?

Introducing the Editing Process

As the above list shows, At-Home writing involves special kinds of thinking before writing and during writing. There is another kind of thinking that happens *after writing* when we might be able to practice *reflecting and editing*. Young writers can learn a great deal about their own thinking through the process of editing when they can look back at what they have written. At-Home writing does not have the same demands as school writing, where the work is judged by the teacher or by a peer in "peer editing," and may receive comments or a grade. This kind of school writing may often be done under the pressures of time or anxiety.

We will take a closer look at editing in Chapter 5. However, this important process can be woven into the At-Home writing activities early on. To begin, here are some simple questions young writers can ask, either right after writing or the next day, when they reread the sentences they have written:

- ♦ What parts seem most clear to me?
- ♦ What words or sentences might I want to change to make them better or clearer?
- ♦ Did I choose the best words for my topic? Which words work especially well?
- ♦ What questions might my reader want to ask about what I wrote?

Editing works best when the young writer understands that *this is part of the whole process*. It's not about "mistakes" but rather about what we are learning about writing by *doing writing*. Parents can support the process by commenting on what you especially noticed, and what changes you are seeing in your child's efforts. Always remember to keep the emphasis on the positive and use any labels that may be appropriate for specific aspects that you noticed in the writing, such as effective word choices or good logical ordering of the ideas. That way, you can help your child develop a positive mindset about this worthwhile process and allay any anxiety that might be associated with editing when it is required at school.

Three Targeted Ways to Reinforce *The Young Writer's Assets*

A. Exploring Practical Purposes for Writing

We can often get children engaged when their writing has a genuine purpose. Children are wonderfully practical. They like to see outcomes and results. And it is a good way to combine early reading and writing practice. Functional writing can be included in a wide variety of situations at home. It can make children feel a part of the operation of the household when they help carry out tasks that involve writing. Such tasks often involve a *recipient*, who can be someone who will read and respond. Best of all, every time children write to communicate, we will see significant language and cognitive development as a result.

A good starting example of functional writing is the thank-you note. Grandparents, aunts and uncles, and family friends are excellent recipients in this regard. In a thank-you note, your child might offer details about how she or he used the gift, or where the gift is kept. He can note how he felt about the gift, and how the gift adds to a collection of other treasures. In today's world of electronic devices, children are familiar with the technology to send emails or texts to family and friends. They may have begun the use of simple narratives to update everyone on important occasions and events. If possible, let the receiver know about your At-Home writing projects. That way, you may be able to prompt an encouraging response to what the child writes. Everybody wins.

B. Promoting Functional Writing with the *Writing Center*

Functional writing often catches on when you are able to establish a *Writing Center* where it can happen. This can be a designated spot where children have easy access to writing materials, and where they can even take responsibility for monitoring and organizing the supplies. Consider this a good investment in practical management skills. It can be a model for collaboration and creativity if the center is also used by Mom and Dad, or sisters and brothers. Many families have a center for a family computer, but for our young writers, this writing center should be equipped with the basics: *pencils*, *notepads*, and *paper*. The computer can be added as needed.

Functional Writing Ideas to Start With

- ◆ The shopping list for Mom or Dad, with details to describe one or two items.
- ◆ The to-do list with commentary for the week or for the weekend. Details can be added to explain why the task is important or necessary.
- ◆ A letter or email to Grandma and Grandpa telling them about what you are learning in science class or an after-school activity.
- ◆ A thank-you note to Grandma and Grandpa thanking them for a birthday present or a recent visit.
- ◆ A request to Mom or Dad about an activity you would like to do. Explain what and why.
- ◆ A persuasive note to Mom or Dad about something you want to get or give. Explain what and why.
- ◆ A note to Grandpa about why he should come to family game night or to hear someone in the family who plays a musical instrument (especially if Grandpa is a good singer).
- ◆ The list of proposed activities for your perfect birthday party.
- ◆ A list of things around the house that you would change. Tell what they are, and why and how they might be changed.

C. Promoting Writing Fluency with the "*Quick-Write*"

As young writers gain practice and confidence, you can begin to talk about writing fluency. *Writing fluency* can be defined as a stage where writing seems to flow more readily, where the child no longer ponders each and every letter for each and every word as he or she writes. Writing has become more "automatic." All of the separate parts of the process begin to come together: forming the letters, spelling the word, and deciding how the words fit together to make the sentences. As these separate parts become more fluent, the young writer is able to dedicate more mental energy to the *overall contents of the message*. This can be a very creative moment for your child, in which the message itself is all-important and at the center of attention.

Instructions for the *Quick-Write*

The *Quick-Write* is designed to promote writing fluency. It works well with young writers who are starting to show confidence with writing. It also works well if and when the young child might be showing some resistance or hesitation about writing. It fits into At-Home writing because it can be individualized, and it also can be done in collaboration with a writing partner. It provides a collection of spontaneous writing samples that offer a window into your child's *writing progress,* especially when the samples are dated and saved.

The procedure is easy to follow. You need writing material, a pencil, and a stopwatch or timing device. You explain it this way: *"I will give you a choice of two topics, or you can choose the topic. You are going to write as much as you can, as fast as you can, for eight minutes. No erasing. Just line out anything you wrote that you don't want. Don't worry about a topic sentence. The idea is to take the topic and see where your writing will lead you. When I tell you time is up, finish your sentence, then stop and count your words. Write the number of words on your page, along with today's date."*

As soon as the words are counted, have your child read aloud what was written, and talk about whether there were any surprises. *Did the writing end up as you thought it would? Did you change directions as new ideas came to you?* This kind of writing is very different from *planned writing,* where you try to brainstorm your key ideas before you begin, and you plan the order and the kinds of sentences. That's the reason this is sometimes called *"Straight-Ahead Writing."* We will discuss elements of planned writing, such as the *topic sentence,* in Chapter 5.

What to Watch For

When you first begin the *Quick-Write,* make sure the proposed topic is a topic that your child *knows something about.* You can increase the time amount later, as your child gets the idea. When your child reads the sentences aloud, note whether she or he does some spontaneous editing or makes changes to clear up any confusion. More formal editing can come later if desired.

The idea of the word count is not to turn this into a competition, though that might happen. It's just one simple measure of *output,* and it relates well to the familiarity of the topic. The more words written, the more background knowledge is being shown by the writer. This is an important idea for children to understand, as they may feel inadequate when they can't write "a lot." They may set a goal to increase the number of words at another time, though this is not necessarily the only goal. As we pay more attention to vocabulary and grammar (Chapter 5), we may want to note how many of the words are colorful adjectives, action verbs, or different kinds of nouns.

Variations on the *Quick-Write*

1. *Quick-Write* three times a week. Write as much as you can, as fast as you can, for six to eight minutes. You can increase the time to seven to ten minutes as you wish. You can think of your own topic, or Mom or Dad could suggest a topic. It must be a topic you know something about, and hopefully, a topic that matters to you or that you are definitely interested in. Because you are using a timer, instead of stopping to erase something you want to change, just make a light line through it and go on.
2. On days that you don't do a *Quick-Write,* you can edit the one from the previous day. Look for grammar, spelling, or word choice items that need to be changed or could be improved.
3. On days that you don't do a *Quick-Write,* you can review ones from previous days. Note word choices or sentences that you are particularly *pleased with*. Draw a smiley face.
4. Take a *Quick-Write* topic from a previous day and write about it again. Notice the differences from the first version. Talk about why and how the two versions are different.
5. Paired *Quick-Write.* Find a writing partner, and both write on the same topic for the same amount of time. Share what you wrote. Note similarities and differences if they seem interesting.
6. Paired *Quick-Write.* Find a writing partner. Each one gives the other a topic to write about. It may be helpful if each partner provides two topics so there is a choice. Both write on their topic for the same amount of time. Share what you wrote.

When Eliza, a seventh grader, wrote her first *Quick-Write*, she had used only simple sentences with no subordinate clauses, and no complex sentences, though I knew her English teacher was teaching them about how to write complex sentences with subordinate clauses. When she finished the *Quick-Write*, I just said, *"Go through and count your **subordinate clauses**."* There weren't any. She was stunned. By the third try, suddenly subordinate clauses were blooming everywhere, and her writing looked like the writing of a seventh grader instead of a fourth grader. This little story illustrates the way that well-designed writing activities, no matter how simple they seem, have great benefits in helping children become comfortable and proficient writers.

Benefits of the *Quick-Write*

- ◆ Provides another way to look at writing output.
- ◆ Promotes the kind of thinking we call *self-monitoring*.
- ◆ Introduces new ways to evaluate writing output besides the number of words, such as kinds of sentences or word choice.
- ◆ Generates options for other vocabulary words that go with the topic.

Experimenting with Different Forms of Writing

The Personal Journal. Many dedicated writers got their start by keeping a journal. In fact, many professional and eventually famous writers used their personal journals to record the thoughts and ideas that later became books, plays, and movies. Journals and letters can become the story itself. We know a good deal about some of the early explorers and their explorations, such as the crew of Sir Ernest Shackleton's ship, the *Endurance*, and their voyage to attempt the land crossing of Antarctica, because of the journals they kept and preserved. And in Chapter 3, we have already presented the idea of the *Family Response Journal*.

A personal journal may not appeal to every child. It may not appeal to the girl who would rather throw a ball against the garage door with her friend from school. It may not appeal to the boy who has his nose in a book written by a favorite author.

Some older children connect the journal with writing tasks from school, where they must document the steps of a science project or document their thoughts as they read an assigned book. But if the activities of Chapter 3 have become entwined with the regular home activities, it is not a great stretch to consider the *Personal Journal.*

It often gets started with a gift. A grandmother or friend may send a bound notebook that simply begs to have something written in it. Or it may start with a book that your child reads that is based on letters or a journal. They will eventually read Anne Frank's diaries, but that is another story and may be very daunting indeed because of its historical importance. Our goal is to make the personal journal connected to the familiar, just as we have done with all the other activities suggested here.

Journal Stories. There are many children's books that feature journals or are written in the form of letters to someone who may provide inspiration to your young writer. Check out *Dear Mr. Henshaw,* by Beverly Cleary, for the upper elementary readers. See *The Gardener,* by Sarah Stewart, for a delightful story told through both pictures and letters for all ages. When children read such books by famous authors, they may be inspired to try a journal story of their own.

Wordless Picture Books. Another genre that may inspire writing is the wordless picture book. These books are often geared to the very young by telling a story through engaging pictures only, or with few words. Once our young writers figure out the storyline, they may enjoy putting the whole story, or parts of it *into their own words.* Here are some good examples: *Egg* by Kevin Henkes; *A Ball for Daisy* by Chris Raschka; *Flora and the Flamingo* by Molly Idle; *Mr. Wuffles!* by David Wiesner; *You Can't Take a Balloon into the Metropolitan Museum* by Jacqueline Preiss Weitzman and Robin Preiss Glasser; and *Imagine!* by Raul Colon.

◆ *Egg* has a number of features that appeal to young readers and writers. It is a "pattern book" that develops its story with the use of repeated (but simple) single words that lead us from one surprise to another. Children can write the tale using the words provided on the page, as well as their own words that explain what the little birds are doing. They can write about how the surprise creature in the fourth egg is feeling as the story unfolds. The ending pleases readers of all ages.

♦ *A Ball for Daisy* builds upon our familiarity with dogs and how dogs can become attached to a favorite toy. Young writers can explain in human terms how a new doggie friend can more than make up for a lost toy.

♦ *Flora and the Flamingo* will appeal to the young writer who is also a dancer at heart. Flora can echo the poses of the flamingo and show both the grace and humor of moving through space beautifully. There are even pop-up surprises that show the two of them soaring together.

♦ *Mr. Wuffles!* introduces us to a curious cat who chances upon a tiny spaceship full of equally curious aliens. These tiny creatures set about exploring Mr. Wuffles's world and speaking to each other in words that are spelled with beautifully geometric symbols and lots of exclamation marks. The action is complicated, but the pictures tell the whole adventure, including how the little creatures make their own pictures of the alien cat's world. Mr. Wuffles tries to capture them, but alas, they seem to get away. Or do they? Your young writer might want to write this story in a series of chapters, or maybe just focus on selected pages.

♦ In *You Can't Take a Balloon into the Metropolitan Museum*, the balloon that you can't take into the museum escapes from the museum guard and sets off on an exciting journey through the neighborhood, through Central Park, through the Plaza Hotel, and even through an opera at the Lincoln Center. The balloon's journey is mirrored in the great works of art being viewed inside the museum by the young owner of the balloon and her grandmother. Everyone and everything, including the elephant who was on stage for the opera, seems to return by the end, back to where they belong, and the balloon returns to the hands of the little girl who is none the wiser! Your young writer might want to write about what the balloon saw as it floated through New York City.

◆ In *Imagine!* we follow a young skateboarder through the streets of New York, until, one afternoon, he comes to the Museum of Modern Art and goes inside for the first time. As he passes through the galleries, some of the images from very famous paintings spring into action, and even allow the boy to step into the painting and join the musicians shown there. Soon there is a procession of the musicians, the boy, and even a lion and a dog making their way through famous New York City landmarks and enjoying a New York hot dog in Central Park. The boy makes sure all his companions return to their proper paintings in the museum before he brings his day to a surprising end.

As you can see from this brief selection, there are many ways to engage our young writers. These wordless or almost wordless picture books are rich in ideas and stories told through appealing images. They are rich in emotion, suspense, and surprise. Your young writer may have the very words that add to, explain, or even extend the stories told by the pictures. You will note that these six example books are closely connected to the familiar or may open wonderful new doors to new places to explore. They may invite your writer to try an original story, told through pictures, words, or both.

Bibliography

Alexander, Caroline. *The Endurance: Shackleton's Legendary Antarctic Expedition*. New York: Alfred A. Knopf, 1999.

Cleary, Beverly. *Dear Mr. Henshaw*. New York: HarperCollins, 1983.

Colon, Raul. *Imagine!* New York: Simon & Schuster Books for Young Readers, 2018.

Esbensen, Barbara J. *Baby Whales Drink Milk. Let's Read and Find Out Science*. New York: HarperCollins, 1994.

Henkes, Kevin. *egg*. New York: HarperCollins, 2017.

Idle, Molly. *Flora and the Flamingo*. San Francisco: Chronicle Books, LLC, 2013.

Raschka, Chris. *A Ball for Daisy*. New York: Schwartz & Wade, 2011.

Stewart, Sarah. *The Gardener*. New York: Farrar, Straus, Giroux, 1997.

Weitzman, Jacqueline Preiss and Glasser, Robin Preiss. *You Can't Take A Balloon into the Metropolitan Museum*. New York: Dial Books for Young Readers, 1998.

Wiesner, David. *Mr. Wuffles!* Boston, New York: Clarion Books, Houghton Mifflin Harcourt, 2013.

5

The Writer's Toolbox

Words, Sentences, and Paragraphs

Activity Level: Grade 2–6+

EASY ACCESS NOTES FOR CHAPTER 5: WHAT YOU WILL LEARN

♦ The Writer's Toolbox: An Easy Reference for Answering Grammar Questions That Come Up.
♦ Parts of Speech: Defined and Explained with Charts and Examples of Usage.
♦ Words with Multiple Functions: Examples and Exercises.
♦ Grammar and Kinds of Sentences: Examples of Use.
♦ Clauses and How They Work in Sentences.
♦ Different Kinds of Paragraphs: Where to Find Good Examples.
♦ Practicing Different Kinds of Paragraphs: Planned Writing Steps with Writing Prompts.
♦ How Writing Promotes Thinking Skills.
♦ The Editing Process Using the Writer's Toolbox: Three Stages of Editing (For Young Writers).

What Is the *Writer's Toolbox*?

A writer's tools aren't just pencils and paper, or a computer. We will use the model of the *Writer's Toolbox* to explain the resources

DOI: 10.4324/9781003452683-7

that children need to help them become writers. Like the *Writer's Assets*, tools and toolboxes don't just happen accidentally. They can be planned, designed, and improved over time. This is especially true in the case of grammar tools. Parents can be a part of the toolbox team by being a source of grammar information that can be delivered on the spot, just when it is needed.

For many parents, the grammar information they were taught in their school days may be a part of the distant past, and something they have not had to use much lately. The purpose of Chapter 5 is to give you *an easy reference* for answering the grammar questions that might come up in connection with school assignments and At-Home writing activities. Grammar terminology is usually introduced in school by second or third grade, and children are ready by then to use grammar tools to talk about their own writing. In fact, having these tools may increase their level of awareness of what and how they write, and may well increase the pride of ownership in what they have produced. It also provides a way for parents to reinforce children's learning when you apply the *grammar labels* to specific operations in writing and achievements that you observe.

Grammar Rules and Parts of Speech

Children are first introduced to grammar in their Language Arts classes when the teacher explains about *Parts of Speech*. Before learning about *Parts of Speech*, children may think that a word is "just a word." Now they are introduced to the idea that we can group words together, based on *how we use those words* when we talk, write, and think. These groups have names that help children learn about the different ways *that words function*. There are groups like the *nouns* that children relate to immediately because nouns are the *names* of persons, places, things, and ideas. Starting from when they first learn to talk, children easily relate to the function of naming. There are other groups, like prepositions and conjunctions, that are more abstract and that may take more practice to catch on to. But *the idea of the groups* is usually easy for a child to understand.

Next, the teacher may explain about *Grammar Rules*: the patterns that help us understand what words mean and how to use them in sentences. It is important to note here that we are not introducing a whole set of "rules" for children to memorize. Instead, we are giving labels to groups of words and patterns *that children already know how to use when they communicate.* These labels serve as tools to help writers understand how language is structured and organized and to see how that structure works when they write. Knowing about *parts of speech* can help children decide how to choose the words to place in their sentences. They might even see ways to experiment with different kinds of words and word combinations.

Parts of Speech

The *Parts of Speech* are listed here, and we will discuss them one at a time:

- ◆ Nouns.
- ◆ Pronouns.
- ◆ Verbs.
- ◆ Adjectives.
- ◆ Adverbs.
- ◆ Prepositions.
- ◆ Conjunctions.
- ◆ Interjections.

Nouns. Nouns are the "heavy lifters" in a language. We need lots of them, because of the work they do. Nouns are the words that name (or label) persons, places, and things. Nouns are used to label items we can see and touch, such as *milk, doggie, ball, shoe, sister,* or *bed.* These nouns are called *concrete nouns.* Nouns also label ideas, feelings, and qualities that are in our minds but that we cannot see or touch. These nouns are called *abstract nouns,* such as *time, happiness, friendship, honesty, fairness,* or *memory.* We need a great many nouns because our world is full of things we need to talk about, learn about, ask for, point to, or remember.

Pronouns. Pronouns are words that take the place of nouns. This group is much smaller in number, but pronouns work very hard indeed. They help us avoid repeating the nouns, which takes a lot of time if we are in a hurry, and even when we are not.

Take this simple sentence from Mary: *"I think I would like to bring my new volleyball to the beach when we meet our school friends there."* Without pronouns, we would have to say: "*Mary* thinks *Mary* would like to bring *Mary's* new volleyball to the beach when *Mary and Sally* meet *Mary and Sally's* school friends there." You can see how useful pronouns are.

To show how often we use pronouns, you might tell your child that pronouns were almost the first words they learned to say: *"It's mine." "Give it to me." "I saw you."* Then you might say, *"I bet you can't talk for two minutes without using a pronoun."* Chances are your child will say, *"Yes, I can."* And you say, *"But you just used a pronoun! You said 'I.'"* Then you can make a game of talking without using pronouns. Make sure you set a time limit. This is harder than you think, and it may raise some questions about which words the pronouns are taking the place of, especially when we use the pronouns "you" or *"it."* Children can be reassured that they already knew a lot about pronouns even before they learned the name of this group. **Table 5.1 and Table 5.2** show **the *Personal Pronouns*.**

TABLE 5.1 Singular Pronouns

	Subjects	*Objects*	*Possessives*
First person	I	me	my, mine
Second person	you	you	your, yours
Third person	he, she, it	him, her, it	his, her, hers, its

TABLE 5.2 Plural Pronouns

	Subjects	*Objects*	*Possessives*
First person	we	us	our, ours
Second person	you	you	your, yours
Third person	they	them	their, theirs

We use personal pronouns to refer to ourselves, other persons, and things. There are pronouns we use to ask questions: *who, what, which.* Some pronouns are placeholders until we come up with the specific noun we want to refer to: *someone, something, anything, nothing, everyone, anybody, nobody.* These placeholders are called *indefinite pronouns.* Some pronouns show possession: *your, yours, my, her, his, their.* Children make good use of pronouns when they start a sentence with a noun and then use a pronoun to refer back to that noun later in the same sentence: **Dad** *went out to buy* **his** *coffee, and* **he** *came back ten minutes later.*

Verbs. Verbs are also "heavy lifters" because they are the words that tell what is happening. They are action words: *run, dance, kick, eat, shout, jump, sneeze.* The action can be something we can see, hear, and feel, such as *run, dance, kick,* and *sneeze.* In addition, the action can be mental, something that happens in our mind, such as *study, wonder, imagine, remember,* and *think.* Another group of verbs are called "state of being" verbs, such as *is, am, are, was,* and *were.* They are usually followed by a noun or an adjective: *Beth* **is** *a doctor. Brad* **was** *a coach. Beth* **is** *really hungry. Brad* **was** *very helpful.* The *state of being* verbs, which also include verbs such as *appear, seem, be,* and so on are called "linking verbs" because they link the subject to a noun or adjective, as shown in the examples above.

Verbs form the part of the sentence called the *predicate* and are usually easy for young writers to identify. They can make sentences very colorful and lively. Verbs are often preceded by smaller words called *helping verbs,* which tell us when the action happened or when it might happen: *will fly, had seen, might go, is wondering.* The helping verbs are used by all of us to indicate the three verb tenses: *present, past,* and *future.*

At first, the helping verbs may be confusing to young writers, because several of them can be main verbs, all on their own, such as *is, was, has, had: Our dog* **is** *still a puppy. He* **has** *a red bike. They* **had** *chickens in the back yard.* When they act as helping verbs, they come before the main verb: *Sue* **is walking** *very slowly. Nancy* **was laughing** *at the birds. Rick* **has discovered** *where to find fossils. They* **had left** *the cat at the vet. Tomorrow we* **might go** *to the park.*

Adjectives. Adjectives describe or modify nouns and pronouns. They tell us all about the size, shape, color, and the number of the nouns they modify. Adjectives answer the questions *"Which one?"*, *"What kind of...?"*, and *"How many?"* We say the *blue* book; the *rotten* egg; *two little* birds. Adjectives generally come before the noun they modify, unless they are following a *linking verb* such as *is, am, are, was, were*: The book *is blue*. The egg *was rotten*. The birds *were little*.

Young writers are often encouraged to avoid the "empty" adjectives, the ones that don't give you much specific information, such as *big, nice, good, great, bad*, and so on. These words are fine as shorthand when you are chatting with friends or texting, but in writing, our young writers should experiment with "informative adjectives," such as *enormous, pleasant, delicious, outstanding, precise, frightful*, and so on.

Adverbs. Adverbs modify or limit verbs. They tell *where, when, why, how*, and *to what extent* or *under what conditions the action happens*. With adverbs, writers can describe an action more exactly, more colorfully, and more completely. Young writers can often easily identify adverbs because many of them end in the suffix *'ly.'* With practice, they catch on to how we can change an adjective to an adverb just by adding *'ly.'* This change can give them more power as a writer: *precise→precisely, happy→happily, vivid→vividly, smooth→smoothly.*

There are adverbs that limit verbs: *nearly, often, seldom, almost, everywhere*. These adverbs can seem less easy to spot, because they can come before the verb, after the verb, or even between the helping verb and the main verb: He *always sneezes* when he wakes up. He *goes* to the movies *often*. She *had quickly washed* all the dishes before she left.

There are nouns that can function as adverbs. Here are two examples: *He came **yesterday*** (tells when). *I went **home*** (tells where). And here are the same words used as nouns: ***Yesterday** was the best day in my life. My **home** was flooded in the storm.* And *not* and *never* are always adverbs. They modify the verb to make it negative. I *do not like* peanut butter. She *will never finish* that project.

Prepositions. A preposition is a word that shows a relationship between a noun or pronoun and some other word in the sentence. Prepositions are often puzzling to young writers, though by first and second grade they are using most of the common prepositions quite confidently and correctly. When we try to define what a preposition is, we have to explain the word in terms of *how it relates to other words in the sentence.* Prepositions have meaning, but not necessarily a definition, because their meaning depends on how they are used: **on** *the phone,* **on** *my back,* **on** *time.* Prepositions are found at the beginning of a *prepositional phrase.* The preposition is followed by a noun or pronoun that is the *object of the preposition.* The prepositional phrase can modify a noun or a verb, but it cannot *contain* a verb.

Some classroom teachers have students memorize the list of prepositions in Table 5.3. Sometimes they learn a whole song with all of the prepositions, kind of like the alphabet song where the list of 26 letters is set to music. But it is actually more valuable if children can *identify* the prepositions and connect them to their object *when they are used in sentences.*

Once they understand about prepositional phrases, the next step is to determine whether the prepositional phrase modifies a noun or verb. If it modifies a noun, it is called an *adjective phrase:* "the dog **with the spotted nose.**" The phrase tells which dog. If it modifies a verb, it is called an *adverb phrase:* "*The cow jumped* **over the moon.**" The phrase tells where the cow jumped.

Once young writers can identify a prepositional phrase accurately, you might try having them find the phrases in other print material, both fiction and non-fiction. Then cross out the prepositional phrases to see what is left. They are often surprised to see how much information and how much meaning is contributed by prepositional phrases. Prepositional phrases are a little like pronouns, in that you can't talk for very long or write very much without them. Writers will also note that prepositions don't like to stand alone, but you will spot some in the chart below that do stand alone, without a noun or pronoun following them. When they are working alone, without an object, they are working as adverbs, without an object. We can say, "*When can you come* **over**?" (adverb). We can also say, "*There was a rainbow* **over** *the mountain*" (preposition) (Table 5.3).

TABLE 5.3 The Common Prepositions

about	before	except	onto	underneath
above	behind	for	outside	until
across	below	from	over	up
after	beneath	in	past	upon
against	beside	inside	since	with
along	between	into	through	within
among	beyond	near	throughout	without
around	by	of	to	
as	down	off	toward	
at	during	on	under	

Conjunctions. Conjunctions are words that join words or groups of words: *and, but, or, nor, for, yet*. The words they join must be the same part of speech: nouns with nouns, verbs with verbs, and adjectives with adjectives. There are also conjunctions that come in pairs: *neither…nor, either…or, both…and, not only…but also, whether…or*. Note that "for" can also be a preposition: "*I got a car for my birthday*." When it is used as a conjunction, it means "because." "*She was very proud, for she had finished the marathon in record time*."

Interjections. This is a small but colorful group of words. These words express surprise or sudden emotion and are often followed by an exclamation mark. They may not really have a relationship with the rest of the sentence. They are just stuck there, usually at the beginning. We use them in conversation when our listener probably already knows what we are talking about: *Ouch! Oh, no! Hey! Oops!* In chapter books, they are used to make dialogue more lively.

Words with Multiple Functions

Once your child gets the idea of the different parts of speech, you can begin to call attention to the words that can have *multiple functions*. There are words that can be a noun, a verb, and an adjective, depending on how they are used. Many of these example words are familiar and can be used to practice the different functions:

The word "*watch*."

♦ *My **watch** tells me what time it is. (noun)*
♦ *We all **watch** the football game on Monday night. (verb)*
♦ *Our golden retriever is a good **watch** dog. (adjective)*

The word "*spring*."

♦ *We got water from the **spring**. (noun)*
♦ *The outfielder could **spring** really high to catch those fly balls. (verb)*
♦ *I am waiting for the **spring** flowers. (adjective)*

Even more complicated words can show how this works, like the word "*program*."

♦ *The **program** lasted for one hour. (noun)*
♦ *Mom will **program** the computer. (verb)*
♦ *The **program** notes told me about the composer. (adjective)*

As children learn more complex vocabulary, they may begin to spot examples themselves. To illustrate the variable functions of common everyday words, ask your child if he or she can think of five words that can function as nouns, verbs, and adjectives. Start off with some good examples, to show how it works:

Talk

♦ *I gave a **talk** in my science class. (noun)*
♦ *Can we **talk** about the dog? (verb)*
♦ *She has a job as a **talk** show host. (adjective)*

Bike

♦ *My new **bike** is pink. (noun)*
♦ *Every day I **bike** to work. (verb)*
♦ *They cleared everyone off the **bike** path. (adjective)*

Hand

♦ *I brush my teeth with my right* **hand***. (noun)*
♦ *When you have a minute, could you* **hand** *me the scissors? (verb)*
♦ *The new* **hand** *soap you brought smells fine. (adjective)*

Work

♦ *The* **work** *at the repair shop will take all day. (noun)*
♦ *I* **work** *at the farmers' market most weekends. (verb)*
♦ *He tore a hole in his new* **work** *shirt. (adjective)*

You will find many more words that have both a noun and a verb form, even some unexpected ones. Encourage your child to collect as many examples as possible, as a kind of game. The *Word Wall* is useful here, which is another good reason to keep it going. But also pay attention to the words that can be only a verb (*breathe*), or only a noun (*director*), or only an adverb (*often*). The small function words (pronouns, prepositions, and conjunctions), and many of the adverbs, generally have only one job.

Grammar and Kinds of Sentences

When children first learn to talk, they find out quickly that the things they say (called *utterances*) can have *different purposes*. Experts who study child language note that children learn to do this early on by listening, observing, and imitating the language users around them. They don't have to be "taught." Kids figure out that we use one kind of sentence to tell about something, or make a statement: *I can't find my shoe. The doggie got out. The milk spilled.* But we use a very different kind of sentence to ask questions about what we want to know: *Where is my shoe? What kind of sandwich can I have? Why is it so dark?* Children can easily tell from tone of voice or from the situation that these are two different kinds of sentences. In grammar terms, the statements are called *declarative sentences*, and the questions are called *interrogative sentences*.

Two other types of sentences are known by their common names, commands and exclamations, or in grammar terms, *imperative sentences* and *exclamatory sentences*. Children learn early on about commands because they both give them and receive them: *Help me with my buttons. Give me an apple. Pick up your shoes. Open the front door.* Commands are a big part of the give and take of family life. Commands are often a focus when we first instruct children about having good manners or treating each other kindly: S*ay please when you ask Grandma to help you.*

In the same way, children learn about exclamations through the give and take of family life but may not always identify them as a separate kind of sentence. Sometimes they are both commands and exclamations: *Get the cat off the table! Watch out for the cars!* When they first encounter exclamations in the dialogue of the little books that they read or listen to, they may notice that this kind of sentence is followed by an exclamation mark that tells the reader or listener that the sentence is said loudly, or with strong emotion.

Knowing about the four kinds of sentences can be a big help to our young writers. First of all, they can build the awareness that *language is something we can talk about, using language.* They can think about how language works for us, both as it is happening and after it happens. When children begin to do their own writing, we can talk with them about how they use language when they write. As they become more aware of the different functions of language, they increase their ability to analyze their own writing. We can encourage them to experiment with different ways to express their meaning. For example, when we write about something we did not know or realize, we can use a declarative sentence: *"I didn't know the dog was still in the car."* Or we might express it as a question: *"How was I supposed to know the dog was still in the car?"*

In addition, when children know about the four kinds of sentences, they have an important framework for understanding the structure of sentences. They can be introduced to the ideas of *subject* and *predicate*, and they will come to expect to find these two elements when they read and write sentences. They will know that the subject is *what the sentence is about.* They will expect the predicate to tell *what the subject is or does.* In other words, they will gradually develop a "sense of sentence." This sense of sentence will gradually become more apparent in their writing. In school writing, the teacher will introduce the idea of the *complete sentence,* in other words, a sentence with both a subject and predicate. In At-Home writing, we tend to be more forgiving of *incomplete sentences* as our young writers gradually figure out how best to express their own ideas. Incomplete sentences are often detected and corrected when children listen to us read aloud what they have dictated or written, or when we engage in the editing process.

When we build the grammar foundation, we also help children make a very strong link between the language they read in books and the language forms they are becoming more confident with when they talk and write. We can say, *"Why did the boy in the story show his surprise by asking three questions in a row? How did the questions help us know how he was feeling?"* We will note here that when children experience the language of books, they become exposed to multiple forms of sentences and the many ways that meaning can be conveyed by sentences of all kinds (even in some cases, deliberately incomplete sentences!).

What Is a Clause, and How Do Clauses Work?

What is a clause, and is it just another kind of sentence? Teachers introduce clauses by grouping them into two groups: *independent, or main clauses,* and *dependent, or subordinate clauses.* All clauses have to have a *subject,* which tells what the clause is about, and a *predicate,* which contains a verb and tells something about what the subject is or does. Main clauses stand on their own because they express a "complete thought." Subordinate clauses also have both subject and verb, but they do not express a complete thought. They must be attached to a main clause so that together the two clauses express a complete thought. When a subordinate clause shows up by itself in something we wrote, it would be called a *fragment.*

One of the important differences between written and spoken language is that we often speak in subordinate clauses, especially around the family or other familiars, because our listener already knows something about what we are talking about. As children gain more experience with writing, they get better at deciding when a sentence is "complete," and when it is not, particularly when we help them with the editing process. Keep these labels and these distinctions in mind when you have the opportunity to give feedback about your child's writing. When you can give this sort of informative feedback, your comments are less likely to be experienced as criticism or the calling out of mistakes, and more likely to be seen as *helpful information*.

Here are some examples of main clauses:

- ◆ The mailman will arrive at 2:00 PM.
- ◆ You should eat fresh vegetables every day.
- ◆ The clock in the kitchen has stopped.
- ◆ I plan to read a new book every week during the summer.

Here are some examples of subordinate clauses (fragments). See if you can spot what is missing:

- ◆ after the rain stopped falling.
- ◆ unless you can find the football.
- ◆ if we can't have the picnic on Sunday.
- ◆ because the students all did well on the spelling test.

Subordinate clauses have three jobs:

- ◆ **Adjective clauses** follow a noun and modify the noun: *Mt. Everest,* **which is the highest mountain in the world,** *is a favorite of serious climbers.*
- ◆ **Adverb clauses** modify the verb and tell where, when, why, how, and to what extent or under what conditions the action happens: ***After the rain stopped falling,*** *we all ran outdoors.* Adverb clauses can either begin or end a sentence, whereas the adjective clause must follow its noun.

◆ **Noun clauses** function like nouns: *We tried to decide **what we should do about the dog**. **What he wants** is a new bicycle.*

There are other aspects of grammar that we will not cover in this reference section. Parents who want or need to delve deeper into grammar can do so with workbooks from educational publishers, such as *Rules of the Game*, from Educators Publishing Service. For our purposes with At-Home writing, the basic elements presented here will be enough to give you the confidence necessary to read and respond to your children's writing in a positive and informative manner. As you practice labeling, you will see more and more opportunities to teach and learn about grammar.

Kinds of Paragraphs

Learning about parts of speech and kinds of sentences is good preparation for the next step, where we discuss the idea of how to write different kinds of paragraphs. This is a very important step in writing. We will use the ideas we have introduced so far as we build background about paragraphs. With this background, you will be able to go on to the suggested activities, which are suitable for young children to practice on. Keep in mind that it is as important to be able to use labels for the kinds of paragraphs as it is to label parts of speech and kinds of sentences.

By second grade, children have probably heard the word "paragraph" in connection with school reading, or with At-Home reading. Language Arts programs will introduce the different kinds of paragraphs by around third grade or fourth grade. But even before that, children are exposed to different kinds of paragraphs in children's science books and other non-fiction reading materials. In a book about whales, for example, they may read the section that compares marine mammals with fish and are thus introduced to the idea of *compare/contrast*. They might have included a comparison in a paragraph of their own, comparing two sports, or two kinds of cookies, using the signal words for comparisons: *unlike, just like, different from, similar to, bigger than.*

In other science books, they may read about the way a tadpole turns into a frog or a caterpillar into a butterfly. Here they are introduced to the idea of a sequence or steps in order. They have learned the signal words for steps in order: *first, next, then, finally*. They might have already written sentences about a sequence or process when they wrote their set of directions to follow in Chapter 3.

A paragraph can consist of four to five sentences about a topic or an event. You will know when your child seems ready to tackle an entire paragraph because she or he will have a lot to tell. For example, he may write several sentences about something that happened at school or at a picnic. This is likely to be a *sequence* paragraph. Or he may have found out about a new topic, such as how vets are trained to take care of large animals. This kind of paragraph, called *topic/detail*, would contain sentences that describe or explain the main topic. Some writers will think about announcing the topic of their paragraph with a *topic sentence* at the beginning of the paragraph. When this happens naturally, it can be a real pleasure to be the parent who is on hand to label the item with the right label, and then use that sentence as a marker for subsequent paragraph writing. If no topic sentence appears, it is completely appropriate to suggest that such a sentence can lead the reader to better understand the entire paragraph and to model some trial topic sentences that might fit.

Practicing the Different Kinds of Paragraphs

Once your child has a good amount of information to write, the next step would be to introduce the idea that a writer can organize a paragraph in different ways, depending on the topic or the purpose of the paragraph. It is good to begin with two of the most common types of paragraphs, compare/contrast and sequence, because children have usually been exposed to them in their reading. With practice, young writers can explore other important forms of paragraphs. They will find lots of opportunities to use these forms because they are useful when we write about our own experiences or about information we have learned. *All forms of paragraph development, as practiced at home, can contribute to your child's confidence with the planned writing activities that are expected at school within the writing curriculum.*

The Planned Writing steps are intended to help the writer focus on the purpose and structure of the paragraph. The process generally begins with a listing of the key ideas, often called the "brainstorming list." This list helps writers examine what they already know that can be included in the paragraph (or essay). Ideas may need to be added based on *further research*. Many teachers utilize forms of *graphic organizers* like "idea maps" that enable the writer to see how the key ideas relate to one another, in order to prioritize and sequence how the ideas will be used. This process can help to form a topic sentence and sort out the various kinds of supporting details in order of importance. All of these steps involve the critical thinking skills that are key to successful writing. When you are able to observe your young writer engage in this process, you are able to gather important clues as to their progress toward building future confidence and competence in writing. You can label and reinforce these steps appropriately.

We will introduce some of the more common forms of paragraph development that are easily understood by young readers and writers. The descriptions of the different types of paragraphs are followed by prompts and ideas to practice with. Each form involves practice with ways to enable children to organize their thinking.

- ◆ Time order/Sequence.
- ◆ Cause/Effect.
- ◆ Problem/Solution.
- ◆ Examples and Illustrations.
- ◆ Compare/Contrast.
- ◆ Reason/Persuasion.

Time Order/Sequence. When your child writes about something that happened, often by turning it into a "story," she is likely to use time order. Many of the stories children read or hear will tell about events that happen in time, so this is a pattern they recognize and understand very well. It is natural for them to adopt a time order for a short paragraph or even a series of paragraphs. In the classroom, they may have already been introduced to the idea of the *narrator* who tells the story using the time order in which events happen.

In narrative writing, writers use vocabulary words that signal specific times, such as *days of the week, special days like birthdays*, or *names of the months*. In addition, they can use specific time reference words: *yesterday, tomorrow, soon, later, right away, now, then*, and *never*. Children who have read or listened to chapter books are very familiar with how stories are organized, and they may have already produced their own narratives when they describe something that happened. Even a very short story relies on time order.

Sequence is closely related to time order, and your child might have some examples of activities that have steps in order but that don't happen at a particular time. They may remember how steps in order worked when they did the direction-following activity in Chapter 3. This kind of paragraph involves good planning and observing the logical order of *how steps are related to each other in a sequence.*

Cause/Effect. The cause/effect relationship may be introduced formally in children's science classes or in the beginning science books that have sparked their interests. If you are just getting started with this idea, and you want to make it part of how you talk about paragraphs, start with an example of a real event that actually happened: *Dad left the ice cream carton out on the counter (cause); the ice cream melted (effect). David forgot to put the puppy back inside his room (cause); the puppy dug up one of Mom's tomato plants (effect).* The good stories they read or hear in chapter books contain many examples of cause/effect as part of the story.

Every household will have examples of actions and their consequences. If your child just happens to write about something that illustrates cause and effect, it is a perfect teaching moment to label the relationship, and then look around for other examples that you could write about. And then you can connect to the many ways we see cause/effect in science books and other forms of information.

Problem/Solution. The problem/solution relationship offers similar writing opportunities. Children will have no trouble coming up with examples of problems that they experience or observe. The solutions that they write about might be real and practical. Or they may take us into a fantasy world where complicated problems get magically solved. In either case, the writing opportunities are plentiful.

Examples and Illustrations. A paragraph that gives an example or illustration might seem more academic than the previous types we have described. However, the process of giving an example is often a part of the *classroom teacher's tool set*, and therefore children have already been exposed to this important teaching technique. They may be able to recall some examples of *how teachers use examples* to help them understand what they are learning about. They will recognize the sentence that starts this way: *"Let me give you an example…"*

Compare/Contrast. A compare/contrast paragraph is used to highlight important characteristics of the two items being compared. The idea of comparisons is pervasive in both fiction and non-fiction materials that children encounter through wide reading. This pattern is a tool for them to include in their writing toolbox because of its universal range of applications and because children understand it so well. You will learn more about how this form is found in all kinds of writing and thinking, in Chapter 10 on Critical Thinking.

Reason Paragraph/Persuasion Paragraph. In the upper elementary grades, children will encounter the reason paragraph, where they explain *why* something happens, or *why* they should take or not take certain actions. It is a short step from the reason paragraph to the persuasion paragraph. Most children take to persuasion readily, as they use it all the time on their parents. When they *write* a persuasion paragraph, they have to organize their key points in order of importance and think about their intended audience. Persuading a younger brother uses different reasons than persuading a grandparent. This exercise causes writers to consider *the point of view of their reader.*

Other Forms of Paragraph Development. Children's writing can include *classification and definition*, which we often find in science books that discuss animal *categories*, such as rodents,

TABLE 5.4 Reference List of Types of Paragraphs

Time order, sequence, process	Examples and illustrations
Compare/contrast	Cause/effect
Problem/solution	Narration
Reason	Description
Persuasion	Definition

water birds, or marine mammals. *Narration* and *description* are also typically encountered in their book reading. Working with these types of paragraphs at home provides added comprehension benefits when young readers encounter these patterns in both fiction and non-fiction books. Classroom teachers frequently provide models in the classroom. The main types of paragraphs found in non-fiction and fiction writing are listed in Table 5.4.

You will find models of all of these forms in children's books, although they will not generally be labeled for you as such. Writers mark these relationships through the use of *signal words* that tell you that you are reading about a sequence or a comparison or some other form. Additionally, these forms can also be found in well-designed workbooks from educational publishers. There is a compelling reason for introducing your young writer to these useful types of paragraphs. You are contributing to the formation of reasoning and problem-solving skills, which are called "critical thinking skills." Chapter 10 explores critical thinking and shows how it fits into the At-Home Model.

Prompts for Writing Different Kinds of Paragraphs

The topics below are included to help you get started. The best topics for your own child will depend, as usual, upon his or her age and interests.

Time order, sequence, process. Write a paragraph that shows:

◆ The steps in order (sequence) for washing your hands before setting the table.

- The time order for the steps it took to get the groceries that were on the shopping list into the shopping cart, and how much time you allowed for each item.
- The steps in order for how to get ready to make scrambled eggs for breakfast.
- The sequence of steps you took to learn how to ride your bike and use the brakes.

Compare/contrast. Write a paragraph that:

- Tells how otters and seals are alike, and how they are different.
- Tells how ice hockey and soccer are alike, and how they are different.
- Tells how cookies and cakes are alike, and how they are different.
- Compares roller skates and ice skates.
- Compares skateboards and snowboards.

Problem/solution. Write a paragraph about:

- A problem that someone might have while doing a school science project, and how it might be solved.
- A problem that you might have with a skateboard or a bicycle, and how it might be solved.
- A problem the babysitter had, and how it was solved (or not).
- A problem that might happen to a zookeeper at a zoo, and how it might be solved.

Reason. Write a paragraph that:

- Gives the reasons why we might want to learn a second language.
- Tells why it is a good idea to learn to swim.
- Gives the reasons why we should help our friends when they need help.
- Tells what theme park you would recommend, and why.

◆ Tells why you should learn to play a musical instrument, and what instrument you would recommend.

Persuasion. Write a paragraph that:

◆ Persuades a friend to go with you to do a new activity.
◆ Persuades your school principal to add new equipment to the playground.
◆ Persuades your city council to add a skateboard area to one of the city parks.
◆ Gives good reasons why everybody should know how to cook breakfast.
◆ Gives good reasons why you should wear a helmet when you ride your bike.

Examples and illustrations. Write a paragraph that gives:

◆ Three examples of a good deed.
◆ Three examples of ways to be helpful around the house.
◆ An example of a gift your mom (or any other family member) would like.
◆ Three examples of things that are fun to collect. Be sure to include examples of what you like to collect and tell why.
◆ Three examples of foods that are good to take on a picnic. Tell why your examples fit a picnic.
◆ An example of an unusual pet your family might like.
◆ Three examples of important "School Rules."

Cause/effect. Write a paragraph that shows:

◆ What happens if you forget to feed the dog.
◆ What happens if you make a loud noise when the baby is sleeping.
◆ What happens if you forget to put your dirty clothes in the laundry basket.
◆ What happens if you forget to water the plants in your science experiment.

Narrative. Tell a story about:

- How you met your best friend, and what you like to do together.
- How you made your grandma or grandad happy or surprised.
- A pet that kept surprising you.
- How you learned to roller skate, tie your shoes, or play the piano.
- The day when everything seemed to go wrong, and how it all ended.

Description (Chapter 7 has further practice with writing descriptions). Write a paragraph that:

- Describes a place that makes you feel calm and peaceful.
- Describes a picture or photograph that made you want to jump into the picture.
- Describes your perfect room of your own.

Definition. Write a paragraph that:

- Gives a definition of "good sport."
- Gives a definition of "best friend."
- Gives a definition of "fast foods."
- Gives a definition of "a good deed."

How Writing Promotes Thinking

In addition to strengthening the components of the Writer's Toolbox, the process of writing itself plays a role in promoting children's thinking skills. When children write, they engage in thinking skills that are used in all of learning. This list is to help you explore "thinking about thinking" as it applies to your young writer. As you read through the list, think about specific moments when you have observed children using examples of this kind of thinking, either with your assistance, or all on their own. Chapter 10 will focus in-depth on children's *critical thinking*.

♦ **Decision-Making**. This skill is used when we decide which topic to write about, and when we decide what to say about our topic.

♦ **Applying Background Knowledge**. We use our background knowledge when we decide if we have enough to say and if we can provide the important details. We use our retrieval skills when we search for and choose what we want to say about our topic.

♦ **Organizing and Prioritizing**. First, we search for and find the information we need. Then we must organize it so that it will make sense to our reader. This involves putting the information in order, and deciding what comes first, what comes next, and what we will tell at the end.

♦ **Taking Perspective**. When we think about what our reader needs to know, or might want to know, we have to *take the perspective of another person*. This important skill is one that young learners will use not only in writing but also in reading, and in daily life, and it typically increases with practice and with experience.

♦ **Word Choice**. We have to select from our available vocabulary for just the right words to explain our idea. Sometimes there might be more than one way to explain what we want to say, and so we can experiment with different kinds of words. Many words have more than one meaning, and we have to figure out the exact words that work best to explain our topic or idea.

♦ **Imagination and Creativity**. Both imagination and creativity play a role when we experiment with expressing a new idea, or when we try out a new combination of words. We use both when we try out new forms of writing, such as telling different kinds of stories or telling stories from different perspectives. We will experiment with these forms in Chapter 7.

♦ **Voice**. Writers talk about *finding their voice* through writing. Often, we don't know what we think about something until we write about it. This aspect of writing involves self-awareness, which helps us to estimate what we know and how well we know it. Self-awareness also helps us clarify what we think and why we think so. We sometimes go in a circle or loop, coming back to something we had thought previously, but with new eyes that help us *understand our own ideas* even better than before.

◆ **Developing Effective Communication**. Communicating with words, sentences, and paragraphs is an ongoing process for both young writers and adults. We have examined the kinds of sentences, the types of paragraphs, and all other aspects of writing so that young writers will develop the *experience* and *confidence* that contribute to effective communication.

As you look back at the list above, you will note many operations that teachers introduce as part of school learning. Parents can be assured that all your efforts with these ideas and these activities at home will contribute to building the thinking skills that will last your child for a lifetime of learning.

How to Approach Editing Using the Writer's Toolbox Tools

The Three Stages of Editing (For Young Writers)

All young writers must be taught the purpose and the importance of editing. For some children, editing can be a sensitive process and it must be handled with patience and encouragement so that they do not interpret it as a form of negative feedback. Editing is not about finding what is wrong with your writing. In fact, if it is handled in a positive manner, children can come away with the knowledge that they are gaining strength and improving their skills as a writer. We will look at some general guidelines that will be applied in different ways depending on the age of the writer, and what kind of writing is being edited. It is important to recognize that many young writers feel protective about what they have written, so our job is to develop the strategies that make editing an integrated part of the whole process of writing. We will introduce editing in three stages.

Stage 1. This stage simply involves having your child read aloud what she wrote to listen to those words being spoken.

Often at this stage, she will note where words may have been left out or sentences that don't quite make sense and will self-correct spontaneously. As a parent, you will note whether your child experiences stress or frustration with this process. If so, you can give a word of praise or ask a question for clarification. You can point out, again, that *writing is a process*, and we can add or change when we look back at what we wrote. At this early point in editing, we keep things positive to encourage persistence.

Stage 2. If your child reacts with courage and interest, you may be ready to proceed to the second stage. This involves examining the writing to see where we might add to or change the wording to make it better. This is a complex step because much depends on what has been written, the age of the writer, and how much time and patience you both have.

If you, as a parent, feel skilled at commenting on things like word choice, the order of the sentences, or parts that seem incomplete, you might start with what we call the *feedback agreement*. You can say: *"Are you okay with getting some feedback from me, as I was reading/hearing what you wrote? This is so that I can share what I think worked well and what I liked about your writing. We can talk about some parts where we could add or change, to make your sentences even better."* Your feedback agreement can also set the stage for you to provide an appropriate label on the occasion when a child might correct an incomplete sentence and provide an alternative that contains both a subject and predicate as needed (also known as Informative Feedback).

If the idea of rewriting seems too daunting, you could offer to type the writing on your computer, so that you can print it out and then make changes to the print copy. Use comments like *"When I read this part, it made me think…"* or questions like *"What were you thinking in your mind when you wrote this part?"*

This stage of editing takes practice and a lot of trust. By now you both may agree that what has been written is really good enough to work on further to make it even better. You might want to send it along to another family member to show what skills have been achieved. You are at Stage 3.

Stage 3. At the third stage, you note that when writers want a finished piece of writing, it is all about editing, rewriting, and editing again. All good writers do this, and the more we do it, the better we get at it. If you can, it's a good idea to use the computer to make print copies for the editing process. For some writers, it's easier to edit and make changes to a printed copy. This makes editing easier, but it still takes thought, patience, and persistence.

At the third stage, the goal is to get a product that has been worked and reworked, so that when we look at it again next week, or next month, we are proud of the effort. The third stage is not often reached in the busy classroom, where students may find there is not enough time to go back and really edit their work. It is sometimes difficult to get beyond the first draft.

In many ways, Stage 3 may be the parent's reward and the child's reward for work well done. This stage will show how the At-Home writing activities and writing tips have been successful because they have promoted an interest in, and a commitment to, writing that we all can be proud of. With the computer, we have the means to print good writing in a form that can be dated, collected, and shared. We have a trail of progress and documents of growth. Some families may have the means to turn out "books" and "articles" that can be illustrated or bound. The possibilities are endless with current technology. And meanwhile, you have made an investment in writing skills that will serve your child for a lifetime of learning.

Reference

Page, Mary, Guthrie, Peter, and Sable, Sloan. *Rules of the Game*, *Books 1–3*. Cambridge and Toronto: Educators Publishing Service, 2002.

6

Connecting Writing to Book Reading

Activity Level: Grade 2–5+

How Books Can Inspire Home Writing

The initial activities in *There's a Writer in Our House!* are home-centered for a good reason. Activities built into familiar situations and a familiar environment can make young writers feel comfortable and confident as they write about what they already know.

DOI: 10.4324/9781003452683-8

This is a natural starting point to get young writers engaged. In addition, the activities have been carefully designed to guide parents so that they can help their children develop the new skills they will need as writers. These activities take maximum advantage of children's background knowledge, strengths, and interests as starting points to build a solid foundation for new skills.

Family-based activities can be supplemented by another important source that we can connect to writing, *the books that children are reading or listening to.* For many children, a life-long reading habit starts with story books and information books that are written especially for young readers. As children read books in school, with the family, or on their own, they are building important background knowledge that comes mainly from books. Children hear and read stories about places and people that may be just like what they are familiar with, or more different than they can even imagine. In addition, books introduce information about the wide world that can be known *only through books.* This important benefit of book reading needs to be consistently emphasized because *reading is key to increasing background knowledge.*

Parents can capitalize on children's emerging interests by providing books that relate to existing interests and that introduce new information to help their minds grow. Trips to the library or the bookstore offer opportunities to explore new topics, see engaging pictures, and encounter stimulating ideas. Book reading allows young readers not only to try out their new reading skills but also to gain more information, *all on their own.* We now focus on book reading as a natural link to encourage and inspire writing.

Non-Fiction Books

In this chapter, we begin with activities that are specifically tailored *to information books.* This kind of writing activity has a different purpose than writing in response to fiction, and it develops a different set of writing skills. Writing responses to fiction will be explored in the sections to follow, where we can touch on elements of literature, such as how we are affected by characters and plots. Keep in mind that both non-fiction and fiction books are equally important sources of information for the young reader, even though their purposes appear to be different. Think about what young readers learn about life on a farm from reading or hearing *Charlotte's Web*!

School Writing Linked to Non-Fiction Book Reading

In the school classroom, writing lessons are frequently connected to the books that children read for class instruction in areas such as social studies and science. For example, they might be given the task of responding to specific book topics in a question-answer format. They must identify the correct information and then interpret it or summarize it as the answer. They may be asked questions about factual information, such as dates or names of important persons and places. The questions may require students to explain a key concept or vocabulary term. Sometimes students may just write down the same words as used in the textbook or the workbook, which may or may not indicate how well they have *absorbed the information.*

As they progress through the grades, students are given more complex forms of writing, such as essay questions. They might have to discuss a process, make a comparison, or explain a cause/effect relationship. These question-and-answer tasks all offer valuable training in academic learning. Parents may need to assist by giving help with how to interpret the questions or express the answers, or by checking the written work before it is ready to turn in.

At-Home Writing and Non-Fiction Book Reading

Beginning readers and writers are on the brink of a useful discovery. They are gradually learning to see reading and writing as two sides of the same coin, and not as separate and independent activities. Even very young children can understand that the words they are reading in a book were written *by somebody who knows how to write and has something to tell about a topic we might be interested in.* They will see that they, too, have the power to write thoughts and ideas in words that can be read by *somebody else*! At-Home writing can capitalize upon the fact that many children become eager writers when they can write about topics that interest them, from otters to butterflies to volcanoes.

There are many excellent sources for non-fiction materials written at an appropriate level for children. The *I Can Read* science books for early readers are a particularly good source for children who like learning about different sorts of animals or the natural world. Other sources include children's magazines such as *FACES* and *Cobblestone*, available through Cricket Media. Publications such as *National Geographic* have magazines for children, as does the National Wildlife Federation with its long-running *Ranger Rick*.

Writing Responses to Non-Fiction Books and Materials

If you have already begun exploring these kinds of information books with your child, you will see that writing can be connected to reading in a natural way during reading time. Imagine that you are sitting together to talk about the new information you are finding in a favorite book or magazine. In that moment, you can bring out a sheet of paper to write down some new facts and new ideas. You do this kind of writing with the book right in front of you so that you both can consult the book for how to spell the new words or science terms. You can encourage your child to dictate sentences for you to write, or your child can do the writing. At first, children might be inclined to write down exact sentences using the book's words, but gradually the art of *restating or paraphrasing* can be introduced when you say, *"How would you say that in your own words?"*

Useful Prompts and Sentence Starters

The following prompts can be used while you are reading along and come to a midway stopping point where there is something interesting that deserves comment, or after you have read a complete section or article. They are general in nature, to help you get started, and they can apply to a wide range of books and topics.

- ♦ Write about *something new* you learned that you did not already know.
- ♦ Write a sentence using a *new word* that you understand how to use because the book explained it.
- ♦ Write about something you read that *connects* to something you already know. You can explain the connection.
- ♦ Write about a *surprising fact*. Say why it is surprising.
- ♦ Write about *a picture* in the book. See if you can tell why the picture shows what the book tells you about.
- ♦ Write *a question* that you would ask the author to get more information.
- ♦ Write about *some other topics* this book makes us curious about. For example, did we start with dolphins and then want to go on to read about other marine mammals?
- ♦ Write about something *you could tell about this topic* to a younger child, like a little brother, sister, or cousin.

If you need some "sentence starters," try these:

- ♦ *I didn't know that…*
- ♦ *This picture really showed me…*
- ♦ *This book tells all about…*
- ♦ *This article taught me…*
- ♦ *This author knows a lot about…*
- ♦ *I would ask the author to tell me more about…*
- ♦ *This author seems to really like…*
- ♦ *When I read about the barn owl (or possums or iguanas), I wanted to know more about…*
- ♦ *If I could write another chapter for this book, it would be about…*

Using the Writing/Reading Link to Explain What You Have Learned

Non-fiction books are a good source to practice writing explanations, because the focus is on information and ideas, and you can use specific vocabulary from the book. To begin, you and your child together can select a "key" word from the book for your child to explain in writing. If you are reading about snakes and how snakes move, you might choose a word like "glide" or "slither" to explain in detail. This may lead to more technical words, such as "side-winding" that require added detail. The child's version need not be elegant, but it should be accurate, based on the information in the book. This can begin an early habit of *restating and reinforcing the new information your child has learned.* Remember that if the topic is highly technical and precise definitions are required for the explanation, you may need to use the specific vocabulary of the book, and then use more personal vocabulary *to make comments or observations.*

If your child has developed a deeper interest in a specific topic, you can explore how that topic links to information that may be found in other related sources. This is where *the background and the interests of the parent* can become useful to guide the child to see how different topics can connect in many interesting ways to each other. Or the focus might land on topics that are equally new to both parent and child, in which case some time can be spent on the computer or at the library to do a search of how one topic might connect to other areas of interest. All parties benefit from the search technologies that make information so easily accessible today, and the young writers benefit when the new information adds background to their writing repertoire. When this kind of activity is practiced at home with topics that are self-selected, your child may build a level of confidence that will be important when the topics are assigned in the classroom and there is less room for individual choice.

Using Pictures as Prompts

Children's science books are often well-illustrated with drawings and photographs of the animal, the volcano, or the rainforest in question. Animals in their natural habitats are often caught on camera doing things that make us curious or make us laugh. You can respond to animal pictures by writing answers to prompts such as these:

- ◆ *What do you think this animal is paying attention to?*
- ◆ *What did he just do?*
- ◆ *What is he going to do next?*

Here are some questions that a child might answer for pictures of natural places such as national parks, oceans, lakes, glaciers, or waterfalls:

- ♦ *If you were in this place, write about what you might be looking at most closely. What else would you want to see?*
- ♦ *If you were in this place, write about what you would expect to see just outside the edge of this picture.*
- ♦ *If you were in this place, write about what you would be sure to carry with you, and why?*

Making Book Recommendations

Children are often eager to share their opinions about a book, especially if they are used to having classroom discussions about the characters, what happens in the book, and how it all turned out. In school, your child may have been shown how to editorialize by writing an opinion about the book's contents, and why he or she liked or did not like the book.

These prompts encourage children to think more deeply about the book and to go beyond what they liked or did not like:

- ♦ *This book made me think about…*
- ♦ *This book made me wonder…*
- ♦ *I think the author is trying to…*
- ♦ *This author thinks it is important to know about…*

Your child might recommend the book to specific friends or family members and may even spot ways to make comparisons between books. Here are some sample comments you might share as models:

- ♦ *My friend Jason would like this book because it shows how kittens grow up.*
- ♦ *Grandma is always interested in how people use the plants around them to make up new recipes so she would like this book.*
- ♦ *This book had the best comments by the writer about how primates behave with their babies.*

- *The short book about snails didn't explain why snail bait works, but the longer book did.*
- *This book would make a good present for Eduardo to help him organize his shell collection.*

Writing Your Own Questions about the Book You Are Reading

Adults give children lots of experience in *answering questions*. Once they start school, they are in that position on a daily basis, when they answer the teacher's questions. At home, children learn early on about asking questions because they figure out that's the way they get their needs met. The questions kids ask are often procedural, about what is happening around the house: *when, where, how*, and especially *why*.

When children learn to read information books, the most-asked question they hear is, "*What is it **about**?*" However, parents can promote a *different level of curiosity* when you engage together in the back-and-forth of questioning and answering. When you make the link between writing and reading, you can turn questioning in a new direction *by encouraging children to pose the questions*. This can be done in a purposeful and systematic way, as you will see. It is important to note that this kind of question-asking promotes a key element of critical thinking, which we call *inquiry*. Inquiry promotes *curiosity*. Inquiry encourages children to ask varied questions, as well as follow-up questions. When you participate in question-asking with your children, you signal to them that *inquiry is an important state of mind for learning*.

Three Types of Questions for Children to Explore

Start noting the types of questions that your children are already asking. You may spot the following three forms of questions, and when you identify and label them, you will help your child develop a greater awareness of *the purposes and kinds of questions*.

In addition to the three forms of questions noted here, which connect to information-based reading, you will find a full discussion of the role of questions in *Critical Thinking* in Chapter 10, with activities to practice a broad range of question types that are introduced.

1. *Fact Questions*. These are questions about facts or information stated directly in the text. The answer is "right there." Fact question examples might include:
   ◆ *Where do rattlesnakes live?*
   ◆ *How many kinds of butterflies live in the Midwestern states of North America?*
   ◆ *Which butterflies migrate and where do they go?*
   ◆ *What animal is a close relative of the badger?*
   ◆ *How fast can a cheetah run?*
   ◆ *What is the oldest National Park?*
   ◆ *Which African countries grow cacao trees?*

2. *Thinking Questions*. These questions require us to make some kind of connection that is suggested by the book but may not be directly stated. They require us to "think and search." Your child might be able to ask about some comparisons, such as how similar animals search for food, or how different insects defend themselves. As they gain a background in science and geography, they may even see how very different animals can have similarities, such as how they use listening to survive, or how animals from different parts of the world can behave in similar ways. In the same way, your child might spot a cause/effect relationship to ask about. Examples might include:
   ◆ *Why should people be careful not to make loud noises around the nesting birds?*
   ◆ *Why should people watch their step in the tide pools?*
   ◆ *Why do different animals have different ways of moving their babies?*
   ◆ *What are the main reasons birds migrate?*

3. *On-Your-Own Questions*. These questions require further research, beyond what is directly stated, requiring the reader to go to another source. Examples might include:

◆ *What other animals besides manatees are endangered by people in boats?*

◆ *What other desert plants offer shelter to birds and reptiles?*

◆ *Are there species of fish in the ocean that we never see? If so, why do we never see them?*

There are many benefits for the child who is encouraged to ask and write questions about books. First, children may have the idea that only adults are qualified to ask questions about material that we read. In school, it's the teacher who is the *questioner-in-chief*. At home, it's the parents. Children can be shown that they, too, have the power to ask good questions. Second, when children ask questions about what they are reading, they tend to become more engaged readers. They learn to go *beyond the information given*.

Finally, when children engage in question-asking, they begin to learn the essential nature of inquiry. There is a great step taken when a child advances from the simple *What* and *Where* questions, to the *How* and *Why* questions. It is the step taken when children are able to use new fact-based information to think about the more complex ways in which facts relate to or connect with each other. Using their knowledge and ideas, they can ponder advanced logical relationships such as reasons, processes, comparisons, cause/effect, sequences, and other relationships that are discussed in Chapter 5. At-Home activities provide many opportunities to explore and practice how to use these patterns in writing.

At-Home Writing and Children's Literature

The great works of children's literature are, for many children, the entry point into becoming a life-long reader. Teachers, families, and librarians have served as traditional sources for the books that each culture values as being of special importance to childhood. For many children, the first exposure to the world of books takes place upon the lap of a family member, whether it is a parent, grandparent, uncle or aunt, big sister or brother, or anyone else in the family who can read. These shared experiences open doors to imagination, exploration, mystery, humor, and the people and places that exist beyond our immediate world. Book reading can offer both stimulation and solace, and often both at once. It is no surprise then, that there are hundreds of books written to promote book reading by children, such as *How to Raise a Reader* by Pamela Paul and Maria Russo (2019). There are many ways that At-Home writing and At-Home reading can contribute to engaging children with literature.

The Book Critic

Experiences with children's literature can involve not only the books children read on their own, but also books that are shared through listening to a parent or teacher reading aloud, or through an audio tape of the book. No matter what kind of experience, children can be encouraged to offer an opinion. In school, children are often asked to write a book report that "sells" the book. They may be asked to make a poster or a picture showing an "important part" of the book. When these instructional activities involve writing, especially writing about the book from an unusual perspective, they contribute significantly to a child's writing repertoire. Parents can be watchful for such activities that might come home from school.

Many school districts and classrooms offer lists of "Ways of Reporting on Books." Such lists will include activities that stick very close to the story in question, but may also have other approaches that become favorites because they are so imaginative:

♦ *Tell about a part of the story that you think could not really have happened.*

♦ *Write a letter to one of the characters and ask that character some good questions.*

♦ *Write an account of what you would have done, if you had been one of the characters, instead of what the book's character did.*

♦ *If you could meet or have lunch with X (a character in the book), what activity would you want to do together?*

- ◆ *If you could interview (or have lunch with) the author, write what you would ask.*
- ◆ *What do you think happened right after the last page of this book?*
- ◆ *Compare two or more books written about the same kind of situation.*
- ◆ *Compare two books written by the same author.*

Be the Expert: Information-Based Writing about Your Own Topic

Young readers take very naturally to reading information books such as the early science books, or children's magazines that feature timely and interesting topics. These kinds of books are generally written by expert authors who have a genuine interest in the topic, whether it's sharks, bats, or the leaf-cutter ants that eat the leaves of the cacao trees. Many a young scientist has evolved from these early interests, and this kind of information-based material serves as an excellent model *for young writers.*

In Chapter 4 we noted two special types of books that often prompt a written response. The first was the *wordless picture book* where the child could write the words that tell the story, and the second was the book in which *the story is told through letters.* Both of these kinds of books can prompt a child to engage in the kind of writing we call "creative writing," which is a bit different from writing a response to a non-fiction book. However, there is one additional way a child might share ideas that were prompted by book reading. If your child has developed some specific interests, for example, in science topics, sports topics, or cooking topics, you might suggest *writing an information article.* With appropriate background, children can use their own knowledge to write about a topic in their "area of expertise."

Children as young as third and fourth graders might write the following:

- ◆ *A guide to my neighborhood.*
- ◆ *A guide to my school.*

- *A guide to my church.*
- *Getting the kitchen ready to bake brownies.*
- *A guide to caring for a fish in an aquarium.*
- *How to make a new puppy feel at home.*
- *Small pets for small spaces.*
- *Best plants for a small garden.*
- *Best games for a rainy afternoon.*
- *How to take care of your new soccer shoes.*
- *Most interesting ways to win a baseball game.*
- *Best activities to help my sister babysit the four-year-old next door.*

These topics maintain the focus on information that is known and based upon direct experience. Information writing can lead to further research on such topics as how to train a puppy, or how to clean the fish aquarium, but the starting point is *what the writer knows.* This kind of writing firmly reinforces the idea that people who write books are starting with what they know and are interested in. Be aware that this kind of writing involves more planning and research, and to be done well also requires editing. Your child might come to realize the amount of research and organizing a writer must do in order to write a book, and indeed, these early writing ideas may result in later years in a book based upon the inspiration of these efforts!

Your Intended Audience

Writing to explain ideas or information about different topics is an excellent exercise at any level. An exercise in varying the way information is presented may offer your child a good additional challenge. As children become aware of the nature of books, they have probably noted that some books are intended just for children, and some are just for adults. Though they might not use this term, they have become aware of the *difficulty level* of books. When your child is ready, you can introduce the idea of the "intended audience," that is, who the book or article is written for. You might say, *"Would Sissy (age 7) be interested in reading about this? Would Grandma or Grandpa be interested in reading about this?"* It would then be a natural transition to suggest taking one of the available topics and *writing about it twice*: one explanation of the topic for Grandma or any other grown-up, and one explanation of the same topic for a younger sister, brother, cousin, or friend.

Early researchers in child language development found that young children are able, at a very early age, to adopt a "register" that is adjusted to meet the language abilities of listeners of different ages. That is, even by the ages of four to six years, children are able to adapt their language to *the needs of the listener*. They use simpler sentences and simpler words for their younger siblings than they use for parents and grandparents, and they do this by imitation, without direct instruction from anyone. We can use this remarkable ability that children possess to explore how they could apply this understanding *when they write*. You might explore whether this holds true for your child.

Start with what to write for a grown-up person: *"Let's pretend that Grandma has never learned about how snails move. Could you write down how the snail uses its foot to push itself along?"* After everyone agrees about the explanation (this may be the occasion for light editing), then go on: *"Let's put this writing aside and pretend that Sissy wants to know the same thing, only she isn't as grown up as Grandma. You might have to make the sentences easier for Sissy."*

The two versions may offer insights into how we write for different audiences. You can note where your young writer used simpler sentences, or where he or she has selected a more basic vocabulary for the younger reader, even though they may not have done this consciously. They will benefit when you point out what they have done and give them positive feedback for the way they managed this very deliberate and useful strategy. They have modified the message to accommodate the abilities and needs of the readers.

On to Creative Writing

Chapter 7 will take us to the realm of writing that is typically called "creative writing" in the classroom. Sometimes this form of writing can be very daunting to the non-poets and the non-storytellers. Your own family may have a child like this, who is often called "the man of few words," though this can be a characteristic of girls, too. These are often children who are very literal-minded and who may find it difficult to "play" with words, use words for multiple purposes, or use words for dramatic effect. To promote creative thinking in the classroom, creative writing activities are often based on a poem or story that the class reads and studies, as a model, after which the children will be encouraged to produce something similar.

The children's author, Sharon Creech, has given us an engaging "novel," told entirely in lines of poetry, called *Love That Dog*. In this "novel," Jack takes us through his own classroom experience with poetry, in Miss Stretchberry's class (Room 105).

He begins with these lines at the beginning of the school year, on September 13:

> *I don't want to*
> *because boys*
> *don't write poetry.*
> *Girls do.*

Jack continues on September 21:

> *I tried.*
> *Can't do it.*
> *Brain's empty.*

Through the dated entries, we follow Jack's musings about the meaning of the lines of the poems they study in Miss Stretchberry's class. We follow him through his attempts to write his own poems, through his meeting up with a real poet who comes to his class and shares poems, through to a very touching and moving ending that will perhaps give you some perspective on how children think about such things. This little treasure of a book is one that can take your child into the mind of a writer, and that can inspire creativity, At-Home. Using the context of the familiar, in Chapter 7 we will venture into the realm of the creative.

References

Creech, Sharon. *Love That Dog*. New York: Joanna Cotler Books, HarperTrophy, 2001.

Paul, Pamela and Russo, Maria. (Editors, *The New York Times Book Review*). *How to Raise a Reader*. New York: Workman Publishing, 2019.

Getting Creative

Activity Level: 6+ years

EASY ACCESS NOTES FOR CHAPTER 7: WHAT YOU WILL LEARN

♦ How to Promote Creativity, Beginning with Descriptive Writing.

♦ Why Descriptive Writing is a Useful Starting Point: Describing Objects, Places, and Events.

♦ The Role of the Five Senses: Sight, Sound, Smell, Taste, Feel.

♦ Ideas for Getting Started: Objects First, Places Next, Then Events.

♦ Markers of Growth; Progress Charts for Descriptive Writing (Downloads).

♦ Writing a Story and What to Watch For.

♦ Writing a Poem or a Song, and How to Start.

♦ Word Games for Ages Six and Older: *Hinky Pinky*; *Word Reversals*; *Word Worms*; *Magic Word*.

♦ Tips for Parents about How Best to Offer Encouragement and Ideas that Expand the Activities.

Promoting Creativity with At-Home Writing Activities

When children write at an early age with systematic and informed guidance, we can expect positive impacts on important

DOI: 10.4324/9781003452683-9

developmental areas: their communication and language skills, thinking skills, learning strategies and reading skills, confidence, and curiosity. In Chapter 7, as we invite children to try out their imaginations, we highlight the impact writing can have *on their creativity*. We show how they can use written words to make readers see a picture in their mind to explore kinds of feelings, to make someone laugh out loud, or even to make someone clap their hands in surprise. They can play with words, and they can experiment with all the different things words can do.

Sometimes people think this kind of writing is only for the natural storytellers, or the great poets, or the talented authors, but we will see what can be done when *everyone is included* in At-Home writing. Children may have met this kind of writing at school where it is called *creative writing*. The class is given a prompt and asked to write about "a funny experience" or "a scary moment." Most children are willing to try to write something that fits the prompt, and they may be encouraged to use colorful adjectives or adverbs to make the writing more lively. But there are some who will find this to be a daunting challenge if the prompt does not relate well to who they are or to what they have experienced. Every child can be shown that beyond writing to a prompt, there is a wide variety of ways to use language creatively, share a unique point of view, appreciate the unusual, or show a sense of humor. Children often develop an ability to play with words when they experiment with the writing activities that are offered in Chapter 7.

Most children love riddles and word jokes, no matter how corny. Children who have loved the books of Dr. Seuss or the poems of Shel Silverstein know how much humor can be found in rhyming words and silly sentences. If your child delights in songs and nursery rhymes, you may have added your own poems and songs to the *Writing Wall*, the *Journal*, or the *Written Conversations*. To make their writing more permanent, children can be given their own notebooks or journals where they can record their creative ideas through these activities *for writing descriptions, writing a story, writing a poem or a song, and playing word games.*

Writing Descriptions: Objects, Places, and Events

Writing descriptions is a good starting point for several reasons. First, this kind of writing can involve a concrete object or place, and it can incorporate the use of the five senses to provide a foundation for the written details. It is an especially accessible kind of writing for the child who is good at observation and feels comfortable with a more factual kind of writing. It's a kind of writing that is guaranteed to improve word choice and the powers of observation. Descriptive writing is often very satisfying to the reluctant writer because he or she can focus on the details that are *clearly observable*. Finally, it offers a writing task that can be broken down into small steps for the writer who might be easily overwhelmed.

To write a description of just about anything, we turn to the five senses: *sight, sound, smell, taste,* and *feel*. Each of our senses contributes a different form of information about what we are describing. Sometimes the sense of sight will dominate, for example, clouds or a rainbow. Sometimes the sense of smell will dominate: the rose garden or the corral where the ponies live. Sometimes it's the sound: Grandma's clock or a cousin's motorcycle. Sometimes the sense of touch will dominate: the new kitty or a perfectly square ice cube. And, of course, if we are describing something we eat, we include taste: tangy fresh-made lemonade or a rich chocolate chip cookie.

1. Describing an Object

When we describe objects, we can depend on the five senses, no matter which one (or ones) may dominate. We will use color and shape to describe how the object *looks*, and we may compare it to another, similar object. Some objects make a *sound*, such as a musical instrument, a clock, or a bird. Many objects have a characteristic *smell*, such as a candle or a hamster. Other objects can be *tasted* or at least put in the mouth, such as an ice cube or a grape. And if our object is available to the touch, we can describe how it *feels*, often with a simple adjective: *sticky, sharp, smooth,* or *bumpy*.

Along with using our senses for our description, we may also bring in other characteristics of our object, place, or event. We may write about how the object works, that is, its *function*. We may write about why the object is in our house when we describe its *purpose*. We may note how the object looks from more than one point of view, and thus consider *perspective*. And of course, if we have chosen an object that we may have strong feelings about, we can talk about how the object *makes us feel*. This kind of writing can be amusing, frustrating, and inspiring, often all at the same time.

Writing a description of an object is a test of our ability to choose just the right word. In addition, when children try out this kind of writing, they often use their powers of observation in new ways that they may not yet have tried out. They have to provide details in such a way that another person would be able to "see" what they are writing about. For the items that we can see, we need the word that will convey an image, a color, or a shape, depending on whether we are up close or far away. This is true whether we are describing a toy, a food, a piece of sports equipment, or our very own room.

It's Time to Jump Right In

With the activities suggested, we begin with objects that are familiar to help your child catch on to describing. You can start with this list of household objects that we can all recognize easily. As interests change or as your writer becomes more confident, you will think of items to add that may be harder to recognize, such as the items that are seldom used or that no one pays attention to anymore. To add even more to the challenge of the activity, you can turn this into a *guessing game* by having your writer write the description *without naming the object*. You or another family member must guess what it is from the descriptive clues. Please note that you must be prepared for when it is *your turn* to write the description, and your child must guess the object. Many of these activities can easily be made *reciprocal*.

TABLE 7.1 Familiar Objects in My House

◆ Toothbrush	◆ Shopping bag
◆ Shoe	◆ Kitchen knife
◆ Pillow	◆ Pet's food dish
◆ Mirror	◆ Toy animal
◆ Front door	◆ Soccer ball
◆ Coat hanger	◆ Bar of soap
◆ Ice cube	◆ Alarm clock

TABLE 7.2 Descriptive Details of Objects Using the Five Senses

◆ Color	◆ Smell
◆ Shape	◆ Sound
◆ Size (as measured, or as compared with…)	◆ Taste (only if appropriate!)
◆ Texture	◆ What it looks like from more than one point of view

TABLE 7.3 Descriptive Details That Go Beyond Appearances

◆ Parts	◆ Who it belongs to
◆ Weight	◆ How long we have had it
◆ Function	◆ Why it is special (or treasured, or annoying)
◆ How it works	
◆ Why it is here in my house	

Based on the five senses, the writer establishes the initial information that helps identify the object. In addition, when your child writes about *"How it works, Why it is here in my house,* and *What it looks like from more than one point of view,"* they must go beyond the object's appearance and *make some interpretations.* These interpretations may well lead to stating some opinions that add even more flavor and color to the physical description. In other words, your writer may begin to think about *why the object is important,* which matters just as much as telling what the object looks, feels, and tastes like.

The list of household objects is just to get you started. Children will have a lot to add as you go along. They can be encouraged to include objects that they find curious or puzzling, such as family treasures that have been around the house for a while. Their fresh ideas may prompt the grown-ups to see things from a new perspective.

2. Describing a Place

When you practice descriptive writing by describing objects, you have made a good start to attempting something that is more complicated: *a description of a specific place*. This is a worthwhile challenge for young writers because they will find, first of all, that they will think about the chosen place in a new way *when they begin to write about it*. Their skills of observation will expand, and they will be able to include new and more powerful words. Topics will vary, depending on where you live. You may write about *a beach or a river, a quiet street or a busy road, a place in nature, a place in your busy community*, or *a place in your house*. You can pick the place depending on how it feels, or how it makes you feel: *a peaceful place, an energetic place, a boring place, a puzzling place, a mysterious place.*

Before you begin writing, spend some time talking about the task. When your young writers set out to describe a place, they may at first be overwhelmed by the sheer number of things there are to write about. You can say, *"You might have looked at this space a hundred times, but there may be some things here that you will decide to focus your writing on, especially if you have not noticed them very much before. They might be important details for your description."* Or you can say, *"There might be some details that are important to you, but they would not be something that Dad would pay attention to. **You get to make the decision.**"*

A familiar topic for many children is "A Room in My House."

- ◆ Start with a walk around the space, to get a sense of what stands out.
- ◆ Make a list of what is there to see. Are there things there that you cannot see, such as items in a drawer or cupboard, that are important to the space?
- ◆ Think about perspective and angle of view. Do you look mostly up, down, or just across to see the space?
- ◆ Think about how the objects within the space relate to each other: close enough to touch, distant, stacked, or beautifully arranged together.
- ◆ Why are some items in the space close together, while other items are far apart?

♦ Think about what details are most important to the space, that is, details that would help identify the space and help us tell this space from all other spaces.

Different Ideas for Place Description

This kind of writing exercise can be divided into sections, so it does not become too complicated.

♦ Write about what you can see from standing in just one spot in this space.
♦ Tell what you can see when you lie down in this space.
♦ If it is an indoor space, write about what might catch your attention if you could look down on the space from the ceiling or other high point such as a light fixture.
♦ You could explain what the different objects are made of, or how they function.
♦ You could record favorite or recent memories of the space, to show how the space makes you feel.
♦ You could include observations about what you saw in the space, or what you learned about the space, that you had not thought about or noticed before.
♦ You could recommend this space to someone who would really enjoy or appreciate it. Say who and why.

Your young writer can test the success of these first two types of descriptive writing by asking a friendly reader to see if he or she can visualize what is being described. This kind of writing can easily become collaborative by inviting your friendly readers to contribute descriptive details of their own. Take note of whether your writer organizes the descriptive details in a systematic manner, or just writes the details as they are noticed.

3. Describing an Event

Describing an event is the most complex kind of descriptive writing, and you can see why. There are so many ways to look at an event. This is where young writers can learn about *point of view*.

They can think about *the perspective of the writer,* and how two different writers might describe the same event in two very different ways.

This simple checklist will help you get started. You will recognize that these are also the elements of telling a good story!

◆ Who?
◆ When?
◆ Where?
◆ What?
◆ Why?

Have your child choose an event that had some *importance or impact* for him or her. You could discuss together what parts of the event seemed to stand out and why. When you write about an event that happens *in time,* you will be using *Narrative Writing,* the basis of all storytelling.

If your child has been a reader of good stories, writing one's own narrative may seem daunting at first. So many things need to be included for it to make sense. If they show any concern about writing something this complicated, be reassuring. It won't feel perfect the first time. But a first draft offers lots of opportunities for discussion and revision if you care to try for a second draft. For now, it's perfectly fine to just date that first draft and set it aside. It may contain some gems of observation that we may come back to at another time to expand or elaborate.

Begin with the familiar. Remember that even when life seems quiet, events happen all the time, every day, so there are usually lots to choose from. If your family is interested in the daily news, you can start with a discussion about what makes an event "newsworthy." But not all events that you might choose to write about have to be the kind of event that would make the front page of the newspaper. If you begin with "the eyes of a child," you can explore the more immediate and important daily events that get our attention. There are always special events, like birthdays or trips, but your child could just as easily turn an ordinary event into something *worth telling about in writing.* Your role as the parent here may be to simply encourage and promote the efforts to capture a real-time moment in written words and to value the effort it took, as well as the written description that may result.

If you need an idea for the kind of event to choose, it's useful to look for the unexpected, just because *the unexpected is interesting*. Sometimes a good title can get the creative juices flowing. Topics from the *Family Response Journal* activity, or from *Paired/Shared* writing might still be around, such as *Surprise of the Day* or *A Lesson Learned*. Some children can be challenged to take a routine event, like shopping for shoes, and use their description of that event to show it in a new light. They might describe an event in the shoe store from the point of view of the tired shoe salesman helping a fussy kid, or from the point of view of the mom who would rather be buying the new shoes for herself!

Letter writing can often promote an interest in describing events. If your child is fortunate enough to have a close relative or friend who lives in a different town, or even in a different neighborhood, sending news of family events can become a life-long and valuable form of communicating. The checklist with the "5 Ws" (at the beginning of this section on describing an event) can give a dependable structure that not only shares the important elements of an event, but also leads to our ability *to create stories*, which is another form of creative writing that can flow from this activity.

Markers of Growth: What You Can Learn from Your Child's Descriptive Writing

There are many benefits to you as a parent when children begin this kind of writing. Besides giving satisfaction to all participants, these drafts of descriptive writing have important information about your child's developing skills. If you are fortunate to have an enthusiastic writer, you may now have dated writing samples that you can look back at for other markers of growth. Here are some things to watch for, and a simple chart for recording progress markers.

◆ **Word choice**. Is your child starting to use good descriptive words, like adjectives? Has your writer included specific names of things? You might see good *labels* of items (common nouns) or names of specific persons and places (proper nouns). Are there good *action words* (verbs) that show the specific kinds of actions that your child can now describe?

◆ **Kinds of sentences**. Note the kinds of sentences he or she writes. Are they mainly the short statements we call *declarative sentences*, or are they experimenting with longer sentences that may include a *question* or two, or an *exclamation* about something that is unexpected?

◆ **Number of words and sentences**. As your child's confidence grows, you may find an overall increase in the total number of words being used, the number of different words, as well as the number of sentences about a given topic.

◆ **Number of topics**. There may be a single topic or there may be multiple topics, with good details about each one. Sometimes the writing may even reach "book" length, showing your child's ability to maintain focus and develop a topic, as might be required for a school writing assignment.

◆ **Signs that your child values this kind of writing**. For parents, there is high value in a child's early writing, which you value through "parent eyes." Be sure your child understands that these early writings, which may look "babyish" when viewed through more critical eyes, are worthy of collecting and reviewing. We save and appreciate them because they are the historical record, the evidence of the beginning of a writing habit. Therefore, we watch for signs that the child is also learning to value and appreciate the efforts. Parents can encourage a special place to collect the writing, such as a notebook or folder. Your child may even come up with a worthy title: *My Life as a Writer!*

Progress Charts for Descriptive Writing: Object, Place, and Event

This kind of progress chart is meant to be informal. We are not "measuring" progress, which would suggest there is some kind of metric or standard for writing that could apply regardless of the age or interests of the child. Rather, the purpose here is to record descriptive notes that offer details of the areas you are observing. For example, under *Varieties of Words*, you can note examples of specific noun labels, pronouns used appropriately, or well-chosen adjectives. Under *Varieties of Sentences*, you can note the use of more complex sentences or signal words that connect ideas to each other within the sentences.

TABLE 7.4 Descriptive Writing: Object

Marker	Time #1	Time #2	Time #3	Time #4
Varieties of words:				
◆ Specific nouns				
◆ Action verbs				
◆ Adjectives/adverbs				
Varieties of sentences:				
◆ Complete sentences				
◆ Simple declarative sentences				
◆ Compound sentences, with clauses				
Number of sentences				
Number of words				
Behaviors:				
◆ Responds well to task				
◆ Willing to spend time				
◆ Makes improvements and corrections				
◆ Shows persistence				

TABLE 7.5 Descriptive Writing: Place

Marker	Time #1	Time #2	Time #3	Time #4
Varieties of words:				
◆ Specific nouns				
◆ Action verbs				
Adjectives/adverbs				
Varieties of sentences:				
◆ Complete sentences				
◆ Simple declarative sentences				
Compound sentences, with clauses				
Number of sentences				
Number of words				
Behaviors:				
◆ Responds well to task				
◆ Willing to spend time				
◆ Makes improvements and corrections				
◆ Shows persistence				

TABLE 7.6 Descriptive Writing: Event

Marker	Time #1	Time #2	Time #3	Time #4
Varieties of words:				
◆ Specific nouns				
◆ Action verbs				
Adjectives/adverbs				
Varieties of sentences:				
◆ Complete sentences				
◆ Simple declarative sentences				
Compound sentences, with clauses				
Number of sentences				
Number of words				
Behaviors:				
◆ Responds well to task				
◆ Willing to spend time				
◆ Makes improvements and corrections				
◆ Shows persistence				

Writing a Story

If your child has written a description of an event, you have all the pieces in place for *story writing*. All cultures share their customs, traditions, history, and wisdom through stories. Through children's stories, we transmit ideas and beliefs about childhood, and cultural knowledge and values from one generation to the next. In addition, children are often first introduced *to written language* when we read them stories from books. Experts on child language development all stress the importance of reading aloud to children, with a focus on holding the book for the child to see and reading in the kind of "storytelling" voice that grabs a child's attention. This can happen very early in the life of a child, even before the child can speak and talk. After all, children are surrounded by *the sounds of language* well before they are born!

Thus, it would be very natural to encourage children to write their own stories. Stories could begin with a tale about daily life within the family, about a visitor to your home, about a new pet in the house, or about an unexpected event. The story could involve new interests that are emerging in your child's life, such as swimming lessons or learning a musical instrument. Many young children show an early interest in collecting things, such as rocks, plants, or shells. They may discover watching birds with small field glasses or planting seeds to see them sprout. They may explore drawing their own pictures or taking pictures with a camera. These early interests can be the basis of stories and are often a precursor to compelling interests that continue into adulthood.

When children write their stories about such topics, they share their personal connections to the wider world of family events, school learning, or childhood activities. When a child shows an interest in story writing, you can introduce the ideas of *the elements of a story*: the setting, the characters, the main problem (or conflict) of the story, and how it was solved (or not!). Encourage your child to identify these elements in a story they have already read, so that they can see the importance of each element. Your child will already have this useful background if such items have been discussed *in the classroom*, often in connection with the children's literature they are studying and discussing.

A child's tale might involve the fantastic and the imaginary. Some children invent imaginary friends and have adventures.

Some children pick up on characters from current TV programs, videos, or children's movies. Whether about the familiar or the imaginary, children's stories offer a delightful way to capture their emerging view of the world. If you do have a storyteller, there are two ways to capture the stories. The child who has gained confidence in her own handwriting can write for herself, with a bit of assistance from parents to help spell the new words. Or the story can be dictated to a willing grown-up who may write the words, or type the story on the computer, print it out, and thus make a book for the child to illustrate. Many early readers became *lifelong readers* by writing and reading their own stories.

What to Watch For

Parents may have questions about a "story" their child has written. What do you do if the story does not follow the usual pattern for a story, with a beginning, a middle, and an end? There might be characters who come and go, with no clear connection to the storyline. Or there may be no storyline at all. Children's early stories can be thought of as *simple narratives*. Your child is just telling a tale, and the tale may not follow the expected path.

Children's stories should be valued for just what they are: a storyteller's attempt to tell a good tale, no matter where it may lead. If your child seems interested, you can introduce the idea of more than one event in the story (this would correspond to the idea of "chapters" or "plot"), by asking, *"What happened next?"* Follow the child's lead. You could add more to the story right now or put it aside for later consideration. Just be sure the story is dated, so that you can come back to it later if you choose.

Watch for important elements of storytelling that may emerge. Besides the events in the storyline, your child may include descriptions of places, which would identify the *setting* of the story. This would be an outcome of your practice in describing places. You can note specific details about how the place looks or feels. As children develop a sense of time, you might find details about real time or imaginary time. The books that children read or listen to have probably introduced them to the idea of a *character*. The main character in your child's story might be a child who is the same age as the writer, or a special family member such as a grandmother. The main character might also be an animal, as children encounter stories about a brave dog, a small mouse, or a pig named Wilbur and a spider named Charlotte!

Even very young children understand the ideas of *mystery or conflict* that are at the heart of every good story. The mystery in a child's story does not have to be on the scale of the *Harry Potter* books but can be as simple as the disappearance of the dog's dish or where Mom lost her gardening hat! If your writers have attempted a story with a mystery, it is good to reassure them that *not all mysteries get solved*. One good story often leads to another. The important lesson to be gained from the story-writing experience is that stories are often a way to tell a truth about life: *all experiences that we have can be shaped into a story that reveals who we are, what we pay attention to, what we think is important, or what we want to become.*

Writing a Poem or a Song

Poem writing often begins with reading poetry written by well-known poets, or by singing songs that have rhyming. Children learn chants to sing along with playground activities such as jump rope. Many children's school, church, and camp activities have poetry and song. If your child can invent poems, be sure to encourage them to capture their poems in writing. The sections to follow offer writing activities that can involve *rhyming words, if your child enjoys rhyming.*

Starting with a Title
Many great songs or poems have begun with just a title. If your child loves Dr. Seuss, she could change *The Cat in the Hat* to *The Fox in the Box* or *The Dog on a Log. The Bug on the Rug* could drive Mom crazy or make her laugh. You could make up names of creatures for a poem: *Sneetches, Wockets,* and *Nizzards* all have lasted for a long time for readers of Dr. Seuss. Shel Silverstein has specialized in poems about Outrageous Things: *"How not to have to dry the dishes"* or *"How to make a swing with no rope or board or nails"* (hint: grow a long mustache that you can drape over the limb of a tree and swing from it!). Remember that all great poets

have understood the art of *borrowing other poets' ideas* and making them even better!

Some titles are just two rhyming words (see also the section on *Hinky Pinky*, to follow) that suggest a whole situation: *"The Wet Vet," "The Rookie Cookie,"* or *"The Dragon Wagon."* Much depends on the age and interests of your child, but no matter what their interests are, children are frequently inspired by hearing the words of the really great children's poets.

Parents who read poems aloud to their children will often notice how easily children begin to memorize poetry. As you may remember from your own childhood, the reasons that poems and songs are easily remembered by children stem from the very nature of the rhythm of the lines, and the melody of the rhyming words. That's the whole basis of the nursery rhymes that children grow up on. These patterns of poetry and song become available in a child's mind for the invention of new poems and songs. If this is the case with your child, you can encourage her to add a line or two to an existing nursery rhyme. If that catches on, you can be there to help her write down the "new" poem. These and other poems can involve "made up" words that contribute to the rhythm and rhyme, which may require your help with some inventive spelling.

As you expose your child to more children's poetry, take note of which rhymes persist in memory, not only for your child but for yourself. If you are not certain of where to start, begin with the classics: Robert Louis Stevenson, Dr. Seuss, Shel Silverstein, Jack Prelutsky, and many others. You may promote a lifelong habit that will delight your children through life, whether or not they ever write their own poetry.

Word Games for Ages Six and Older

Hinky Pinky

The *Hinky Pinky* is a rhyming pair of two-syllable words that can be guessed from a clue. For example, if I ask you what is a five-cent cucumber, you answer, *"a Nickel Pickle."* If I ask you what is the violin in the center, you answer, *"the Middle Fiddle."* A fake horse is a *"Phony Pony."* A sports closet is a *"Soccer Locker."* A fortunate water bird is a *"Lucky Ducky."*

If the rhyming words are just one syllable, that's a *Hink Pink*. If I ask you what is a large feline, you answer, a *"Fat Cat."* If I ask you what is a black bird that does not fly fast, you answer, a *"Slow Crow."* A drenched dog is a *"Wet Pet."* Sky-colored footwear is a *"Blue Shoe."* A tidy road is a *"Neat Street."* You get the idea.

For slightly more complicated word pairs, you may try a *Hinkety Pinkety*, where your rhyming words have three syllables. If I ask you what is a babyish reptile, you answer, an *"Infantile Crocodile."* If I ask you what is an albino primate, you answer, a *"Vanilla Gorilla."* If you start this game, be prepared for some outrageous combinations.

Part of the fun is the *Hinky Pinky* itself, but there is a great challenge in selecting the best words *for the clue*. To create a good clue, think about how well you need to select synonyms for each part of your *Hinky Pinky*. Think about the words that are literally synonyms, such as "infantile" for "babyish," or "fiddle" for "violin." Other choices may be more of a stretch until we see what two words are being linked together: "albino" with "vanilla." *Hinky Pinky* pairs deserve a place of their own on the *Word Wall*.

Word Reversals

This is a good game for children who are starting to notice how a word's meaning can change depending on how it relates to other words. This game involves a pair of words, of any number of syllables, that are commonly connected and make sense together, both forward and backward. Take a look at the examples below and think about what you as a parent could introduce to your child as a fun way to explore and play with word relationships. Some of the ideas here depend upon a broader base of experience background than a younger child has (as yet) had a chance to develop. Still, it's a good starting point to get children to think about how words *relate to each other*. The successful pairs involve words that can each function as both nouns and adjectives, or both nouns and verbs, and that make sense when paired both forward and backward.

Most of us have noted that a *Venetian Blind* is not the same as a *Blind Venetian*. A *Crime Novel* is different from a *Novel Crime*. There are some more in Table 7.7.

TABLE 7.7 Word Reversals

Head cold – Cold head	Dish Soap – Soap Dish
Dirt cheap – Cheap dirt	Box Lunch – Lunch Box
Plate glass – Glass plate	Snow White – White Snow
Entry level – Level entry	Player Piano – Piano Player
Dog toy – Toy dog	Red Light – Light Red
Eye glass – Glass eye	Drum Solo – Solo Drum
Page One – One page	Dress Rehearsal – Rehearsal dress
Home run – Run home	Official playoff – Playoff Official
Pool toy – Toy pool	

Now you try some in Table 7.8.

TABLE 7.8 Word Reversals for You to Try

Back _____ – _____ back		_____ – _____
Pan _____ – _____ pan		_____ – _____
Sword _____ – _____ sword		_____ – _____
Green _____ – _____ Green		_____ – _____
Dog _____ – _____ dog		_____ – _____
Hair _____ – _____ hair		_____ – _____
Foot _____ – _____ foot		_____ – _____
_____ – _____		_____ – _____
_____ – _____		_____ – _____
_____ – _____		_____ – _____
_____ – _____		_____ – _____
_____ – _____		_____ – _____
_____ – _____		_____ – _____
_____ – _____		_____ – _____
_____ – _____		_____ – _____
_____ – _____		_____ – _____
_____ – _____		_____ – _____
_____ – _____		_____ – _____
_____ – _____		_____ – _____

Word Worms

This word activity is appropriate for children in first through fourth grade when they are learning how to manipulate the letters that spell the sounds of a word. It is also a word game for older children who like the challenge of manipulating spelling patterns, as they would in a game of *Scrabble* or *Anagrams*. For most children, school instruction in spelling patterns begins with first grade or earlier, as a way of introducing "phonics," or, as a teacher would describe it, the *letter-sound associations*. Children need this skill for reading when they must "sound out" new words. They also need it for spelling when they must match the sounds they make when saying the word to the letters that represent the sounds. In beginning spelling activities, the child must substitute or replace sound elements in short words, a letter at a time, to make a new word. Any activity that increases this ability can contribute to success in reading, writing, and spelling.

Your child's teacher would note that the *Word Worms* activity is a means for teaching the following beginning reading and spelling skills:

- ◆ Consonant substitution.
- ◆ Vowel substitution.
- ◆ Common spelling patterns.
- ◆ Manipulating or rearranging the sound and letter components in words.
- ◆ High frequency letter clusters that have predictable pronunciation (also known as *syllable units*).

Getting Started

To try out *Word Worms*, you first model the activity to show how it goes. Begin with a three-letter word, such as "cat." You then replace any one (but only one) of the three single letters in the word to create a new word. Here is an example:

cat→sat→mat→man→ran→run→fun→bun→bin→win→ wit→fit→sit→set→let→lot→pot→pet→put→rut→rat→

To increase the challenge, you can try a four-letter starter word:

cost→lost→last→mast→mask→mark→dark→dare→care→ cure→core→corn→worn→word→wore→were→wire→ hire→here→

Word Worms can be a collaborative activity, with two partners taking turns to think up the next word. It can also be a competitive game, in which the players get to make up the rules (see Rules suggestions to follow). Or it can be an engaging individual activity. There are many possible variations.

Beyond four-letter words, things get more difficult because of the patterns of English letter order and because now we must deal with words that may divide into syllables. Try some yourself. This discovery about *regularly occurring letter patterns* will help students understand more about how words are spelled and how they are divided into syllables.

> *liner→lined→mined→miner→mines→pines→pipes→
> popes→ropes→?*

> *soaps→slaps→flaps→flops→floss→gloss→glows→slows
> →plows→plops→?*

Word Worm chains are usually represented as a series of linked "word worms" that can go in a straight line across the page, or that can curl around the page in the shape of a worm.

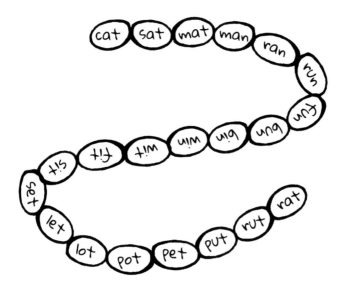

FIGURE 7.1 Three-letter *Word Worm*

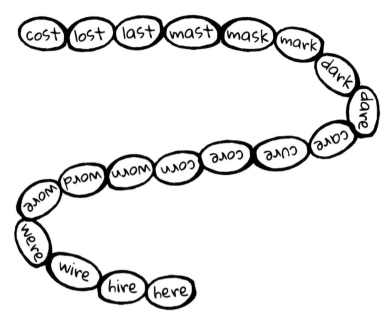

FIGURE 7.2 Four-letter *Word Worm*

Rules and Variations (as agreed upon by the players)

- ♦ No word can be repeated in the chain.
- ♦ Keep a dictionary or computer handy in case your "word" is challenged.
- ♦ A single player can create the longest word chain as an independent activity.
- ♦ Take alternating turns with a parent, teacher, or another child.
- ♦ Make a chain that starts and ends with the same word, i.e., start with *cat* and end with *cat*.
- ♦ Give the start and end words (ex: start with "*cat*," and end with "*end*").
- ♦ Make a chain that uses every letter of the alphabet at least once.

How to Win

- ♦ Stump your partner (i.e., you win when your partner cannot think of a next item for the chain).

- Make a chain using less common letters like *q*, *x*, and *z* (only once).
- Make the longest chain you can with the same starting and ending word (start with *"cat"* and end with *"cat"*) but no repeated words.
- Achieve a *Word Worm* with two-syllable words (even a short worm would do).

Other Variations

Taking individual words from a four-letter *Word Worm* chain, adding a single letter to make a new word:

rent + d = trend	*sand + h = hands*
bond + l = blond	*stop + s = posts* (or *spots*, or *stops*)
band + r = brand	*note + s = stone*
leaf + s = fleas	

You will see many other possibilities as you play this game. It is a quickly completed activity with lots of payoffs. And there are good benefits for children who are first learning how to manipulate word letters and word sounds to create lots of old and new words. They can learn about how flexible our alphabetic system is and how it allows us to move sounds and letters around in different combinations. When children are first learning about *phonics* in school, this game gives real practice in how phonics *works*, without looking like a phonics "drill."

The game can also promote habits that lead to vocabulary development. Your child may propose a possible letter combination that can be pronounced, such as *"mirt,"* and will be challenged to prove that it is a "real" word by checking in the dictionary or computer, and verifying its meaning. Children will catch on quickly to the idea of using rhyming words that end in the same group of letters, as when they change *"same"* to *"name"* to *"game."* Children also learn about how different letter substitutions result in different pronunciations, often to their surprise, as when they change *"new"* to *"sew,"* or *"some"* to *"dome"* or *"were"* to *"here."*

Sample Word Worms

milk→silk→sill→dill→dell→deal→real→meal→meat→
meet→melt→molt→jolt→colt→cost→cast→cash→lash→
bash→base→

coat→boat→beat→best→bust→must→muse→muss→
mass→mast→fast→fact→face→fate→fade→fads→

milk→silk→sill→pill→pile→file→film→firm→farm→
harm→hard→herd→here→hare→rare→rate→rats

dill→dell→deal→real→meal→meat→meet→melt→molt→
jolt→colt→cost→

car→can→fan→fin→pin→pun→nun→run→rut→rot→
not→now→new→sew→set→let→

Magic Word

If you have ever played Anagrams or Scrabble, you will recognize the idea of this game. It builds on the patterns we used with *Word Worms* but with a different goal. The *Magic Word* is unknown to the players, and the goal is to figure out the "magic word" that uses all the letters in the pile *while recording all the smaller words that can be made with that group of letters.*

To play *Magic Word*, you need a set of letter tiles such as you might have in a Scrabble game or for an Anagrams game. The letters should be all upper case. The players need to be able to arrange and rearrange the letters into different combinations. Begin by laying out all the letters of the *Magic Word* in a pile, so that *there is no order to the letters.* For children at ages seven to nine, you would choose a word that is eight to ten letters long. But since part of the game is to see how many smaller words you can make with the letters of the *Magic Word*, there are some special requirements for the letters contained in the *Magic Word* that you choose. See if you can spot the special requirements from these examples of "best choices":

- ◆ battleship
- ◆ presidents
- ◆ wilderness
- ◆ shipwreck
- ◆ snowflakes
- ◆ parachutes
- ◆ arguments
- ◆ carnivores
- ◆ destination

You are correct if you noted that the candidate words all contain at least three vowels, one of which must be "e," and they all contain the letter "s." The "s" allows you to form plural words, and the "e" can transform a short vowel into a long vowel when you add the final "e," as in *"spin"* to *"spine."*

At the start of the game, the player has only the pile of mixed-up letters that form the whole word and does not know what the *Magic Word* is. You begin the game with a sheet of lined binder paper on which you make six columns headed by the numbers two through seven. The parent acts as the scribe to record the words that can be formed in the appropriate column for the number of letters in the word. The idea is to generate as many small words as you can make by combining and recombining the letters. The lists of two to five-letter words will be the longest, with the lists of six and seven-letter words shorter because these are more complex words. When there are five to ten words in each group of the shorter words, you can offer the child the beginning letter of the *Magic Word*: *"Your Magic Word begins with the letter 's' (or p or w, etc.)."*

Often as a result of forming the small words, the child is able to spot the *Magic Word* right away, given the first letter. If, however, she or he is still trying out various possibilities for the beginning of the word, you can respond with, *"The second letter is not 'e' (or whatever letter she just tried and it is not)."* Or, depending on her need to know, you can confirm as appropriate, *"You have the second letter."* As more correct letters are determined, the child is more able to use the spelling patterns of known words to eventually get the *Magic Word*. Meanwhile, you can tally the small words in the columns for what kind of record has been set. The all-time record holders for most smaller words will include words like "shipwreck," "snowflakes," and "carnivores."

TABLE 7.9 Smaller Words Made from the Letters in SHIPWRECK

2	3	4	5	6	7
is	pie	wish	speck	riches	whisper
he	hip	peck	whisk	chirps	
we	sew	wire	spice	wicker	
	pew	hire	price	sicker	
	sir	rich	swipe	picker	
	she	crew	wipes	pricks	
	rip	ship	crews	prices	
	her	hick	screw		
	ice	rick	pecks		
		chip	wires		
		risk	wicks		
		whip	hicks		
		spew	chips		
		rice	whips		
		chew	chews		
		wipe	picks		
		sire	wreck		
		skip	prick		
		wick	chirp		
		sick	crisp		
		pick	Chris		
		wisp			
		wise			

Other Sources for Creative Writing

If you have explored some of the materials that are available for children in the area of writing, you no doubt have found that there are many appealing workbooks and idea books for both parents and teachers that promote involvement in writing. Using the framework of At-Home writing, you will now be able to see what kinds of materials and activities are most likely to appeal to your particular child and which ones best fit your family circumstances.

Watch for the activities that seem to be a good fit because you can then use *your own creative ideas* to expand on what is offered in the published materials. For example, you may see the wide variety of the kinds of "prompts" that are typically suggested to stimulate writing. Some prompts will resonate with your child, while other prompts may produce only a blank look or even confusion. Writing prompts are a bit like the foods we offer to our children in hopes of promoting a balanced diet. Some become immediate favorites. Other foods may take some time to catch on. So we keep on scanning the available ideas, knowing that the ones that catch on "only slightly" could still offer nourishment and will at least point us in the right direction.

Concluding Thoughts on Writing

Ideas for creative writing, and for all writing, can be thought of as "food for the mind." As with the food we offer to children, with writing it is important to keep two important points in focus. The first is the idea of *variety*. Most children thrive on choices, and with At-Home writing, we can provide choices that are tailored to what we have learned and observed about our child. We can promote the ideas that work and hold back on the ones that don't generate enthusiasm. We can also note when we have offered too much, where we may have a child who gets easily overwhelmed by "too-much-ness." We take a step back and simplify.

This leads to the second important idea to keep in focus: *patience*. Sometimes a seed sprouts immediately, and sometimes it takes a long time to find both its roots and its path to the sunshine. In either case, when a parent can give the gift of patience, combined with interest, enthusiasm, and support, we have a very good chance of promoting a lifelong comfort with, and interest in, *being a writer*.

PART 2
The Emerging Reader

8

The At-Home Model for New Readers

The *Language Experience Approach (LEA)*

Activity Level: 5–6+ years

EASY ACCESS NOTES FOR CHAPTER 8: WHAT YOU WILL LEARN

♦ Applying the At-Home Model to Reading: A Brief Background in Emergent Literacy.

♦ Introducing the *Language Experience Approach* (*LEA*), with Personalized Reading Activities.

♦ How *LEA* Benefits Reading Development.

♦ Collecting the Dictated Stories: Steps in Order, Example Stories, What to Watch for.

♦ Activating Children's Own Stories to Build Reading Skills and Confidence.

♦ Example Activities: Sentence Strips, Word Banks, Letter and Sound Matching, Rhyming Words, and Word Categories.

DOI: 10.4324/9781003452683-11

The Writing-Reading Connection

As a long-time educator and clinician, I have been fortunate to observe the many ways parents can interact with their children in learning situations. Based on these observations, I can confidently promote the role that parents can play as their children learn to read and write. *There's a Writer in Our House!* represents a compilation of carefully designed activities to support parents in this important role, with an initial focus on writing. If you have checked out the books for parents who are interested in early literacy, you may have found that the topic of *early reading* seems to receive more attention than early writing. Parents do care about writing, but the resources for helping children with writing are not as plentiful. To address that shortage of materials, my intention in **Part 1**, *The Emerging Writer* has been to offer specific guidance and encouragement so that parents could feel as comfortable with writing as they typically feel when reading with their children.

As you have explored the At-Home Model thus far, you have seen how the suggested activities can be *customized and personalized* to help your child become a writer. The familiar home context helps to develop confidence and comfort with writing, and the activities are intended to build competence through guided practice. And since every writing activity involves *reading*, you might have wondered if the At-Home Model for writing can be used in the same way to customize and personalize *early reading activities*. The answer to that is YES. In **Part 2**, *The Emerging Reader* (Chapters 8–10), you are introduced to a systematic At-Home approach *to boost reading for the beginning reader*. You will see that this approach is based on the same principles you applied to the beginning writer.

A Brief Background in Emergent Literacy

Speech and language specialists provide the framework to understand how child language develops in two domains, *expressive* and *receptive*. Children *hear* language before they are even born.

Listening is in the *receptive* domain. Soon after birth, babies begin to make sounds, their first form of *expressive* language. Both of these forms of language are well documented across cultures by language scholars who note that children go through similar developmental stages regardless of the language spoken in their culture. In typical cases, development proceeds normally and children successfully enter the language community into which they are born. Children learn to understand the language they hear, and they learn to speak to others in the community by imitating others and by participating in shared activities.

Unlike speaking and listening, reading and writing must both be learned through deliberate and systematic instruction because *no child is born knowing how to read and write.* This crucial instruction is the combined responsibility of both home and school. Parents provide the family context for learning, and the school provides trained teachers and a structured Language Arts curriculum. And as we know from studies of home literacy practices, the contributions of the home environment can be enormous. Children might see their first books at home when they see family members reading books and other print sources, and when they are taken to the library or the bookstore. They learn about *school reading* from school-age siblings and other family members. Written text is a part of our environment, ever-present on computers or other screens, as well as on t-shirts, hats, and hoodies. Early on, most children get the idea that reading is something very desirable. They look forward to being able to read.

Early Reading Comes before Early Writing

It makes sense that early reading is learned first. In cultures with widespread literacy practices, children are exposed to written language that they can see and that they can listen to when it is read aloud to them. It is important to note that these early literacy experiences highlight *meaning.* In other words, when children first experience listening to words that are read aloud from books, they are almost always connected to *meaning in some form.*

Books designed for young children are well-illustrated with pictures that support the meaning. The child expects the words to make sense, to "say" something about something, as the words and pictures combine to tell a story.

School instruction generally helps children make the connection between writing and reading. They get it that the words we can read were written by *someone*. I well remember a child who was reading aloud from an early reading book for her assigned homework. The book had very simplified text compared with the children's literature that her parents had been reading to her at home. She came to a line that said, as I recall, *"The fat cat sat on the tan mat."* She looked up at me and said, *"Who **wrote** this stuff?"*

This child was starting to *read like a writer*. The two perspectives of writer and reader mutually reinforce each other, to the benefit of both. Every time children write, they have to read the words and sentences they have just written. As they write, they have to think about which ideas to write about, as well as which words they will choose. When they begin to write longer pieces, they think about the order of the ideas so that their words will make sense to another reader. In the same manner, *they learn to read like a writer* when they encounter more complex paragraphs and chapters written by other writers. They gradually become able to question the writer and even evaluate the quality of what they read. They are beginning the process of *critical thinking*, the foundation of all learning.

Applying the At-Home Model to Reading: Learning to Read Like a Writer

In a society that values literacy, we can agree that every child in every family needs to be able to read effectively. Since the beginning of the public school system in the United States, educators have held ongoing discussions about the various methods for teaching *beginning reading*. As adult readers, we ourselves may well remember our first experiences when we connected spoken sounds and ideas to those marks on the page. As we became readers, we were gradually able to connect the marks on the page to sounds and ideas *because we could read.* We may have made the connection in a classroom where the teacher showed us a printed word and spoke the word. Or we may have been on the lap of a parent or a grandparent or a big sister or brother who was reading aloud from a book, and perhaps pointing to a word as they said the word. We began to figure out that those first words in a book or on a chart were written *by someone who knew how to write and had something to tell us.*

As early as the 1920s, in both the United States and New Zealand, some insightful educators realized that children can be shown how to read *their own words* when they are written down by a grown-up who knows how to write. This remarkable idea was translated into an approach for teaching beginning reading, which came to be known as the *Language Experience Approach* (*LEA*). For decades since, *LEA* has been a well-recognized method for teaching beginning readers (and even non-literate adults) how to read.

Personalized Reading Activities Based on *LEA*

The *Language Experience Approach*, as the name suggests, builds on the personal experiences and the language of the child. As used in a school setting, the child's words and ideas are dictated to the teacher and are recorded exactly as spoken by the child. These "stories" are simply recorded accounts of what children have to say about things that can happen in a child's life. The stories can be used to teach the idea of the *speech-to-print connection* when children have the opportunity to read and reread their stories. In many ways, this beginning reading approach has a natural fit with the At-Home approach to writing. We will focus particularly on reading activities that fit comfortably with your role as a parent, as you use the activities to promote both reading and writing, At-Home. The steps are explicit and easy to follow, and they have been tested by parents and teachers alike.

How *LEA* Benefits Reading Development

Before we begin with specific steps, this overview will high-light the many contributions that *LEA* can make to your child's reading development. You will be able to appreciate why it is an important complement to the work you are already doing with At-Home writing. There is a rich potential here, with activities based on the stories your child dictates for you to write down. As you will see, these activities are designed to support the develop-ment of essential beginning reading skills. More than that, when a child has *ownership of the words and ideas* as recorded in their stories, the learning is more likely to be effective, in much the same way as the At-Home writing activities promoted comfort, confidence, and competence with writing.

Sight Words

We begin with "sight words," that is, the words that we recog-nize immediately *by using visual memory of how the word looks*. In the dictated stories, children will use many of the high fre-quency words that are used over and over again in different contexts and thus become easily recognized. A child's *sight vocabulary* is an important building block in reading devel-opment and a strong component of *LEA*. The dictated stories become immediately available for *rereading*, and rereading the stories reinforces visual memory and contributes to confidence and *reading fluency*. In addition, when we are ready to focus on the alphabetic, or spelling, characteristics of individual words in a systematic way, we can use the known words *for decoding new and different words*.

Phonological Awareness

Once a word enters a child's sight vocabulary, these known words can be used for another important step in learning to read. This step is called "phonological awareness," or "phonemic awareness." These terms refer to the ability to hear and separate out the smallest sound units, called *phonemes*, which together compose an individual word. For example, the word "cat" has three phonemes: the sound of '*c*' at the beginning, the sound of 'a' in the middle, and the sound of 't' at the end. If we are talking about more than one cat, we add another phoneme represented by the letter 's' after the 't' to make the plural form: *cats*. You may recall that we introduced a game called *Word Worms* in Chapter 7, in which we could change one small word to a different word by changing just one letter, or phoneme.

Some children catch on to this principle more quickly and more easily than others. However, every reader *who learns to read in an alphabetic language* has to learn this big idea: we separate out the individual sounds of the word and represent the sound with a symbol (or letter). In fact, sometimes the sound is represented by two or three letters, as is the case with words like *storm, branch,* or *watch*. In the classroom, this is referred to as *phonics instruction*. For the beginning reader, instruction promotes the development of phonological awareness so that the child can eventually understand and independently use the principles of *sound-to-letter* and *letter-to-sound* correspondences.

Reading research over the past 80 years has helped educators better understand how to promote this important awareness in all children so that each child can be successful with phonemic awareness, especially in the early stages of reading. Educators are better able to identify the child for whom this is a difficult operation, and to ensure that the child is given appropriate instruction early on. In the classroom, this early intervention has saved many children from experiencing reading failure.

LEA in School

In many cases, the exposure to letters, words, and sounds will come in the form of lists of "sight words" that the children say and are taught to memorize. In the *LEA* classroom, the words may initially come from a story the teacher reads, but they may also be based upon *an experience in the classroom.* In kindergarten and first grade, children may be given a sheet of paper on which to draw a picture, and then are asked to "tell" about the picture. The teacher records the child's words below the picture, and the child reads the words. Later, with a group story, a whole class or group may provide sentences that tell the story of a classroom experience.

In the *Language Experience Approach,* as we will use it here, our focus will be on dictated accounts by the individual child based on *a home experience* rather than a school experience. *LEA* becomes a systematic way to incorporate these experience charts into the individual child's At-Home reading practices. It's a way to take advantage of all the learning opportunities offered when we use *LEA* at home.

Other Applications of *LEA*

The *Language Experience Approach* is used effectively in a number of instructional settings. The *dictated stories of blind children* can be transcribed into braille so that children can read their own words in braille. *LEA* is used to teach *students with limited English,* for it captures their beginning attempts to use the new vocabulary and grammatical patterns of their second language. *LEA* is used widely, and particularly fittingly, with *non-literate adults* who are becoming *new readers.* Many of these adults are encouraged to become readers through the dictated stories because someone thought that what they had to say was *"important enough to write down."* For many adults, *LEA* is an effective approach because it makes beginning reading *meaningful.*

LEA has a special place for those who work with *struggling readers.* For the child who has not caught on right away, the process of looking at those marks on the page can in fact be almost painful. I remember sitting beside a third grader whose parents had watched him fall further behind in school, especially when it came to reading. When I first placed an open book in front of him to check what he was able to read, he seemed physically unable to even *look* at the page. His eyes were averted, and his gaze was anywhere but on the book. Even with the first few dictated stories he found it hard to look at the paper. However, as he finally made the connection between those written words and what he had just told me, he made a remarkable transition to looking at the words, and then finally, *to reading the words. LEA* was not a quick fix, but he was now on track to be able to practice his reading. *LEA* is a process that benefits many struggling readers even beyond the first or second-grade level.

Using *LEA* with Personalized *At-Home* Activities

The At-Home Model for beginning writers has emphasized the benefits of starting with the familiar to build confidence and comfort with writing. For parents who wish to explore the At-Home approach to reading, transitioning to *LEA* will feel logical and natural because the activities are based on many of the same principles as At-Home writing. The *LEA* stories can be turned into learning activities that are easy for parents to carry out because they require minimal supplies, often just paper, pencil, and scissors. You can also put your computer and printer to good use, as we will see in the following activities sections. It is important to note here that *LEA* activities do not conflict with, nor replace, the beginning reading activities that your child experiences in the school setting. They can be very complementary.

Collecting *LEA* Stories: Steps in Order

The steps for collecting the dictated stories follow a logical order. As before with the writing activities, some parent preparation is involved. Once the stories are collected, you will be able to use them in instructional activities that are designed to help your beginning reader practice the important skills. In Chapter 9 you will find indicators of progress, along with pointers for the child who might be struggling or showing resistance. For the directions that follow, the "child" will be referred to as "he" or "she" alternatively, and the story recorder will be referred to as "you" or "the parent." The age level of your beginning reader may be kindergarten or first grade, although you may also be working with a second or third grader who is still uncertain about *how reading works*.

Step 1: Setting the Stage with a Stimulus

As your first step, it is important to identify what your child is most likely *to talk about*. This is very similar to the pointers that we suggested for promoting your child's At-Home writing. But now we turn the tables. The child gets to talk, and you get to write down what she says. You might say, *"Today we are going to do something different. You are going to tell me a story, and I will write it down, just the way you tell it. Then you can read your very own story."*

You could start with a recent experience or a topic that you know she will have something to say about, such as a favorite toy, a new pet, an interesting activity, or a new friend. Later you will learn how you might *set up* a stimulus, such as cooking something in the kitchen or doing some kind of experiment. But at first, you might say, *"Why don't you tell me about the hamster and I am going to write down what you tell me on this paper. You can watch me write it down."* You, the parent, are now identified as the "scribe" for the child who is telling the story. Write the words using appropriate upper-case and lower-case letters in their print form, written large enough to be seen easily by both of you.

This example story was dictated by Spencer, an entering second grader who had his car collection on the table in front of him:

> *My collection of cars has so many of them. And I like them all. My favorite cars make me happy. If I lose them, they don't make me happy. They are golden. If something hits one car, it might hurt the car. The driver sits on the seat.*
>
> *By Spencer, age 7*

This next story was dictated in a clinic setting by Becky, age six, following a science activity with a thermometer:

> *A thermometer goes up and down. You may put a thermometer in a fish tank. We have a thermometer in our fish tank. You might have a catfish. When you have company, they might look in the fish tank. The guppies learned how to swim. When your mother comes over to feed your fish, she might find one dead. When I was at school, we saw guppies. Our puppy eats things.*
>
> *By Becky, age 6*

This third example was dictated by Jessica, a six-year-old who had many pets and many experiences to tell about:

> *I had a parrot that was on my shoulder. He didn't even bite me. Then I have a crab and I have a snake too. The crab died. It was a little baby crab. And when we went to the beach there was a crab under my mom's bathing suit and it bit her. Then when I was in the sea when I was at the beach, a rock hit me on the foot and my foot bleeded. I put a band-aid on it. Now my owie got all better.*
>
> *By Jessica, age 6*

This final story was dictated by a second grader with limited English, who had been given a frog hand-puppet to tell about:

> *FROG*
> *He is look the frog. He is sit down in the desk. This day is night. He is asleep.*
>
> *By Jose, age 7*

Remember that we use the stimulus as a very informal way to get some words and sentences about the topic. In the beginning, the organization of the sentences is less important, though as you will see from the follow-up activities, we will begin to discuss how the ideas are organized, as they are expressed in the sentences. The message you give to your child from the beginning should be the following: *"The story you have to tell is important enough to write down, and then we can read your story and think about it some more."*

Step 2: Recording the Dictation

As you can see from the examples, we do not expect a child to dictate an experience story that is like a conventional story, with a beginning, a middle, and an end. Children often begin with one idea, and then suddenly switch to another idea entirely. Becky's story began with guppies and ended with her puppy! To get the activity started off, we just need a topic that the child shows some interest in, and that he seems comfortable telling about.

As your child tells his story, you record it exactly as it is dictated. Children who have heard many book stories will often adopt a book-like manner in which to tell their story. Some children may rush along with a great flood of sentences in a more conversational manner. If your child talks quickly, you may need to ask him to slow down a bit or even to repeat the sentence. You might need to explain, *"Watch my pencil so you can see how I make the letters for each word. We can say the words together as I write them down."*

If your child hesitates or seems to get stuck, you can go back and read aloud the sentences you have so far. Many beginning readers are just making the connection between the words we say, and the letters it takes to represent them in print. Making an *LEA* story promotes and reinforces the understanding of the "speech-to-print" connection. It demonstrates directly how much time it takes for the child to say the words, for the scribe to hear the words, and for the words to be written down.

What to Watch For

Here are some things to keep in mind as the story is being told. You may be wondering what to do if your child produces immature or incorrect grammatical forms, such as "He bringed it," or "My foot bleeded." For a word like "bringed," your response will depend a bit upon the age of the child. You can write the word the way she said it and go on. When you read back the story to the child, she may say, *"That's wrong,"* at which point you can say, *"Yes, the right word is 'brought.'"* Then you can write the word with the conventional spelling, and just say, *"This is how we spell that word."* At a later time, you can discuss the appropriate forms of words like "bringed" or "bleeded" as a separate item of interest if your child seems interested and ready for the discussion. The unconventional forms, such as the use of the 'ed' ending applied to the wrong form of the verb, are merely indicators that your child is in the process of experimenting with the various forms of language that he or she is hearing and is learning how and when to apply them in spoken language. These forms drop out of usage because they do not get reinforced.

When a child produces longer, more wandering sentences, it is still important to record the story just as dictated, because if you start changing the words into a more "adult" form, it is then *no longer his story*. The benefit of reading the sentences back to your child as you proceed is that he himself might hear where the words do not make sense and might spontaneously edit. This is a highly desirable outcome when it happens, and you can say, *"Good checking!"*

When You Can Intervene

There are several instances, however, when you may appropriately intervene during the dictation. First, the goal is to record between five and eight sentences. Anything more than that becomes unmanageable for the beginning reader to follow and work with, as you will see when we turn the story into activities. If the story is coming out as one continuous sentence, you may say, *"Let's put a period here, and make this a new sentence."* If, after several sentences, the child switches to a new topic, as Becky did in her story (*"Our puppy eats things"*), you may say, *"That sounds like a new story. Let's save that one for next time."* If the story is showing no signs of ending soon, you may say, *"Let's make that the last sentence and save some for the next story."* On the other hand, you may have a child like Jessica who knew perfectly well that the story was over when her *"owie got all better."*

Step 3: Reading the Story Together with Your Child

When the dictation is concluded, you now say, *"Let me read it to you, just the way you told it to me."* After you do that, you say, *"Is there anything you would like to add, or is it okay?"* The benefit of recording the story with paper and pencil, as opposed to typing it on the computer, is that the child can see very directly the relationship between the marks on the page and the spoken words. She can also see how we can change what the story says if we want to. After any changes are made, you read the entire story again, using your finger to follow along the line of words as you voice them, clearly and slowly.

Inviting Your Child to Read the Story

Now you are ready to invite your child to read his story. Say, *"Would you like to read your story, just the way I read it to you? I will help you."* Some children will read the story readily, as they will already have it memorized. Others may seem as if they are only seeing or hearing it for the first time. Some will proceed confidently, hesitating only now and then, while others will struggle with many of the words, even though they themselves have just dictated them. The observant parent will note these levels of readiness, which give us good information as to *how to proceed with additional stories or experiences.*

It is always appropriate to record more than one account of a given topic. This may provide the additional benefit of repeated encounters with new or *high frequency words.* When words are used frequently and repeatedly, they are reinforced in the child's visual memory and expressive language vocabulary. Many of the common verbs and high frequency words are necessary for almost any story, such as *"were," "these," "them," "up," "down,"* and so on. These are the words that rank very high on teachers' lists of high-frequency words that children need to recognize automatically, on sight.

As you begin to use this process of dictated stories, you will note some important characteristics of your child. She may be eager to add to the collection of stories. She may even suggest some topics that you did not think of. On the other hand, she may not see the point of what you are doing and express some resistance. This resistance frequently dissipates once you begin to activate the stories in the follow-up activities. The key response from you as the parent is *to maintain both patience and interest.* It will pay off.

Children with Differing Levels of Confidence

There are a number of possible strategies for children with differing levels of confidence when they read their stories with you at this beginning stage. You may have a confident reader who seems to remember most of the words. Starting at the beginning of the story, you read along with your child, modeling good expression and pace. When he hesitates, you supply the word and continue on *to maintain the flow of meaning*. You can make a mental note of which words seem to have persisted in memory, particularly if there have been repeated words in the story and he remembers the word each time it appears. Here we see the benefit of a good story stimulus. If we are writing about the hamster, the word "hamster" is likely to be in the story several times. Each time you come to it, drop your voice back and let him say the word independently.

With a less confident child, you will have different expectations. At first, she may only remember selected words. You can make a mental note of which words seem to be easily remembered. Is it a word that appears frequently? Is it a word that seems to have a special meaning *for this child*? Each time you read the story together, she may add additional "known" words that seem to have a pattern, such as how long the word is, or words with similar beginning letters. You will still be there to supply the words slowly and clearly to keep the meaning going. If the dictated story is meaningful to the child, she is more likely to keep the "sense of story." Reading the story multiple times has the benefit of reinforcing the connection between speech and print, thus increasing confidence.

It is possible that you may encounter resistance from the beginning, though it is somewhat unlikely, given that children seem to relish this kind of sustained attention. If your child really does not want to try to read his own story, this may reflect some feelings of uncertainty or even anxiety about the whole process. It is important to keep the interaction relaxed. The child should feel no pressure to read the words perfectly right away, or even on the first several trials. When the stories are short (remember we are trying for only five to eight sentences at a time), we can focus on only the first sentence, or on only the last sentence. Be reassuring, by noting, *I will help you.*" The initial uncertainties often diminish when you explore the follow-up activities that are based on the stories and the words they contain.

Step 4: Activating the Dictated Stories to Support Reading Skills

With the foundation you have developed through the At-Home experiences to support your child's writing, you will start to see many connections to the ways the dictated stories can be tapped *for activities that promote reading skills.* These activities build upon the same strengths of the At-Home approach to writing. They are done at home, they involve the individual interests and strengths of your child, they are tailored to your child, and they take advantage of the familiar environment.

Dictated story activities help parents promote the development of the following reading-based operations:

1. **Sight vocabulary.**
2. **Decoding skills.**
3. **Reading comprehension: Forms of paragraph organization and sentence structure.**

1. Developing Sight Vocabulary

Sight vocabulary, as you will recall, is the term we use for those words that a child knows automatically on sight, often through memorization and frequent exposure, without having to "sound it out." For many children at the beginning stages, their first sight word is their name. All *LEA* stories contain useful, familiar, high frequency words such as common verbs, common adjectives and adverbs, pronouns, and names of common items. As children reread their stories, the visual appearance of the words in the meaningful context of the story allows for increasingly automatic word recognition. Repetition builds confidence and competence.

Activities with the Known Words

There are a number of simple activities that will promote automatic recognition of these words. This is where your computer and printer can provide useful support. You can simply type the dictated story from the paper and pencil version onto your computer. Now both the lines and the words can be easily manipulated. The story should be typed in size 14 font, with double spacing.

After you and your child have read the printed story a few times, give him a pencil and ask him to underline the *"words you know."* These words become important teaching materials in the next step, to follow. Please note that in *LEA* activities, the emphasis is always on the *known words*, which provide the foundation for the subsequent practice activities. The known words are most likely to be names of objects or people (nouns), as well as the action words (verbs), that have become known through repeated exposure. Gradually, the known words will begin to include the small and similar-looking words, such as *"is," "if," "the," "or," "for,"* and so on. You can pay specific attention to those later.

Sequential List

This next follow-up activity is a little more work for you. You will type the story with the words in vertical lists, as opposed to horizontal sentences. You could use the "table" option in Word to make three to four columns of the words. The list still retains the continuous sense of the story as the child reads down the list, but now the words are somewhat "in isolation." They can therefore be recognized on their own merit and not because of their placement in a sentence. Now, give your child the "sequential list" and ask him to once again underline the *"words you know."*

Spencer's story about his car collection as dictated:

> *My collection of cars has so many of them. And I like them all. My favorite cars make me happy. If I lose them, they don't make me happy. They are golden. If something hits one car, it might hurt the car. The driver sits on the seat.*
>
> *By Spencer, age 7*

Using the chart with the sequential list, the child is invited to underline "the words you know." As she does this task, there are some useful behaviors to note. Is she vocalizing the sentences as meaningful units, which she reads aloud with expression? If she comes to a word that she does not underline (because it is not yet a known word *for her*), does she reread the words above or following to recapture the meaning of the whole sentence and thus use context to help her? These behaviors are powerful indicators of the *emerging reader*, who is now developing strategies to figure out new words as they are encountered in other forms of reading.

TABLE 8.1 Spencer's Story with Words in a Sequential List

my	cars	if	By
collection	make	something	Spencer
of	me	hits	age
cars	happy	one	7
has	if	car	
so	I	it	
many	lose	might	
of	them	hurt	
them	they	the	
and	don't	car	
I	make	the	
like	me	driver	
them	happy	sits	
all	they	on	
my	are	the	
favorite	golden	seat	

Scrambled List

The next step is to type *the known words* that your child has underlined from the sequential list into the "scrambled list." The words are listed in any order, hence the name "scrambled list." Now your child no longer has the meaning of the whole sentence context to help identify the words. Using the scrambled list, have her again underline the known words. By this process, the words are gradually withdrawn from context and presented *in isolation*. These words are successfully becoming her sight vocabulary, that is, words that are recognized automatically, at sight, without the reliance on decoding. These words now represent your child's growing mastery of words in their print form. Note that Scrambled Lists will be variable in length, depending on your child's known words. The known words are now available to be used in word recognition activities, such as sentence strips, the child's own Word Bank, matching letters and sounds, rhyming words, and word categorizing (to follow). The possibilities are numerous and do not require expensive materials.

Parents often note, with some concern, that these known words are "just memorized," as if that is a problem, or as if it is not "real reading." However, fluent reading is just that, the automatic and swift recognition, on sight, of thousands of words. Experienced readers do not "decode" the thousands of words they process when reading text unless they encounter a word they have not seen before. When this happens, as it does even for experienced readers, they enlist the next strategy, word decoding ("sounding out"), which brings us to the next step.

2. Developing Word Recognition (Decoding) Skills

Much has been researched and written about the process of word decoding, and how to make it happen for beginning readers. It is not the purpose of this chapter to cover everything that is now known about how decoding works for most children, and why the process sometimes fails. See the *Resources* list at the end of Chapter 9 for further reading. Our purpose here is to suggest some simple activities based on the *LEA* stories that may clarify and make word decoding more successful for the child who is now taking the steps from the dictated stories into real-world reading.

Sentence Strips

You will use your computer for the sentence strips activity. The story can be typed with each sentence on its own separate line (or lines for a longer sentence) in a large print font with double spacing. Now the entire story can be cut into separate sentence strips which can be manipulated in several ways. You or your child can cut up one sentence strip at a time into its separate words. This is a useful exercise to highlight word boundaries, which are not always evident to the child at the beginning stages of reading. Your child can sort the words into the "known" and the "not-so-sure-yet" groups. You can then reassemble the separate words back into the original sentence, or even try out a new arrangement of the words to see if we can make a new and different sentence (adding in other words as needed). The sentence strips add a tactile benefit, as your child manipulates both the single word elements and the whole sentence elements of the story. Additionally, the sentence strips will be useful when we turn to *LEA* stories and *reading comprehension*.

Word Banks

When your child has a collection of about a dozen known words, you can introduce the **Word Bank**. The words can be stored in a small box of the type your grandmother used to store recipes. You can even include the little divider cards that divide the contents alphabetically, which is an excellent way to introduce the idea of *alphabetical order*. Print the known words clearly on small 3×5-inch file cards, one word to a card. Use lower-case lettering unless the word is a proper noun like the name of a person or place. As you observe your child looking at the words and saying them aloud, you might begin to notice how he approaches figuring out the word. If he is already in a kindergarten or first-grade classroom, the chances are that he has been introduced to the idea of vowels and consonants and is probably learning something about the sounds represented by the individual letters. As with the sentence strips, there are additional tactile benefits to handling the word cards.

Matching the Beginning Letters

If you feel confident about showing your child how to sound out a word by starting with the first letter as a clue, go ahead and do so. Remember that the first letter is not always a reliable clue, depending on the following letters of the word (think about words like "honest" and "happy," or "cent" and "cat"). Some parents may remember how difficult this task was for them when they were just catching on to how letters and sounds work. You may want to verify how and when this foundation is being covered by systematic reading instruction programs in school.

Spend some time just observing what your child does with the words on the cards. Your word bank may contain a number of words that begin with the same letter making an identical sound. You can point out that they begin with *the same sound* when that is the case. School instruction will cover the exceptions, but many children are ready to use the word cards to distinguish the sounds of the letter 'c' at the beginning of *cat* and at the beginning of *cent*. Or the sounds of the letter 'g' at the beginning of *get* and *gentle*. Same letter, different sounds. With both the initial 'c' and 'g,' the sound they make is generally determined by the vowel or other letter that follows. Even if you feel that this is an area best left to trained teachers, you are able to observe how your child handles the important process of how to match words using their beginning letters. There will be many opportunities to apply this principle to new words.

Rhyming Words

Watch for words from the dictated stories that can rhyme with other common words. If the word *"cat"* has appeared in a story, it can be transformed into *rat, sat, fat, mat,* and so on. You may have already tried out rhyming groups in a game of *Word Worms* (Chapter 7). An investment in *Scrabble* or *Anagram* letter tiles might be appropriate here, so your child can actually physically manipulate the letter combinations (as you did with the *Magic Word* activity, also in Chapter 7). Many of the common words in stories will represent rhyming possibilities and it is very effective to capitalize on them when they occur. Parents, please note here that the ability to do rhyming is a *well-researched indicator of success* in learning to apply phonics principles to new words. See *Bryant and Bradley* in the *Resources* section at the end of Chapter 9.

If your child is participating in phonics instruction at school, or if you have introduced these letter-sound connections, you can build upon those ideas by grouping any Word Bank words that start the same, end the same, or have the same sounds in the middle (known in school terms as "consonant matching" and "vowel matching"). The value of the *LEA* stories is that children can now see phonics instruction in the context of *words they know* and ideas they can relate to. For additional practice, *Word Bank* words can be alphabetized, both in the box and in card sorting activities.

Word Meanings

When you are practicing word-based activities, always keep in mind that a word represents *a unit of meaning*. Activities that focus on the individual letters and sounds must quickly be supplemented with activities that focus on *the meanings of the words* so that your child can see that phonics activities are not merely "barking at print." Early readers can be shown how to add letters or endings to change the meaning of a word. For example, you can show how to add 's' to make nouns mean more than one (plural). You can call attention to the suffixes, or endings, we attach to verbs to show verb tense and make other forms of the base word: *call, calls, calling, called, caller; teach, teaches, teaching, teacher*. More complex relationships, such as the connections between irregular verbs and their tense endings, can be pointed out when these words occur, particularly if your child is interested. You can show how we change a common word like *"write"* to *"wrote"* to *"written"* to *"writer."*

Word Categories

The word cards can be used to teach another important function of words when you show your child how to group words *by category*. You can group by names of family members or names of holidays. You can group all the words that name animals, tools, or things we can do outdoors. Use this activity to encourage your child to broaden her vocabulary by adding new words that name other members of the category, even if the words have not yet been used in a dictated story. This may happen quite naturally as children are exposed to science lessons and books you read together at home. You can introduce the word *category*, and remind everyone of how we use categories, at home, in the kitchen, in the garden, and in closets. The *Critical Thinking* skill of categorizing is further explored in Chapter 10.

Here is an *LEA* story that lends itself to word-building and word-sorting activities. Note the use of color words, size words, words with rhyming possibilities (*fast, last; name, game; big, dig, pig,* etc.), and the addition of the suffix '*ish.*'

> *I have a big turtle. His name is Tom. He is six inches long. My aunt bought him at a pet store. He is fast crawling. He's brownish, blackish, and yellow. I got him on Easter vacation. His head is long.*
>
> By Patti, age 7

3. Reading Comprehension: Forms of Paragraph Organization and Sentence Structure

Children's experience stories frequently tell about an event. As such, they offer an excellent opportunity to focus on sequencing. When you happen to get such a story, you will have an appropriate activity for sequencing intact sentence strips. As you did previously with the sight words activity, you type the story on the computer with each sentence on its own separate line (or lines). The paper copy can be cut into sentence strips that can be mixed up and reassembled by your child in the proper order. When you use the sentence strips activity in this way, you can now call attention to *the logical ordering of the sentences.*

LEA stories of events show the child's increasing mastery of *time order* and may include time signal words such as *next, then, finally,* or *yesterday.* A story might include a pattern of *cause and effect*, where one event causes another event to happen. A story might give *reasons* for why something did happen or should happen. When you spot these patterns, they can easily become the topic of further discussion. In Chapter 10, we explore ways to highlight these patterns through the At-Home activities that promote *critical thinking.*

The sentence strip format thus allows for additional analysis of the internal order, whether it is time order, cause/effect order, or some other form of logical ordering. When you revisit the story in sentence strip form, you may observe insightful editing or reordering by your child. He might see a place where more detail could be added, and you can ask, *"What else can you tell about that?"* This question introduces the idea of *elaboration*, a skill that will also be important for school discussions and school writing. When children catch on to how to elaborate, they often bring in other details from their background information, and they may also introduce additional vocabulary in this way.

Here are two stories that lend themselves to sentence strip activities:

Christine's Story

Yesterday my mom and me were making brownies. When I was licking out the pan the pudding was all over my face. Then my sister woke up. Then it was all over her face. Then when it was done I ate two brownies with my little sister and my brother.

By Christine, age 6

Jason's Story

When the seeds grow bigger, we are going to take the flowers home. We put seeds in the cups. We put some dirt in it and some stones in it. When the flowers come up, they will have roots on them.

By Jason, age 6

Christine's story is full of time order words and a recognizable steps-in-order sequence pattern (with a small cause/effect example in sentence two). Jason's seeds story is an example of a sequence in nature that can be the basis of similar science experiences. Jason might be encouraged to note that the first sentence he dictated for the story is really the last thing that happened, and with the strips, he can easily change the order. He might want to add sentences at the beginning so that he could list the items that were needed to do the experiment.

If your child can follow along with this kind of analysis, it is an excellent indicator that he has truly read the sentences and understands what they mean. You can now say, *"Hand me the sentence that tells about the container,"* giving a clue as to which sentence he should look for. Or *"Hand me the sentence that has a word that means the same as **soil**."* These exercises promote good problem-solving based on both word meaning and whole sentence meaning. In addition, to do this activity successfully, the child is developing the skill of *scanning* the sentence strips to search for a specific word or combination of words. A good rule here is *Don't leave the story too soon.*

You can use the sentence strips to focus on *the amount of information* in an individual sentence or story. You might ask, *"Could you tell me about what happened after we were all done with the brownies?"* You might ask, *"Can you find a sentence that needs a little more information? What else could you tell me about the flowers on the plant?"* Sentence strips also allow for a specific focus on the structure of the individual sentence. You might ask, *"Can you find any questions in **your** sentence strips?"* You might ask, *"Can you find a sentence that tells just one idea? Do you see a sentence that tells two ideas?"* You can use these kinds of questions to call attention to *the structure and content of the sentences.* This can be done without having to delve into complex grammar instruction about subjects and predicates unless you have already talked about subjects and verbs (depending on the age and grade level of the child). You may be surprised at how well children can view their own sentences from an analytic point of view.

Other Possibilities for Maximizing the Benefits of *LEA* Dictated Stories

If you feel that we must have milked the dictated stories for every possible benefit that can be imagined, read on. Because of their high meaning value to your child, we want to be sure that we don't overlook the benefits that can come from expanding the application of the dictated stories to other areas of reading development. For example, any discussion of reading achievement for young readers must include consideration of the importance of background knowledge. Similarly, success in reading comprehension is clearly connected to the breadth and depth of the reader's vocabulary. And parents will benefit from the perspective of knowing the markers of growth and how to keep the stories going. Finally, how can these techniques benefit children who might be struggling readers? Chapter 9 develops all these themes for you.

9

Expanding Reading Development with the *Language Experience Approach*

Activity Level: 5–6+ years

EASY ACCESS NOTES FOR CHAPTER 9: WHAT YOU WILL LEARN

♦ *LEA* Stories as a Source for Building Background Knowledge and Promoting Concept Development.

♦ Transition Points to Additional Early Reading and Writing Activities: Reinforcing the Reading-Writing Loop.

♦ Benefits of Keeping the Dictated Stories Going, with Suggestions.

♦ Markers of Growth: What to Do if You Don't See the Expected (or Hoped-for) Progress.

♦ *LEA* Stories for Remediation of Struggling Readers.

♦ Importance of *LEA* Stories That Are Collected, Over Time.

DOI: 10.4324/9781003452683-12

Building Background Knowledge and Promoting Concept Development with *LEA* Stories

The procedures and methods for capturing dictated stories are designed to make the approach as natural and as convenient as possible so that parents will be encouraged to use the approach for maximum benefit. It is important to note that the benefits do not end when you have gathered a few stories and used them to enhance beginning reading skills. There are many more educational opportunities that can be explored.

Here are a few examples. *LEA* stories can be used to promote concept development by helping children extend what they already know about a topic, through utilizing the power of a stimulus based on your child's experiences and interests. Experience stories can be based on science experiments, cooking experiences, field trips, or books that you read together about topics your child is curious about. Children can learn the important skill of *retelling or explaining* using their expanding vocabularies that reflect new information they are learning. The stories can be used to develop a sense of *internal organization*, as your child is encouraged to talk about the topic and add essential and interesting details. *A child's own views of the topic can be encouraged*, often to the delight and amazement of the scribe!

As an engaged parent, you can build on concepts that may emerge in the dictated stories by carefully selecting books for your young reader that just happen to contain many of the same words that have been expressed in the dictated story. Thus, an *LEA* story about a pet guinea pig can be paired with a beginning science book on the same topic. The confidence built from reading the words repeatedly in the *LEA* story transfers quickly to reading the same words in other print materials. You can increase the network of vocabulary words surrounding the topic as you add new and related words. Word meanings can be extended. You can arouse your child's curiosity to learn more about this topic and related topics. This is "real reading" that is full of meaning for your young reader. And most importantly for parents to understand, as children progress through the different levels of education, their success as learners and readers is increasingly tied to the extent and depth of their background knowledge. The more they know, the better they are able to succeed as their education continues.

Transition Points to Additional Early Reading and Writing Activities

◆ Your child can be encouraged to read the dictated stories aloud to share them with family members.

◆ Children can find known words in pattern books or try their own pattern stories, such as *Brown Bear, Brown Bear, What Do You See?* (Bill Martin Jr. series).

◆ Dictated stories can branch out into poetry and songs.

◆ Dictated stories can link to the many family activities that are supported by language, such as concentration games, rhyming games, family storytelling, and computer games with a strong language basis.

Book Making

Parents will see many advantages in collecting the dictated stories over time and preserving them in folders or binding them into books. Dictated story collections provide documentation of growth in important areas. You will see new vocabulary items appear. You may see how stories become more organized around a topic or an event. Watch how sentences may become longer and more complex. Your child may experiment with different types of sentences such as questions and exclamations. You may see the appearance of clauses and interesting prepositional phrases. Dictated storybooks often become family treasures to be enjoyed and shared by all members of the family. Both the scribe and the storyteller must remind each other *to date each story for the historical record!*

Reinforcing the Reading/Writing Loop

In many cases with *LEA*, there will come a point when the child takes over. He will reach for the pencil and say, "I can write it." This growing sense of independence can be supported by the **Word Bank**, which by now may contain many of the words needed for him to write on his own. The *Word Bank* can be supplemented with a published *Beginner's Dictionary*, with which he can now look up both spellings and meanings. Creative writing can be encouraged in much the same manner as the dictated stories were initially begun, with a good stimulus object, activity, or idea. You may refer to the opening chapters of this book to be reminded of many of those stimulus activities, such as the creative writing activities that involve imagination and wordplay in Chapter 7.

Reviewing the Writer's Toolbox

Chapter 5 presented background information for parents about areas of grammar such as parts of speech and types of sentences, as well as some of the major forms of paragraph organization. While **There's a Writer in Our House!** is not intended as a structured workbook in these skills, once you are confident about the main patterns of paragraph organization, you might find that these ideas fit well with patterns that are often used by children quite spontaneously in their *LEA* stories. We have seen the steps-in-order pattern when children describe an event or process. If your child is comfortable with the process of dictating, you might suggest a topic that lends itself to using one of the main patterns, such as compare/contrast. You might begin with this: *"Why don't you tell me about how Maryam's birthday party was like yours? What did you both do that was the same?" "When you saw Ricardo's car collection, what did you notice was different from your car collection?"*

If your child shows interest in exploring some of the common organization patterns like comparisons, **please note that many children are able to develop greater fluency with spoken**

language when they know there is a "scribe" to record their dictation. Think about the child who finds that the sheer management of the many aspects of writing can be overwhelming: forming the letters, trying to remember the spelling, keeping track of the organization of the sentence, deciding which words to choose, deciding which detail to include, knowing where to begin or where to end up. Many a child "of few words" has suddenly had a great deal to say when given the support of a scribe, and when they have specific organization patterns to target in the dictation.

Watch for other ways to introduce the ideas of paragraph organization informally into your conversations about the *LEA* stories, or about books that you are reading. For our At-Home activities, it is probably enough to highlight the examples when you spot one of the main paragraph organization patterns, which can occur in either a fictional story or a non-fiction dictation that is information-based. The most important benefit to your child is that *you help build awareness of how information is typically organized.* Chapter 10 emphasizes the role of this awareness when we focus on *critical thinking.* If awareness is truly developing in your child's mind, you may have the joy of hearing a spontaneous comment when he or she makes a good connection to one of the paragraph organization patterns.

Benefits of Keeping the Stories Going If Your Child Maintains Interest

Early literacy activities provide a wealth of information about the development of your child. Parent observations in the At-Home context are particularly valuable. You will see development in a different way than one might observe in the classroom where your child is part of a larger group. You may also find that your observations are supported and supplemented by the teacher at school when you have periodic parent-teacher conferences. The purpose of the following section is to note the markers that indicate the kind of progress that could be expected, or at least is very likely. We will also note markers *that may suggest a need to take a closer look.* The following diagnostic markers apply to many aspects of a child's overall language development based on the work with the dictated stories and the follow-up activities.

Progress Markers to Watch for While You Are Collecting the Stories. *These Markers are based on both the contents of the dictated stories and on your child's behaviors and confidence levels that you can observe.*

Awareness of One's Own Language Output

- ♦ Can store sentences in memory and repeat the sentences for you to write down in cases when words were spoken too rapidly for you to write.
- ♦ Is increasingly able to repeat the original thought exactly.
- ♦ When the story is read back, is able to spontaneously add words or change the original forms of words or sentences to make them better, as in noting an immature form such as "bringed."

Awareness of the Process for Writing the Dictations

- ♦ Watches as the story is written down.
- ♦ Follows the progress of the pencil with a sense of what it takes to produce the written symbols that represent the words and thoughts.
- ♦ Deliberately paces the dictation to match your ability to record the words.

Vocabulary Breadth and Depth

- ♦ Introduces new terms for items and actions based on the stimulus activities that you have provided and may have discussed together.

◆ May comment specifically about the words that are used, may observe that the word is "new," or may note the source of the word.

◆ Shows evidence that the new words have entered into the child's permanent vocabulary by using them in other contexts.

Ability to Produce Specific Vocabulary Words for the Story, Such as Appropriate Nouns, Verbs, Adjectives, and So On

◆ Shows evidence of greater word-finding skills from existing permanent vocabulary.

◆ When searching for a word to express the intended meaning, shows evidence of word-searching strategies in response to specific questions that you might ask to clarify meaning: *"Are you trying to tell me about how the bicycle fell over?"*

◆ Makes comments about where and when the word was learned, or whether the word has come up in another context.

◆ May note that the word also was used in a previous story.

Ability to Produce a Coherent Story, with Thoughts That Are Organized in a Clear Way

◆ Shows the ability to adopt the idea of *story*, and to imitate the story format of the stories they hear.

◆ May incorporate conventional language such as *"Once upon a time…"* to begin the story.

◆ Shows a more deliberate internal organization of the story or the use of well-sequenced sentences.

◆ Is beginning to use appropriate conjunctions and other words that link events together, such as *when, then,* or *after that.*

Appearance of More Complex Sentence Structures

♦ Makes consistent use of simple sentences with basic subject-verb construction.
♦ Is beginning to introduce added details, elaborating single ideas appropriately.
♦ Uses compound sentences: *"The dog was looking for his stick, but he couldn't find it."*
♦ Introduces complex sentences, with a subordinate clause added to the main clause: *"When we go to the beach, we take our own chairs."*
♦ Experiments with different types of sentences in addition to declarative sentences, such as questions or exclamations.

Ability to Read Back the Story after You Have Both Confirmed the Dictation

♦ When reading the story aloud, shows that the story has been stored in memory.
♦ Shows awareness of how the written words express the idea she or he had in mind.

Ability to Locate Specific Words

♦ When prompted following the dictation, can locate specific words in the written text.
♦ When prompted, can find repeated occurrences of specific words.
♦ Can find words that have the same beginning (or ending) letters.
♦ Can find a word that is a synonym of a word clue that you give.
♦ Shows indicators about further story activities that he or she might now benefit from if you have the time or

opportunity to introduce them, such as writing about a related stimulus activity.

Growth Markers Over Time

As you can see from the above growth markers, there are multiple benefits to both parent and child from continuing to collect dictated stories over time if you and your child are able to maintain interest. Dictated stories offer valuable information from at least two sources: first, from the texts of the stories themselves, and second, from the behaviors and the confidence you might observe while collecting the stories. Additional important benefits can be noted from the saved stories, based on the elements listed above. Your child's maturing vocabulary will be very evident. You will see longer and more complex sentences. You will note stories that are more deliberately and better organized (*story coherence*).

As you observe the behavior during the dictation experience, you might note a growing awareness of the writing-thinking process, in the way your child paces the dictation to match your ability to write down the words. You may see that she can hold sentences or ideas in memory or actively organize the words to make a good sentence. You may hear her self-correct a sentence during the dictation in order to make it better. Or she might change the wording when you first read back the story for confirmation.

If you are interested in tracking such markers, you might note the new words that are added or even keep track of the number of different words within the story. You can note the length of a sentence and whether it contains subordinate clauses (Chapter 5). You can count the number of sentences related to the main topic or the number of topics within a story. Many of these markers will also appear during the independent or paired writing activities that have been introduced in the previous chapters. With many children, a key indicator of growth in *LEA* is that moment when they seize the pencil and say, "*I can write it.*"

Appearance of "Borrowed Stories"

When children listen to stories or read book stories on their own, you may find that some of these well-told or familiar tales begin to show up in the dictations. This may present a dilemma for you as the parent if your child seems to be "borrowing" story ideas from other sources. In this case, there is no single appropriate response that applies to all children. Much depends on the age of the child and the level of confidence that has been shown with dictating stories. It may be enough for you to comment, *"That sounds like the story we were reading yesterday."*

You may continue to record the story for the child and use the child's own language for the activities we have already described. You may note when you do the next dictation, *"I would love to hear your OWN story today."* You might take the opportunity to suggest a new topic for a story. You might also note (with private delight) that your child's adaptation of a borrowed story is indeed better than the original in ways that only your child could imagine! In all cases, show your child how much you value the stories and continue to collect them.

What to Do If You Don't See the Expected (or Hoped-for) Progress

The dictated stories have significant value in documenting language development. They provide early markers of *language processing issues* that may indicate a referral to the student study team at school, a speech/language specialist, or an educational therapist. Children with language processing difficulties, especially in *expressive language*, may produce words and sentences that seem confused and disorganized. These children often cannot hold in mind the sentences that they have just said. They may be unable to repeat the utterance when asked to do so. They may be unable to respond successfully to their own dictated sentences and work with them in the instructional activities if the sentences do not provide sufficient structure to allow them to restate or clarify the meaning. From this point of view, *LEA* stories serve as an excellent diagnostic tool, *as they help us capture verbal output for systematic examination.*

Children with expressive language impairments often need speech/language intervention *before LEA can be used successfully.* In this case, the therapist and parent can team up to tailor the activity to the child's needs in expressive language development. The "experience story" can be as simple as a single sentence, often as a caption for a picture the child might draw. It can be a dictated comment or two about an object such as a toy or pet. This practice still helps the child make the connection between speech and print. It also offers ongoing documentation of the child's language output that is useful both for *evaluation* and for *tracking progress.* Parents gain an added sensitivity to how well their child is using language to communicate, which increases the potential for At-Home reading and writing collaboration.

LEA Stories Can Play an Important Role in Remedial Instruction

The *Language Experience Approach* has a well-established history in remediation, as well as in the field of adult literacy. The dictated stories of struggling readers, both younger and older, offer not only a tool for instruction but also a significant source of diagnostic information. When used in speech/language therapy or educational therapy, the stories provide an opportunity to observe many elements of expressive language. These would include the following critical elements that a specialist would note: the child's ability to form coherent sentences, the understanding of grammatical elements, breadth and depth of vocabulary, the extent of background knowledge, and the ability to retrieve relevant knowledge when it is needed.

Critical thinking and executive functioning skills are often revealed in whether the child is either able or unable to stick to the topic. The stories can show the ability to utilize and maintain a logical sequence, and to use the words that signal logical relationships such as time order, cause/effect, or comparisons. Important cognitive functions such as maintenance of attention, short-term memory, and problem-solving are all evident. Multiple aspects of a child's cognitive development which are relevant to successful progress through the educational system can be observed and treated diagnostically as appropriate. The parent observations and the data from the dictated stories can lead to appropriate referrals to specific professionals as needed.

For moderately or severely remedial students in speech/language therapy or educational therapy, dictated stories can "jump start" the acquisition of a functional sight vocabulary. In the case of older students, dictated stories can involve topics at the student's interest level in areas such as science and history, or in after-school activities such as music and sports. These students often advance quickly to recording their own stories, especially with the use of the computer or voice-activated and other assistive technology.

This example of an *LEA* story was taken in a clinic setting with a third-grade remedial reader:

> *Greg is smart. And he is not dumb. I go to Mountain Side School, grade three. Born at one o'clock in the morning, adopted the next day at 2:30. And when my eyes opened, I was two months old. When I first learned how to walk, I was two years old. The end.*

Note that this experience story is rich in biographical detail that enabled the therapist to begin the reading instruction with many good insights into Greg's world and his sense of self. Even though the time sequence is based on Greg's early memories, the story could become the beginning of work on time concepts, in addition to the work on sentence organization and elaboration. His subsequent stories were informative indeed with this story as a baseline!

Many adult literacy programs are based on *LEA*. Adults are often initially encouraged to dictate letters to family members or friends, which can then be sent with the hopes of receiving a response. One adult in such a program noted that her dictated letter was *"the first time anyone thought that what I had to say was important enough to write down!"* This individualized and personalized instruction can be a powerful motivator for an adult to stay with the task of becoming a *new reader*.

The *Language Experience Approach*, with its long history at all levels of education, has much to offer to children and parents, and to teachers and specialists who are involved in providing reading education. It is an approach based almost entirely on the positive. *LEA* can be used to validate and extend even the most minimal level of reading skill, expressive language, and experience background. The stories themselves give a powerful message to the storyteller, that no matter what their age or level of education, their experience stories and the way they tell them are important enough to write down. The stories record the way they think and the way they see the world. The benefits to parents, caregivers, and teachers are considerable when they become active participants in the diagnostic and instructional process. The ultimate benefit, of course, goes to the children and adults who are able to successfully join the *community of readers* using their own language, their own experiences, and their own stories.

References

Martin, Bill, Jr., and Carle, Eric, illustrator. *Brown Bear, Brown Bear, What Do You See?* (And many additional pattern books.). New York: Henry Holt and Co., 1996.

Resources: Sources for Beginning Reading and the *Language Experience Approach*

Aukerman, Robert C. *Approaches to Beginning Reading*, 2nd Ed. New York: John Wiley and Sons, 1984. ISBN 0-471-03693-5.

Bear, D. R., Invernizzi, M., Templeton, S., and Templeton, F. *Words Their Way: Word Study for Phonics, Vocabulary, and Spelling Instruction*, 6th Ed. Old Tappan, NJ: Pearson, 2015.

Bryant, Peter, and Bradley, Lynette. *Children's Reading Problems*. New York, NY: Basil Blackwell Ltd., 1985. ISBN 0-631-13682-7.

Cullinan, Bernice. *Pen in Hand: Children Become Writers*. Newark, DE: International Reading Association, 1993. ISBN 0-87207-383-1.

Cunningham, P. M. *Phonics They Use: Words for Reading and Writing*, 6th Ed. Old Tappan, NJ: Pearson, 2012.

Dixon, Carol N., and Nessel, Denise. *Language Experience Approach to Reading and Writing: LEA for ESL*. Hayward, CA: The Alemany Press, 1983. ISBN 0-88084-037-4.

Gambrell, L. B. "Exploring the Connection Between Oral Language and Early Reading." *The Reading Teacher*, 57(5), 490–492, 2004.

Goodman, Ken. *What's Whole in Whole Language*. Portsmouth, NH, Heinemann, 1986. ISBN 0-435-08254-x.

Goodman, Yetta M., Ed. *How Children Construct Literacy*. Newark, DE: International Reading Association, 1990. ISBN 0-87207-534-6.

Moats, Louisa Cook. *Speech to Print: Language Essentials for Teachers*, 3rd Ed. Baltimore, MD: Paul H. Brooks Publishing Co., 2020.

Morrow, Lesley, Ed. *Family Literacy: Connections in Schools and Communities*. Newark, DE: International Reading Association, 1995. ISBN 0-87207-127-8.

Strickland, Dorothy S., and Morrow, Lesley Mandel, Eds. *Emerging Literacy: Young Children Learn to Read and Write*. Newark, DE: International Reading Association, 1989. ISBN 0-87207-351-3.

Vacca, J. L., Vacca, R. T., and Gove, Mary K. *Reading and Learning to Read*, 2nd Ed. New York, New York: HarperCollins, 1991. ISBN 0-673-46358-3.

Vacca, R. T., and Rasinski, T. V. *Case Studies in Whole Language*. Fort Worth: Harcourt Brace Jovanovich, 1992. ISBN 0-03-052254-4.

10

Building Critical Thinking Skills At-Home

Activity Level: Children 5+ Years and Their Parents

EASY ACCESS NOTES FOR CHAPTER 10: WHAT YOU WILL LEARN

- ♦ How Critical Thinking Begins at Home.
- ♦ Three Kinds of Critical Thinking Activities That Can Thrive At-Home.
- ♦ Part 1. Questioning: How Questions Function at School and at Home.
- ♦ Different Kinds of Questions and Activities to Promote Them.
- ♦ A Checklist for Question Practice (Download).
- ♦ Applying What We Have Learned to School Questions.
- ♦ Part 2. Making Comparisons: Starting with Similarities; Activities for Practice.
- ♦ Ways to Think About Differences with the *Compare/Contrast "T" Chart*.
- ♦ Part 3. Categorizing: Starting Off with an Informal Evaluation Exercise.
- ♦ Introducing the Category Rule and Category Labels.
- ♦ Adding Category Members to Labeled Categories.
- ♦ Categorizing at School: Academic Applications That Show How Categorizing Functions in Learning and Remembering.

DOI: 10.4324/9781003452683-13

Critical Thinking Begins at Home

Parents may expect *critical thinking* to be part of school learning, starting in the early years of education. Yet anyone who has been around young children knows that they are already capable of thinking critically. Beginning with their earliest efforts to use language to communicate, children can be observed to ask thoughtful *questions*. They can make *inferences* about what their parents are thinking or feeling based upon body language and other clues. They can make *comparisons* when they detect how items or actions can be similar to each other and different from each other. They can group objects together into *categories* based upon common characteristics. They can readily understand how events can happen *in order*, even when their sense of time has not yet fully matured. They can weigh the evidence and reach *conclusions*. They can be *persuasive* to get what they want. They can tell *when something is silly and when something is serious*.

The family At-Home activities are designed to provide young children with a lively learning laboratory for developing an awareness of how critical thinking works. As a parent, you can highlight critical thinking by applying *specific and accurate labels* to the critical thinking operations. You can promote these skills in a systematic way through targeted activities that involve both reading and writing. This chapter shows you how to do that.

The thinking ability of young children has been the subject of much scholarly writing and academic research, from the work of Piaget in the last century, to the work of today's neuroscientists and executive function researchers. It is not the purpose of this chapter to provide an exhaustive discussion of all that we know today about children's thinking. Rather, we will take a look at how critical thinking fits into the frameworks we have already developed for At-Home writing and reading. **In other words, what does critical thinking look like in the context of the familiar?** As you engage in activities that promote critical thinking operations, you will see frequent opportunities to label these operations *so that they become thinking tools for the growing minds of your children*.

Three Kinds of Critical Thinking Activities That Can Thrive At-Home

Three kinds of critical thinking activities have been selected because they lend themselves to activities that fit comfortably At-Home: *questioning*, *making comparisons*, and *categorizing*. These three areas belong to a larger group of formal critical thinking skills that children encounter through schooling and are especially useful for us to consider because of the way they can be customized and personalized. You will note that the activities are based on experiences that have been "right there" the whole time, and now you will be able to turn them into guided learning experiences. You will continue to incorporate children's background knowledge. You will tailor the learning activities to what they are interested in. And you will explore how parents and children can collaborate. With these activities as a starting point, through the creativity of parent/child partnerships, many more activities are likely to develop and thrive. Some of your activities will show up in dictated stories, and some may enter the *Family Response Journal*. Some, hopefully, may even result in books such as this one, written by someone **At-Home** to share even more family-based activities and ideas!

Parents have a special role in encouraging and guiding many important critical thinking operations in children. First of all, this does not always involve formal teaching, as we would expect in a structured classroom with a formal curriculum, although these activities do occur in classrooms. Second, you may find yourself redefining some of the ways you interact with your children as you engage in the ongoing work of raising kids and running a household. You will become more of a "trail guide" who leads the way but who also points out the important features of the landscape.

Third, you may find that your commitment to engaging in critical thinking will strengthen as you see your children's confidence grow with practice. You will become expert at learning from them along the way. And finally, you will find, as you did with the beginning chapters on At-Home writing, that you will become very creative in spotting and seizing the opportunities for guided learning in critical thinking, At-Home.

Critical Thinking Part 1

Questioning

Questions All Around Us

As a parent, it is not likely that you sat down one day to train your child in how to ask questions. You did not even have to give your child *a reason to ask questions.* In most households, children are surrounded by language in much the same way they are surrounded by the air they breathe. And most children take to language in the same natural way they take to breathing, by participating in the action around them. They observe and react to what is happening. They watch and listen. They take note. They imitate.

And here is what they observe. They hear the big people use certain groups of words (we think of these utterances as *sentences*) that often contain a rising tone at the end, or that have an emphasis on the first sound that is made. They may observe that certain utterances get a more immediate response. They may observe that some of these response-getting utterances contain only a single sound: *Why? What? When? How? Where?*

Studies of child language development across different cultural groups and different communities show similarities in the way children learn language by imitating others in the language community. In these studies, children are often described as *Little Linguists* because of their ability to observe and incorporate language patterns. Thus, they learn early on that there is a difference between *asking and telling.* They learn the pattern of intonation when a question is asked, and they learn how and when to imitate that intonation. In most families, this learning takes place so naturally that we hardly notice it, and we as parents do not make a special effort to *teach* question-asking. Indeed, in the case of a very persistent and vocal child, we may find ourselves saying, *"Stop asking so many questions!"*

What Do Children Need to Know?

Given that most children learn about asking questions in the natural course of learning to talk, why would questioning be a focus point in a chapter on critical thinking? Don't they already know enough about questioning? The answer here has to do with degrees of awareness. They have already learned the label, when we say, *"Stop asking so many questions!"* or when we say, *"That's a good question."* To focus on questioning as a critical thinking skill, you first *raise awareness of questioning* in the child's mind. You can already easily say, *"That's a good question."* But you have not told the child what makes it a *good* question. Specific At-Home activities can bring attention to questioning in the same way you brought your children's attention to the process of writing and to the process of reading their dictated stories.

Focus Points for the Questioning Activities

- ◆ What are the main functions of questions when we communicate?
- ◆ What are the different kinds of questions?
- ◆ How are questions used for different purposes?

How Questions Function at School and At-Home

Children's early school instruction in reading and writing builds their awareness of language itself. Even very young learners use *language* to learn about *language*. They learn to think about words in a whole new way, as units of meaning that have labels and component parts (letters and sounds). *Word awareness* develops gradually over time. With word awareness, they are able to build the foundation for the awareness of *whole sentences*, which have component parts and different functions. In second and third grade, children are introduced to the idea of the four kinds of sentences: statements, questions, commands, and exclamations. And by then they have had several years of experience with both asking and answering questions.

We don't have to wait for school to take the lead with the special terminology we use to talk about questions. At-Home, parents have great opportunities to focus on questions as they happen, *for functional reasons*. You don't have to purchase a workbook with a lesson on questions because you can *seize the questions* as they happen. You watch for examples of questions that occur in conversations, in a dictated story, or in any other activity that relates to reading or writing. You can write down the question itself, along with the word "question," and you are ready for the conversation about question terminology, depending on the age and grade level of your child, and depending on what you have found out that they are learning in school.

You start at the very beginning, with the word "question" itself, leading with a question: *"Do you know what a **question** is?"* It might seem like asking for the obvious, but it is important to know what kind of understanding your child has for that key term. You might already have the word "question" written on a card (hint, hint), so you can look at it together.

The responses you get to the question about questions will set the stage for the discussions about the functions and kinds of questions. For example, your child may reply that a question is what we say when we want to know something: *"What time is it?"* A question is what we say when we want something: *"Can I have chocolate milk?"* We ask a question when we want to know the reason for something: *"Why can't I go with Grandma?"* Sometimes we ask a question when we just want to stay up a little longer: *"Can I have a drink of water?"*

You can go on to talk about why questions are important when we are talking to each other. You might say, *"Did you ask any questions today when you were with your friend? Do you remember why you asked the question?"* You can explore how we use questions both at home and at school. You might say, *"Did your teacher ask any questions at school today? Did you get to **answer** the question? Did you get to **ask** a question?"* You can talk about different situations when we use questions. You might say, *"Did you ask Daddy any questions when you went to the hardware store? Do you remember what you asked him?" "Did Grandpa ask you any questions after the game? Do you remember what he asked you about?"* Based on this kind of discussion, you are ready to get more specific.

Kinds of Questions

You can now go on to discuss the types, or forms, of questions. The "start words" for many questions are useful here: **Who, What, Where, When, Why, How.** By school age, children are familiar with questions that begin with these words, but they may not yet have identified the *kind of information* that these words are asking for. Questions that begin with the words *Who, What, Where,* and *When* can usually be referred to as *Fact Questions* because the information they are requesting is often given in the form of a fact: *Who is coming to the party? What are we having for dinner? Where did you put my shirt? When are Grandma and Grandpa coming?*

In contrast, the questions that begin with *Why* and *How* are asking for something more complicated, and the answers are usually longer. *Why* questions ask for the *reasons* for something. *How* questions ask for information about a *process* or *procedure*, or for information about an experience. For this reason, these last two question types are often referred to as *Thinking Questions.* The differences in these types of questions will become clearer to your child when you practice the application activities that follow.

We will note here that these words at the beginning of questions are also words that can occur within sentences where they have a different purpose and *do not ask a question.* In grammar terms, these words are functioning to begin certain kinds of clauses and are typically labeled as *relative pronouns.* They are likely to be encountered and analyzed in upper elementary or middle school English lessons.

- *I saw the man **who** delivers the mail.*
- *I found out **what** the teacher was surprised about.*
- *We parked the bikes **where** they would not get wet.*
- *It all depends on **when** we get there.*
- *Dad found out **why** the car would not start.*
- *Mom figured out **how** to get the box open.*

Activities to Practice All Kinds of Questions

The following activities are meant to be unstructured and conversational. They can begin with a topic that has come up in conversation or they can follow from a question you hear your child ask. They can even be carried over into one of the writing activities, depending on how much time you have and how much interest they spark in your child. Remember that the focus here is on the questions only, and how we use them. The *answers to the questions* can come later – when we have time.

For parents who like a little more structure to the activities, a simple checklist might be helpful and even inspirational. It can be found in the table following the discussion of each question type. There are columns in which to record the dates when you first tried the question practice, and a column to record the date if you did it again. This kind of checklist might prompt you to record the questions on another piece of paper, which would give you an opportunity to see if there are changes in what kinds of questions your child can think of or what kinds of questions have a high frequency.

WHO questions. When you ask a "Who" question, what kind of answer do you expect? Your child will note that you get *the name of a person* such as a family member or friend. In some families, it might occasionally be the name of the dog or cat! For many children, the answer will be obvious, but since we are in the process of raising awareness, *the obvious is very useful*. For this form of question, you might practice using just names of family members or people you already know. You can model some patterns for your child, and then have your child try out this form of question. Remember that we will save the answers for later.

- ◆ *Who does Grandma like to play bridge with?*
- ◆ *Who has a birthday in March?*
- ◆ *Who has a piano lesson on Friday?*
- ◆ *Who always sits in the front seat of the car?*

WHAT questions. When we ask a "What" question, we expect a much more complicated kind of answer. It could be a single object, for *"What is in the box?"* But it could be a whole set of actions or events: *"What are we going to do if it rains on Monday?"* Thus, we can look at the many purposes of *what* questions and how they differ from *who* questions. To apply this form of question, you might start out with examples using just a simple object: *"What is on the cover of the book?" "What do you want for lunch?" "What is the dog barking at?"* In this process, your child may begin to understand more fully the purpose of questioning, and how we use questions in many different situations.

WHEN questions. "When" questions generally refer to points in time, specific dates, or hypothetical time. As you and your child work with examples of *when* questions, point out that *when* can refer to three kinds of time frames: *past*, *present*, and *future*.

- ◆ *When did you lose your shoe?* (past)
- ◆ *When is the best time to make the cookies?* (present)
- ◆ *When will the movie start?* (future)

"When" questions can also refer to anticipation or expectations (hypothetical questions): *"When will you have your homework finished?" "When can you help me?"* This is another form of *question awareness* to explore together.

WHERE questions. "Where" questions seek information that relates to place or location. Children will realize the great functionality of such questions in daily life, as we frequently have to locate something or go somewhere. Examples of such daily life questions will be easy to think of. Watch for questions that demand exact information, such as *"Where is the volleyball?"* versus those that are hypothetical: *"Where shall we put the new computer?"*

WHY questions. This form of questioning seems to be a favorite of young children. Mostly we are proud of them for wanting to search for the reasons to explain a puzzle or to understand a situation. Sometimes the "Why" question is used to buy time or prolong an argument. But no matter the purpose of the *why* question, the topic can still produce a great many examples of how to apply the form. You may observe even further understanding and application of this useful type of question as you dig deeper into the topic of questioning.

Young children will be able to see the differences between the "Why" questions they might ask a best friend, versus the "Why" question to a parent, versus the "Why" question to a teacher.

You might say, *"Think of a 'why' question you could ask Ricardo (best friend). Could you ask your teacher that same question? Why, or why not?"* This might prompt some discussion about how a "Why" question to a best friend is different from a "Why" question to a teacher!

HOW questions. This form of questioning may be the most complex of the group in terms of answers because it usually asks about steps in order, some kind of process, some kind of state or feeling, or some kind of logical relationship: *"How did you feel when the lights went off?"* We might be referring to cause/effect relationships: *"How did the lamp get broken?"* We might be referring to compare/contrast relationships: *"How is a car different from a truck?"* If these discussions spark an interest, you will find that the question checklist gains added value as a way of documenting your discussions of the varieties and purposes of questions, as well as their great value in human communication, At-Home and elsewhere.

Application Activities

The application activities here are intended to promote a parent's own growing awareness *of each child's repertoire of questions*. And equally importantly, the questioning activities may in fact promote a greater *sense of inquiry* in your child's mind. You may note that the content of the questions begins to transition from being mainly procedural questions about the conduct of daily life to being *genuine forms of information seeking*. These latter kinds of questions indicate the development of the kind of inquiry that builds background knowledge. The questions may prompt some good collaboration between parent and child *as to how you might both search for answers and further information.*

Questions with Different Purposes

Questions to make a request, ask permission, or show courtesy and politeness. As you and your child explore questioning, you will note another major category of questions that do not use the six key words that we have discussed above. These questions begin with a verb form called a *helping verb*: may, did, can, have, could, might, would, will, and so on. *"May I go with Grandma?"*

TABLE 10.1 A Checklist for Question Practice

Question type	Example prompts	Date of practice #1	Date of practice #2
WHO	◆ A *who* question about Mom or Dad ◆ A *who* question about a sister or brother ◆ A *who* question about a favorite teacher or coach ◆ A *who* question about the neighbor down the hallway or down the street ◆ A *who* question involving a pet		
WHAT	◆ A *what* question about an object in the room ◆ A *what* question about an item in the kitchen ◆ A *what* question about something a child could make ◆ A *what* question about something that happened today ◆ A *what* question about a gift you want to give to a friend		
WHEN	◆ A *when* question about a family event that may happen in the future ◆ A *when* question about something that has already happened ◆ A *when* question about something you would like to do ◆ A *when* question about something that happened to a brother or sister or friend		
WHERE	◆ A *where* question about a possible activity ◆ A *where* question about a missing toy ◆ A *where* question about the location of a park ◆ A *where* question about a place on the map ◆ A *where* question about a place in a story		
WHY	◆ A *why* question about a family tradition ◆ A *why* question about a favorite food ◆ A *why* question about an animal ◆ A *why* question about rain or wind or a kind of storm ◆ A *why* question about a favorite sport or other activity		
HOW	◆ A *how* question about procedures for a possible project ◆ A *how* question about making a favorite food ◆ A *how* question about a sport-related skill ◆ A *how* question about a process in science or in nature ◆ A *how* question about the cause of an accident or a mishap		

"Can Stuart stay for dinner?" These questions include requests and inquiries about the status of various situations. *"Will you please help me?"* *"Did you finish your homework?"* *"Have we got enough apples?"* *"Could you feed the dog before you go?"* These questions help young children navigate their social environments, and get their needs met. And they are among the first forms of language that we use to model good manners, so children are more likely to get those needs met!

You could fill several books with ideas for activities involving questions, but you will very naturally find ideas to fit your own family. To use the At-Home Model to focus on questions, you might use the *Writing Wall* to record some example questions you are likely to hear on a given day or in a given situation, and then discuss some possible responses for the question you are discussing. Sometimes it is a simple Yes or No, and sometimes it's more complicated. But all discussions at home can build awareness for the next important form of questioning, *school-related questions*.

School questions. As we have noted, when children begin formal education, teachers pay attention to *elements of language* in a structured way. Children learn about word boundaries. They learn sound/letter connections. They learn to write a sentence. They also learn to respond to the kinds of questions *that are used to examine and evaluate their learning*. Ideally, they will get direct instruction about the structure of questions and specific question terminology so they are familiar with how these questions are used in the classroom to examine and evaluate.

In the classroom, children may feel that they must pay more attention to *how to answer the question, rather than how to analyze the question itself*. However, if the At-Home activities have been successful in promoting question awareness, there may be an indirect payoff at school in the form of a greater understanding of the purposes of the questions themselves. Your child may now be alert to the idea that a "Who" question is likely to be answered by the name of a person in a book or in a history lesson. A "Why" question requires a *reason* in the answer, and so on. And if your child is ever invited to "make up" a question for a school activity, he has many options to consider, because of the practice with questions At-Home.

Finally, an important payoff to question practice may be a payoff that you do not get to observe directly because it may happen while your child is in school. Classroom instruction offers children a great deal of practice in hearing questions, thinking about questions, and responding to questions. For some children, this can be an anxiety-provoking process. When the question is given as part of classroom discussion, the child may not immediately understand the wording of the question. And even when your child understands the question, he still has to search his memory and retrieve the exact information needed. And then he has to find the exact words *to express the answer.*

Some children experience time pressure, fear of exposure, and even humiliation if they can't come up with an answer quickly. Without the necessary practice and support, in some instances, a child may appear to have a "learning disability" in this kind of situation. *And a child who is experiencing anxiety in such situations is unlikely to want to* **answer** *the question next time, even if she or he knows the answer.* Each time children can practice analyzing and making up questions in the context of the familiar, they are building the confidence and the skill to deal with questioning effectively, no matter where the questions happen. When you provide the labels for the kinds of questions and when you encourage your children to make their own questions, you are helping them to expand their repertoire of critical thinking skills.

Critical Thinking Part 2

Making Comparisons

Child development specialists might suggest that the children with brothers and sisters are the first to learn how to make comparisons: *"He got more ice cream than I did." "She gets to stay up later than I do." "My shoes are bigger than yours."* For children, comparisons that involve amounts of something seem inevitable. But whether siblings are present or not, comparisons are a solid part of real life, with real-world applications. Thus, comparisons are a handy way and a functional way to promote the development of critical thinking.

Step 1: Begin with Similarities

You will begin your comparisons practice by considering the way that things are alike before we consider the differences. In the comparison example about ice cream, the similarity is that you both get some ice cream. In the second example, you both have to go to bed at some point in time. And in the third, you both wear shoes, even if they are different sizes. If you begin a discussion of comparisons, and the first comment focuses on differences (this often results in an argument), you can switch the focus to similarities by asking: *"How are they **like** each other?"* Parents can then begin to list the characteristics that objects or events can share, like size, amount, time, or type. The idea of similarities should be clearly established when you begin to practice this critical thinking skill. When children look for similarities, they are looking at *the important characteristics that define both objects and events.*

Start in just about any location at home: the kitchen, your child's room or closet, or the room where people gather together. You can group things together physically: *the drawer with the spoons; the drawer with the socks; the shelf with the canned goods.* You can group by function: *which foods are best kept in the freezer; which clothes do we wear when it is cold.* You can also note similar activities: *sports that require a ball; sports that involve fast running; activities that require a special place;* and *activities that require a partner or a group.*

When children are explaining how common items like these are the same, they may come up with some surprising views of similarities that we have not thought of. For this reason, their perceptions offer good insights into how they arrived at their ideas. In the event of an unusual opinion that could easily turn into an argument, you can focus on just the specific features that are the same, and you can encourage that kind of inventive thinking. Some issues can best be left *unresolved*, especially when a child has not yet developed the necessary background knowledge or perspective: *"We can come back to that later on!"*

In the At-Home environment, we can look at common items or events and identify their similarities. Some similarities are obvious, such as similar desserts (usually all sweet and eaten after lunch or dinner). But sometimes things that don't seem similar

TABLE 10.2 Activities for Similarities: How Are These Things Alike?

◆ Dog and cat	◆ Singing and talking
◆ Moth and butterfly	◆ Train and airplane
◆ Breakfast and lunch	◆ April and August
◆ Shoes and socks	◆ Calendar and clock
◆ Snow and ice	◆ Swimming and diving

can have similar features, such as a tire and a doughnut (round shape, hole in the center). This may evolve into a game in which children search for items that are very different on the surface but have some characteristics in common. You may find that this kind of exercise causes your child to examine just what we mean when we use the words *"the same."* The section on categorizing, to follow, will also offer some activities to help children identify the common characteristics that are shared by things that are similar.

Your family will be able to make many lists of this sort. Watch for the less obvious similarities that depend on background knowledge, such as *frog* and *butterfly* (both are the outcomes of metamorphosis), or smoke and fog (both are forms of vapor).

Step 2: Ways to Think about Differences

The examples of unusual similarities can lead to the discussion of differences. Here again, we focus on some common characteristics, such as *size, shape, color, function, age, cost, purpose, usefulness,* or *popularity.* You begin with the obvious, such as the physical features of two kinds of reptiles, marine mammals, or birds. Children with good science backgrounds can start with the four-legged animals, and then go on to separate out the ones with paws and the ones with hooves. You can use household items, such as different cooking tools: mixing bowls and blenders both used for mixing but only the blender uses electricity; measuring spoons and measuring cups, both used for measuring but for different kinds of foods and amounts. You can also point out that some things can be different in more than one way. If I compare two pets, I might focus on their size and what they eat. But I might also note what kind of training they require, whether they can live both outdoors and indoors, or whether they are usually caged or able to roam free.

Points of Comparison

Depending on the age and school level of your child, you can now introduce a very important idea about comparisons. You can talk about *the variable characteristics that we use to make a comparison*. Children as young as third grade can be introduced to the idea of *Points of Comparison*. When we compare two fruits, for example, such as oranges and bananas, we would note that both are fruits and both have skins that we don't eat, but we make juice from only one of them. *Points of Comparison* are the features of the two items *by which they can be compared and contrasted*. If we are comparing two tools, for example, we would focus on the function of each tool, the material it is made from, its weight and durability, and whether it is powered by electricity or muscles. Of less importance is the store where we purchased the tool.

If we are comparing two sports, we would look at them in terms of other sports that are similar but not identical, such as the athletic abilities of typical players of the sport. For practice purposes, we would need to think in terms of *significant variables* or *important points of comparison*. Thus, we would be unlikely to ask for a comparison between a dog collar and a garden hose, as they have relatively little in common besides general shape. Finally, with practice of this skill, we would be helping the child understand a broader range of characteristics for a given item, which can go well beyond the obvious. We can explore this range of characteristics with the use of the *Compare/Contrast "T" Chart*.

Step 3: The Compare/Contrast "T" Chart

Your child might find it helpful if you use a structured way to demonstrate and practice compare/contrast as a form of *critical thinking*. You have already taken the first steps: how two things are alike and how they are different. You have practiced on physical items (spoons, foods, etc.) for physical characteristics, and you have also included abstract characteristics (function, usefulness, popularity, etc.). You have talked about how things can be compared using the idea of *points of comparison*.

The simple T chart, or matrix, can be used to introduce structure into this activity. Many elementary students have seen the teacher use the *Venn diagram* with its two intersecting circles to show the areas where the two items are different but show the similarities in the zone of intersection. However, the information in the Venn circles may not be organized to show the *points of comparison* between the two items being compared, and how they match up with each other. In fact, if the points of difference are listed in a random order, the way they relate to or balance each other may not be clear.

To make the *T Chart*, you begin with a three-column chart and write the items you are comparing in the second and third columns. In the left-hand column, you will write the labels for the *points of comparison*. **This column is where the main critical thinking is done**. The *Apples and Oranges* topic is useful as a starter because many kids have heard someone say *"But it's apples and oranges"* when they are arguing that the two items are not really comparable.

This is also a good way to illustrate how many ways we can compare familiar items like two fruits. Children typically will begin with the most obvious characteristics, but they quickly discover there are many other points of comparison, such as the structure of the fruit, whether or not you can eat the skin, or whether you cook the fruit. They can be led to think of other more complex ideas such as what kind of climate the two different fruit trees require, how the fruits are sold or stored, and how they are referred to in literature and legend.

Step 4: At-Home Activities to Highlight Compare/Contrast

- ◆ Using the *T Chart* format, compare two simple concrete items: *apples and oranges, dogs and cats, knives and forks, shoes and socks, hammers and saws, bicycle and tricycle, skateboard and snowboard*.
- ◆ Using the *T Chart* format, compare two complex items: *two sports, two characters in a book, two board games, two musical instruments*.
- ◆ Compare two processes (for children in fourth grade and up): use science or social studies examples, real-life examples like home improvement projects, cooking or art projects, learning to sew, or learning to play the piano.

TABLE 10.3 A Comparison Chart using a Comparison Matrix

Points of comparison	Oranges	Apples
Food category	Fruit	Fruit
Color	Orange color	Red, green, yellow, orange-ish
Shape and size	Round and mostly the same size	Round, with some smaller in diameter, and some larger in diameter
Peel or skin	Not edible, except when cooked in marmalade	Edible
Seeds	In the segments	In the center core
Structure and texture	Divided into segments, can be shared easily	Solid texture, must be cut with a knife to be shared
Juice	Orange juice	Apple juice
How prepared	Eat raw	Raw or cooked (apple sauce, apple pie, etc.)
Where grown	Needs year-round warm climate: southern states	Needs cold winter, warm summer for ripening: northern states
Type of tree	Evergreen	Deciduous
Food storage requirements	Needs refrigeration or will spoil (important to the produce manager at the grocery store)	Keeps for a long time without refrigeration (reference to Johnny Appleseed who brought seeds to the pioneers to grow apples that would keep through the winter)
In literature and legend	— Hint: you can use this space as an opportunity for family research	Symbol of knowledge, temptation; Johnny Appleseed; Golden Apples
California history	First brought by Spanish missionaries from South America; exported from southern California to other states	Imported to southern California from northern California or other states
My own state	The regional climate might require oranges to be imported from somewhere else	Homegrown in yards or orchards if the climate is suitable for the trees

Critical Thinking Part 3

Categorizing

Categorizing may seem to be a very functional, everyday operation to be included with the critical thinking skills. It's just the operation we use when sorting the laundry or loading the dishwasher. Children appear to automatically understand and observe categories. Think about how the kitchen is organized. Think about what we teach them (or try to) about how to sort the laundry and where to put the socks. The ability to categorize seems to emerge early on in child development as a common sense and useful operation.

However, we should not underestimate its contribution to critical thinking. And like other simple-seeming operations, it should not be assumed that a child fully understands how it works, or why it is important. As children get older, any limitations they may have in understanding categories are easy to spot: the messy room, the disorganized backpack, or where things that should belong together don't seem to stay together. Limitations may also emerge in *the way children store knowledge, and in the way they retrieve what they know.*

Categorizing has been included here not only because it fits well with the At-Home Model, but also because there are multiple reasons to highlight categorizing skills among the larger group of critical thinking skills. It is an important skill to support in the early ages because categorizing has broad applications in both the classroom and the real world, even though it is not always taught as a structured skill until somewhat later on in schooling. Categorizing skills impact not only the ability to manage the tasks and items of daily life. As researchers in executive functioning tell us, this skill impacts how the brain organizes data, experiences, and events. Categorizing is a basic element in the cognitive operations that form the basis of learning and thinking, and as parents and teachers we want to address it systematically early on. We don't want to wait until signs of limitations in this critical skill show up in the messy room, the scrambled backpack, the lost homework, or the anxiety that comes from the sense that you can't find something important that has been misplaced.

Introducing Categorizing in Stages

Categorizing can be approached in stages, as you have done with other complex *cognitive operations*, that is, operations that involve your child's thinking. For the younger child, at first, you will not even need to use the words *categorizing* or *categories*. Keep the language simple and related to the At-Home environment where you can focus on the familiar. By the age of four or five, children will be familiar with the idea of *groups*, particularly if they have participated in groups at pre-school, kindergarten, church or other religious venues, or in children's sports, music, and play activities. You will introduce the idea *that all members of the group share something in common or are alike in some way.* This concept is the foundation of categorizing.

Getting Started with an Informal Evaluation

It is useful to begin your work on categorizing with an informal evaluation of how your child understands the idea, right now, using simple grouping tasks that are appropriate to his or her vocabulary or age level. You will take note of whether she can explain why the selected items or words belong together. Can she identify the characteristics that are most important, or critical, to belonging to the group? For example, when Janie (age eight) was shown a list of different motor vehicles (van, car, bus, truck, motorcycle), and was asked what they had in common, she replied, *"They all make noise."* While this is true, her response made clear that she had not yet noted *the essential characteristics they share*: all have wheels and engines, all are used for transporting people and things, and all are driven by a driver. The characteristics in this list of similarities are called *"critical attributes."*

In addition, you will want to observe whether she has begun to acquire *category labels*, that is, the names by which we refer to a category. Janie did not say, as an older child might have, *"They are all **vehicles**."* You will also note whether she can see multiple possible groupings, based upon alternative category rules.

Fortunately, for our purposes, we can examine these understandings informally, using objects that can be found At-Home.

Step 1: Informal Evaluation Tasks

This evaluation exercise uses items that can easily be found around the house and are likely to be items that would be known to a child. First, using a small box as a container, you assemble a number of items that might be in the office area or the kitchen area, such as paper clips, a small screwdriver, a red ribbon, a bookmark, and so on. Make sure there are items that are *sharp*: a pin, a thumb tack, a staple remover, and a sharpened pencil. Include items *made of metal*: a pin, a thumb tack, keys, staples, a screw, and a knife. You might include items that are *red in color*: a ribbon, a bookmark, a first-class stamp, and the box with your supply of staples. You might have items with *print* on them: the staple box, a coin, keys, a stamp, and a pencil. You might have items that have *plastic*: a screwdriver, a staple remover, and a luggage clip.

The exercise you will start off with is typically very effective with the younger ones, who experience it as a game, but you may be surprised at how well it works with some older children who have not considered common characteristics at such a concrete level. Begin by laying out four or five items that are sharp and ask in what way these things are "like each other." Then proceed to the metal group, followed by the plastics group. So far we have explored how they can be grouped based on how they feel (sharp) or what they are made of (material).

The next grouping might be things with red color (or a similar color). The group of items with print words or numbers is more difficult because the common characteristic is less obvious and has less to do with form or function. If you have three to four items that are long and narrow, such as a pencil or a small screwdriver, you can include the characteristic of shape. You now can proceed to a discussion of the labels of the typical features that we used as a basis to form the groups, such as *shape, size, color, material*, and *function*.

If your child seems to be catching on and having fun with this, you can turn the tables. Have him select three or four items that he thinks share a common characteristic, and now it is your turn to guess how they are alike. Be prepared for some ideas that stretch the concept, such as "They all belong to Mom" or "We keep these things in drawers." This might lead to a discussion of whether it is hard or easy to identify the group called "Mom's stuff" as opposed to "things made of metal." The group of "Mom's stuff" or "kept in drawers" might well contain things that are quite unlike each other in any other way, but a good discussion has been started.

Step 2: Introducing the Category Rule

After you have used these concrete objects to establish the idea of common characteristics, you can now introduce the idea of the *category rule*. If you have invited your child to make his own group from the available items, you may have been able to *label* the common characteristic. If the common characteristic has a recognizable label, you now can utilize the category rule for further exploration. You could have your child add new members to the "sharp" category, or the "metal" category. From there, it's an easy next step to start taking note of the evidence of categories in the immediate space (books all together on shelves, toys in boxes, and so on). The kitchen is a good place to practice, or someone's bedroom, or the garage. These are generally functional household categories, easily identified, such as the cupboard where the canned foods are stored, or the drawer with the plastic storage containers.

Step 3: Category Labels

Language plays a major role in all learning, and the role of language is particularly important in the growth and development of critical thinking. As you have observed with your own family, young children are continuing to develop fluency in language, both through experiences and through schooling. You will see this happen right before your eyes when we proceed from common characteristics to introduce *category labels*.

By the ages of three to five years, children are very used to the idea that we give names to things. That's how we know what we are talking about. With the lead-up experiences in categorizing, we have referred to various groups by their category labels, because it is an efficient way to make ourselves understood.

When you were grouping your little collection of office or household items for the informal evaluation, you might have referred to "tools," "dishes," or any number of common household groups. The understanding is already there. Now you can make it formal through *the discussion and use of category labels*.

This is a two-step process. You will first want to emphasize that there is a whole group of words *that name categories* by using group names your children are already familiar with: *pets, toys, snacks, furniture, clothes*, and *games*. The second step is to try listing the members of the category. This activity can turn into a back-and-forth game between parent and child, as you shall see.

There are several points to remember about category labels and category membership. Some categories are what we might call "fixed." That is, there would be general agreement about what belongs in the category, such as *birds, planets*, or *oceans of the world*. There might be other groups we could name for which there might be some disagreement as to what belongs in the group, such as "annoying noises" or even "pets." A big step of growth for a child is to learn the difference between these kinds of groups. Children also may note that there is room here for creativity and inventiveness in such categories as *art materials, building materials*, or *family traditions*.

Adding Category Members to Category Labels

You can also watch as children become more skilled at applying the labels. If you are talking about the group we call "pets," you would be likely to include cats and dogs but probably not bats or skunks. A good marker of critical thinking is the ability of your child to explain why skunks wouldn't belong. Finally, it is important to note that a category label must be informative. You would not have essential clues about the identity of specific items that were in the box labeled "Mom's stuff."

Additionally, you can watch for development in a child's ability to *list the members of the group*. This is a reliable marker *of the growth of background knowledge*. A child might be able to say the word "bird," but be unable to name many of the specific bird species that belong in the group. We want to promote a balance between the ability to label the groups and acquiring a good supply of members in the group. Children often gain confidence from their ability to name lots of birds, flowers, or tools, and for us, it is a measure of their learning.

You will find opportunities to introduce the idea of *sub-categories*, which you can note in a trip to a place such as a grocery store. You can walk along the canned goods aisle and note that the different kinds of canned vegetables are grouped together, even when there are differences within the sub-groups like canned vegetables (tomatoes with tomatoes, beans with beans), as with the soups and the canned fruits. If you have time, and the store is not too crowded, you could explore other forms of grouping and discuss why there might be things that are not made of milk in the "dairy" cases. Similarly, the shoe store will offer sections for sports shoes, sandals, and dress-up shoes.

You can note that some items can share one identifying characteristic but are mostly unlike each other. Thus, we can group a kitchen knife and scissors together because both are sharp and are used to cut things, and that is a desirable and deliberate characteristic of those two items. But a piece of broken glass is also sharp, and that is not desirable if you are the one picking up the pieces of broken glass. These finer distinctions may occur to your child and can be celebrated when they do occur. They may indicate the mind of a child who is truly puzzling over the new idea of *category rule*.

The Role of Categories in Learning

Categories have a significant role in academic learning. As children are exposed to both school instruction and home reading activities that involve science information, they will see immediately that science is all about categories. Science categories represent an important way that we use to organize the new information we are learning. Once we learn the characteristics of *mammals*, for example, we can apply that information to identifying *marine mammals*, or when we contrast mammals with *reptiles*. In the social studies class, children learn about community groups that have developed identifying characteristics over time, or the characteristics of the kinds of plants that are grown for food. This principle applies generally to how knowledge is learned and stored, not just for children but for grown-ups as well.

Finding the Best Places for Exploring Categories and Sub-Categories

Once you have established the frameworks for categorizing, you can explore many ways to promote categorizing, starting with *categorizing field trips*. As noted, you could easily begin with a trip to the grocery store. Here everything you want to buy is organized by category, and each aisle has a sign telling you where you will find the items on your shopping list. You might encounter a few new category labels right away, such as the word *Produce*. You can provide helpful explanations if the label is a new vocabulary word. You might note that the temperature even varies depending on whether you are right by the deli cases, or in the aisle with the paper towels, which don't need to be kept cool.

There are many other places where categorizing is visible and useful. Take a visit to the hardware store and have your child make a list of ten important categories in this kind of store. To bring writing into this activity, you and your child together could make a list of four reasons why categories are important to the customer and four more reasons why categories are important to the people who work at the store and re-stock the shelves. See if you and your child can spot some items that can be placed in more than one category. Tools are a good example because you might have pliers in the kitchen, the office, and the garage (but an electric saw would be most likely to be only a garage tool).

Taking Turns

The At-Home environment is a good place for reciprocal activities, once you and your child have the ground rules for categorizing. By now, you have learned to listen for any category labels that might pop up in family discussions or conversations. For example, if someone mentions the word "pest," you might discuss the characteristics of things that belong to that group, and then go on to list some members that we might already know about or have heard of. Most children have encountered the idea that mice and rats are pests (unless, of course, we have a "pet" mouse or rat), but not all families would add "raccoon" to the group unless they have had a raccoon in the attic.

Now you can take turns. Mom or Dad gives the category label, and the children have to name things that belong in the category. Then it's your child's turn to give the label and your turn to come up with examples of members of the category. You will quickly see the differences in life experiences, and you will also see how often a grown-up can be stumped! Everyone can enjoy this game, and everyone can enjoy the discussion of what fits, what does not fit, and why.

Categorizing at School

As you would recognize from your own schooling, categorizing has many important functions in school. You can use the following examples to help your child identify the process when it is used in homework and other school-based activities. It is important here to contrast school categorizing with the categorizing we found in the hardware store and the grocery store. When you go to a store, the categorizing work has already been done for you. That's so that you can find your way around, and quickly find what you are looking for. In school, the students have to learn what the members of many groups have in common: how all mammals are like each other, how all amphibians are alike, and how all butterflies are alike. In school, we have to learn the category labels: mammals, reptiles, birds, and so on.

But in school, we may also be presented with some words or concepts or specific details, and we have to determine what they have in common, such as when we group words by their sounds or by their meanings. Children might be asked to group adjectives by how they might be used to describe living things or non-living things, persons or animals, real places or mythical places. This is the reason we recognize categorizing as an important *critical thinking skill*.

Academic Applications

- ◆ Categories form an important basis for organizing science knowledge and other aspects of subject area knowledge.
- ◆ In reading comprehension, readers use categorizing when they cluster or group details under an appropriate

label, which helps to identify a key idea about the topic. Examples might include reading in social studies about how different kinds of communities may share similar characteristics.

♦ In reading comprehension, identifying the "main idea" or "theme" involves the use of categorizing when we cluster the ideas that the writer most wants us to think about, such as "friendship," "courage," "creativity," or "resilience."

♦ A group of details about a character in a book may help the reader understand what the character represents in the story.

♦ A group of details about a difficulty in the story helps the reader explain "the problem" or "the conflict."

♦ Children are often asked to group vocabulary words based on characteristics such as "negative" or "positive," "active" or "passive."

♦ In formal writing, children will use the structure of categories to make their plans for key ideas for the paragraph or essay.

♦ The ability to label categories accurately and quickly often enables students to successfully share their interpretation of what they read, after they have finished reading.

♦ Categorizing can be practiced in many domains that are both familiar and new.

♦ Categorizing has broad applications in both the classroom and the real world.

Watch for examples of categorizing exercises that may come home on school-based worksheets or homework assignments. Since your child may learn this skill both directly and indirectly at school, you can observe if there are any examples of how categorizing functions in homework or class assignments, either as a direct focus or as a by-product of the assignment. These observations will be valuable both to you and the teacher. When you are offered a periodic teacher conference or progress update, you can mention the home activities, and share any observations you have made in connection with schoolwork. The home perspective is useful for a teacher to have.

What Categorizing Can Indicate about Your Child's Critical Thinking and Learning

Children who are skilled at categorizing are generally more effective at *storing the information they have learned* because they have a better sense of where to put it. In addition, they can use this strength to *retrieve the information when they need it.* They may show the positive school behaviors of being organized, both with time and with school materials and school assignments. As parents and children discuss these ideas, and as you observe the responses, you may be gaining insights into how this critical thinking tool is functioning to help them be effective learners and successfully functioning students. At-Home is a good context to gather any data that might help explain any areas of difficulty they might be experiencing, such as missed assignments, signs of disorganization, or inability to see key relationships among words and ideas. These signs may indicate a need for further discussion with the teacher or with the learning specialists at school.

Concluding Thoughts about Critical Thinking

At the beginning of the chapter, we noted that the three approaches we have presented here have been selected from a larger group of thinking skills that educators have traditionally called *critical thinking skills.* You may see these ideas also cited in the books or articles you might read about *executive functioning.* These three approaches are highly adaptable to the home environment for two reasons. First, when you do the suggested activities, you will be using language terms and patterns that are already familiar to your child. Second, the activities do not require the more specific terminology that teachers use for some other areas of school instruction. As an example, the skills of making *inferences* or making *generalizations* are not included here because they require a specific language of instruction. We have not addressed the ideas developed for literature analysis, such as metaphors and similes, character analysis, point of view, and story elements. We have not addressed elements of essay or paragraph analysis, such as thesis statements, conclusions, or summaries. These ideas are generally addressed through classroom practice or focused workbooks.

However, there are many benefits to both parents and their children in the three approaches presented here. The activities offer many opportunities to observe and evaluate growth in thinking, particularly if these activities are followed over time. It is very important for parents to play an active role in noting this kind of progress. The periodic report card need not be your sole source of data on school progress and learning progress.

In addition, the activities can help children build an important level of self-awareness of their own thinking skills. They may develop a whole new understanding of something as ordinary as asking a question or knowing how to put items in groups or classes. Most importantly, the activities can set your children on a path *toward developing an internalized set of learning tools*, a set that can be practiced, added to, and expanded over time. For example, students who think that memorizing is their only tool for learning can be highly motivated when shown how using categories can support memory and learning. Students can learn to recognize connections within and among categories. These are important academic benefits.

All the recommended activities have been designed to be challenging, creative, and fun. They can enhance problem-solving skills and self-confidence. Like the activities in the preceding chapters, they may help you and your children discover strengths and talents that are now emerging through practice. You can enjoy them all collaboratively!

A final note: when there seem to be difficulties in grasping any of these three operations, as may happen for some children, you as a parent may provide some indicators that will be useful to the teacher or the school learning specialists. These issues are further addressed in **Part 3**, **Meeting Today's Challenges for Parents**, because they may indicate a need for further evaluation.

Bibliography

Meltzer, Lynn, Editor. *Executive Function in Education: From Theory to Practice*. New York: Guilford Press, 2018.

PART 3

Meeting Today's Challenges for Parents

11

Parents in a Supporting Role

Introduction: Building on What You Have Learned So Far

Books for parents are written at a point in time and usually reflect the values parents are believed to hold at that time for the care and nurturing of their children. Such books also try to address the challenges faced by potential readers of the book in

DOI: 10.4324/9781003452683-15

order to offer guidelines to parents that are both relevant and inspirational.

At the time of this writing, parents continue to struggle with multiple unprecedented challenges that face families and children from the effects of a global pandemic, effects that may last well into the coming years. This pandemic has caused significant restrictions and restructuring to the ways we have been able to educate our children. During a time when teachers were often unable to teach children in person, new responsibilities fell to parents (and grandparents) who had to learn how to help their children, at home, without the benefit of books or research studies to guide them through these specific challenges. Many children have experienced significant learning loss, which is being evaluated and discussed, so that we can fully understand what resources will be needed, including how much time, to help these children compensate for the losses, or even to "catch up."

Although Chapters 1–10 of *There's a Writer in Our House!* were compiled and mostly written pre-pandemic, the At-Home Model seems hopeful, relevant, and useful to parents right now as a timely model for how to go forward, based on activities that help them nurture and promote the literacy skills of reading, writing, and critical thinking. In Chapter 11, we take a breath and an opportunity to reflect on the new skills acquired and the awareness you have built about your own At-Home environment and how it contributes to learning.

You have been introduced to activities that take advantage of opportunities that already exist in the familiar home environment. And as you have tried out the activities for writing, reading, and critical thinking, you have no doubt come up with adaptations based upon *your own creativity* and *your child's own current strengths and interests*. Along the way, you may have noticed that these activities can supplement or even replace some kinds of online and computer-based programs that would not be personalized *in the way you are able to do, At-Home*. You may also have found some surprises in the kinds of information you are able to derive from observing your children in action during focused learning activities.

Parenting is constantly evolving, and parents benefit from having many sources of information, support, and guidance.

As you will see from the sections to follow, the final chapter of this book is intended to show parents *how to best utilize the information you have gathered regarding your own children's individual strengths and needs.* As in previous chapters, the discussions focus on each child's strengths but will offer some additional important perspectives on specific issues that may emerge in the course of exploring the activities. These sections offer strategies you can use when you feel the need for extra help, if things are not going as you had expected or had hoped, including a strategy for helping children self-evaluate their own strengths. The sections focus on what children are typically experiencing in first to fifth grades, though many of the suggestions can be generalized to work beyond the fifth-grade level. The strategies can be personalized and individualized in ways that support and build a wide range of skills that children need as they continue their education.

Section 1

Teaching Children How to Self-Evaluate Their Strengths

Parents make an enormous positive contribution to their children's development when they focus on strengths. In Chapter 1, we introduced the idea of *Informative Feedback,* a process that focuses explicitly on a child's strengths. When you help your children build self-awareness of their own strengths, there is an additional ingredient you can add to this focus. Today's books on parenting often emphasize that a part of the parenting responsibility is the development of *self-concept* or *self-worth.* There is good reason for this. A positive self-concept is a foundation for successful adulthood, no matter what personality or temperament a child turns out to have. Child development researchers may agree that the process depends on the individual child, and they may agree or disagree as to *how* the child may best acquire a sense of self because it is a complex and lengthy process. They may agree or disagree about how to describe the exact role of the parent. However, as a parent, you will find it useful to consider *your child's perspective* in this process, which brings us to *the idea of self-evaluation.* Children are accustomed to being evaluated by others but can be refreshingly honest when asked for their own perspective. If you have these easy preparation steps in mind, you will be better able to explore the self-evaluation process and keep it informal and relaxed.

Advance Preparation: The Self-Evaluation Questionnaire

Step 1: Prepare the following simple questions that a child can easily respond to. The questions can be typed or written on a piece of paper, with spaces following each question for you to record the answers. When you are prepared in this way, you signal to your child that you value their responses to the questions. You can then set up a comfortable situation for asking the questions.

The Self-Evaluation Questionnaire

Date: _____

1. **Tell me something that is easy for you to do.**

_____

_____

_____

_____

_____

_____

_____

_____

2. **Tell me something that is hard for you to do.**

SUPPORT MATERIAL

_____

_____

_____

_____

_____

_____

_____

_____

3. **What are some things you are good at?**

_____

_____

_____

_____

_____

_____

_____

_____

_____

4. **What things can you help other people do?**

_____

_____

_____

_____

_____

_____

_____

_____

5. **If you had a day to choose anything you wanted to do, what would you do?**

_____

_____

_____

_____

_____

_____

_____

_____

_____

6. What is something you like at school?

_____

_____

_____

_____

_____

_____

_____

_____

Step 2: This next step depends on the age of your child. Your goal is to *start a conversation* about your child's perceptions of his or her strengths in language that is familiar and easily understood. You might start the conversation by noting *a recent example* of something your child did that showed an area of strength, such as being able to solve a problem or help someone else in a thoughtful way. She might have shown an emerging interest in something she had not noticed before. She might have asked a really thoughtful question or made an insightful comment about something she is just now learning. *You* may have made an observation at the time that *this action showed a specific* **strength** *that you could give a label to,* using the word "strength," and you may have even followed with an added comment that we can use this word *strength* to refer to other abilities *besides being able to push hard, or to lift heavy things!*

Step 3: With a real-time example to work with, find a minute to sit down with your child. Describe the specific "strength" in words that are descriptive and clear: *"I was noticing that you found a really good solution to help Micah hook up his truck and trailer toys, and I thought that was a good strength to have. I have been thinking that* *we might make a record of the strengths you have right now. Here are some questions that I can ask you, and write down your answers, just like we do when you tell a story and I write it down."* Introducing the questionnaire is likely to follow easily when you have observed a helpful example to set the stage.

If the answers are short, you can be ready with a follow-up question or a helpful hint (without putting words in his mouth): *"When you said skateboarding is easy, tell me about what part of being on the skateboard is easy for you." "When you said you are 'good at games,' tell me what part of playing games, or making up games, you are good at."* If you receive just a short answer to Question 5, you might add: *"Who would you go with? What do you think you might see?"* All the answers that are given can be expanded upon in a similar manner.

Step 4: Think about other occasions for asking the questions. The first time you are able to use the questionnaire, it may get good attention because it's new. However, there can be other occasions for using the "strengths" interview. A birthday is often a moment to mark the passage to a different age. *"Now that you are nine, this might be a good time to see what you think about these questions. We will save your answers and ask the questions again when you are ten."* There are other rituals of childhood that can be incorporated, such as participation in groups that have different levels of advancement, like church, sports, or academic activities. The beginning of a new school year or the end of a school year are excellent points to mark a child's thoughts about personal strengths. It is very likely that they will change over time in interesting ways.

Easy/Hard

You will note that the six questions suggested for the Self-Evaluation Questionnaire, except for Question 2, are all focused on the positives. Question 2, *"Tell me something that is **hard** for you to do,"* is important because it provides balance, and is another window into your child's self-perception. The questions are deliberately simple in wording and are not meant to be overly analytic or psychological. The main purpose is to *begin a dialogue* about one of the important processes of growing up, the *process of self-evaluation*. If you have the opportunity to repeat the questions over time, the notes from the dated conversations offer parents many opportunities to point out changes in self-awareness and self-confidence: *Remember when you said it was really hard to get started in a long book? I wonder if you feel that way now!"*

Finding the Right Time

We have noted that many of the writing activities involve a high level of self-expression from your child. We have noted that writing often helps your child find his or her "voice." The self-evaluation questionnaire, while very valuable to us as parents, may cause certain children discomfort even though the questions are deliberately positive in tone. If you detect that your child is not comfortable with responding, it is important to set the questions aside for another day. You can watch for some moment when things seem to be going well, for whatever reason, when your child might find it easier to respond. You might try humor, or in the spirit of collaboration, you might offer to give your own answers to the same questions. Be sure to ask your child if any of your answers were a surprise! You might also ask your child: *"Can you think of any other questions that I could have asked about your strengths?"* You may be surprised by the answer to that.

This activity is designed to be *descriptive* in nature. For you as a parent, the questions themselves may identify areas of self-perception that you were not aware of until the questions were asked. When the questionnaires are saved over time (dated), they can become a reference point to share with your child about some trends of growth and change that were made clearer, once you asked the questions. **This experience is designed to introduce a child to the important concept of self-evaluation, which itself is an essential part of each child's growth and development.**

Section 2

Important Guidelines for Readers and Writers of All Ages, and for Their Parents

Besides being careful observers, parents can play a key role in supporting their young readers and writers with concepts that will help children understand and appreciate not only the task demands but also their own successes in meeting the task demands. The following general guidelines are designed for parents of children in multiple age ranges, grades K through six. They can be revisited as appropriate, to follow children through many stages of development.

- ◆ **Reading and writing take time**. Do not try to rush your child. Be prepared to spend time if you want to see results. Your efforts will likely be rewarded.
- ◆ **Reading and writing take practice**. Children become proficient readers by reading, and they become proficient writers by writing. Let them know that good readers and writers got to be that way because they practiced, and they may have been fortunate enough to receive feedback.
- ◆ **Read to your child and write to your child**. Children need to hear and see the language of print in real time.
- ◆ To build awareness, **share the ways you use reading and writing** in your home life and your work life. *Let them see you reading and writing.* This is especially important for the child who has not yet caught on to the purposes of reading or writing. It is also a reminder that while our adult minds understand that reading and writing are important, children can effectively receive this message not only through being taught by us but also *through being shown how reading and writing are important to us.*
- ◆ **Focus on the positive**. Watch for what your child is doing right and talk about it when it happens. This can protect a struggling reader from getting discouraged or feeling that he or she might never learn to read or write.
- ◆ **Making predictions is a powerful thinking tool**. Use predicting as part of just about every experience you have with your child: reading with your child, going to the market, going on a field trip or vacation, going to visit your family and your friends. You can ask: *What do you think is going to happen? Why do you think so?* (And afterward, *Did it happen?*).
- ◆ Prepare well for events and activities that your child is involved in that could connect appropriately to reading

and/or writing. Think about how to use labels for activities, places, actions, feelings, and outcomes. Make a special effort to express the events with descriptive comments. **When you can encode experiences into language, they are more likely to be remembered and turned into useful knowledge**.

◆ **Rereading and rewriting have enormous value**, with the added benefits from digging deeper, from seeing what we missed the first time, and from finding the gems of insight and expression *that we can now appreciate even more through looking back*.

◆ **Practice *informative feedback* with your child**. Both struggling readers and writers need accurate information about their performance so that they won't come to believe that they don't do anything right. In both reading and writing, children's struggles can be especially visible and can cause anxiety, humiliation, or shaming when children over-focus on perceived weaknesses. Parents can practice *Labeled Praise* to counter negative feelings when they are observed or suspected.

◆ If you have invested thus far in exploring At-Home activities, and if the practices of customizing and personalizing the learning opportunities in the activities seem meaningful to you and your family, you may well have enjoyed the benefits of the many creative possibilities to be found here. You may have already seen multiple ways to extend the activities beyond their initial purposes in directions that were unforeseen at the beginning of the adventure. This is, of course, the nature of both reading and writing: they can lead us into the unexpected and back again on literacy journeys that can be both shared and private and can be stored in many forms that allow us to revisit and further celebrate what we learned.

When We Encounter Difficulties: A Note about the Upcoming Sections

The titles for Sections 3 and 4 use the words "Reluctant" and "Resistant" to denote a degree of difficulty on the part of the child that is of a somewhat lesser degree than indicated by the word

"Struggling" in the titles of Sections 5 and 6. Both conditions are of concern when observed. However, the intention here is to show that *all learners* experience reluctance and resistance from time to time because learning is hard, especially when it throws us challenges that we did not expect or ask for. The timing of the challenges might be the worst possible. Or there may have been previous learning experiences that were negative in some way and that we were unaware of. As learners ourselves, when we can reflect, and as we mature, we are often able to see the actual benefits of working through the challenges and view them as a valuable part of the learning process. With time, our children may also come to that important and beneficial realization.

The word "Struggling" in the titles of Sections 5 and 6, on the other hand, is used to denote a condition that persists and is not easily overcome without skilled intervention. The condition *must be addressed* to keep it from inhibiting future learning and may require the intervention of a learning specialist.

Section 3

Reaching the Reluctant or Resistant Writer

Possible Causes of Reluctance or Resistance

Parents understand the high value of engaging children in both reading and writing, which is why you are exploring these learning activities in the first place. You also can understand that children vary widely in their abilities to respond to instruction and to encouragement. But no matter how carefully you set the stage and monitor progress, it is likely that you will encounter resistance or reluctance at some point, especially in writing. Writing involves multiple skills that must be orchestrated together to make the process work, and the skills must be in balance with each other. If a child is lagging in just one area, such as remembering the spelling patterns of some of the common words, that might be enough to derail the whole process at times. Thus, dealing with resistance may take some detective work on your part to identify where the problem lies. You will also have to decide *if the resistance is just occasional and situational, or ongoing.*

Let's start with the *signs of resistance* and think about why your child has been or has become resistant. Sometimes a child takes to writing easily and seems to be comfortable with the activities. You assume that all is well. But resistance may appear where there was none before. Evidence for this level of resistance is often found in the immediate situation and will show up in certain behaviors, such as refusing outright to do a writing activity. In this case, it may be something in the new activity that seems to place unexpected or different demands. As you know as a parent, children react in different ways when they face new (and old) challenges. They can often be encouraged to explore the causes when we maintain a positive interest.

Task Demands

Your first step as a good detective is to look at what we call *task demands*, to see if you can see a clue *in the nature of the task*. Sometimes a new task takes more patience. Sometimes a new task takes your child beyond his background knowledge and makes him feel inadequate. Sometimes the task requires a group of words that he is not yet comfortable with using. Or sometimes the task just *looks too hard*.

Here you could offer some reasons that might explain the problem: *"I am wondering if you feel that this writing today takes some words that you are not sure about. I can help you write those words if you tell them to me. We could make a list of the words you need for writing before you even start. They will be right there when you need them."* *"I am wondering if you have forgotten what happened while we were on the hike, and it's too hard to write about it when you don't remember it very well."* You would encourage him to write just about the part he does remember. In other words, you can change, modify, or redirect the task.

Sometimes the writing task itself demands more complicated language. For example, if you were trying out the ideas for different types of paragraphs, such as a paragraph about a sequence of steps, your child might not be clear in her mind about what came first, then next, and then last. If the sequence seems scrambled, then the sentences will also seem scrambled. In this example, you might help her jot down the steps in order with bullet points to clarify the sequence *before trying to write about it.*

After you have thought about the task demands, a second step would be to discuss the task directly and ask your child what part of it she thinks is *too hard*. This could range from the purpose of the task, the sequence of steps of the task, how to begin and end, or even how to tell if you have done the task correctly. This kind of discussion is part of self-evaluation and is closely linked to the process of editing. It can be very enlightening for both parent and child. It offers you a window into the perspective a young writer is developing in regard to his or her own writing. The child who can set foot on the path to self-evaluation is on the road to becoming a writer. Please note here that finding ways to modify task demands is not always easy. It takes experience and patience on your part, and there are likely to be benefits from collaborating with your child in doing this detective work.

Situation and Timing

Besides looking at task demands, consider the issues of situation and timing. To make At-Home writing a success, it is necessary to have buy-in from both parent and child. If it's more important to Mom or Dad to do this writing, no matter what else the child may have in mind to do right then, there is a good chance that resistance will appear. To give the writing activity a chance, it is important to not let it become a battleground. Perhaps timing can be negotiated so that all parties are comfortable. Offer ongoing reassurance that you value both the activity itself and the output that we can look at again later when we have time to enjoy the results of all the good efforts.

Another possible reason for resistance is a little harder to diagnose at home. Often a child can be resistant to a task because it reminds her of a similar task that was done at school or in another setting when she felt inadequate or uncertain. She herself may not understand why the At-Home task reminds her of something negative. Or she just may feel uncomfortable talking about it. This may take a bit more detective work to explore the reasons. It may be a situation that can be resolved with explanation and subsequent encouragement, which is all well and good.

Children always need to be reminded that becoming a writer is a process, and it does not happen all at once. A light touch is helpful here if the child is especially sensitive to real and perceived setbacks. In other words, provide explanations along with a focus on the positive. Emphasize signs of growth and be flexible when you choose what kinds of writing to attempt next.

Other Causes of Resistance

As noted, resistance might be related to the nature of the task, or to the situations and settings of the activities. There are, in addition, several other factors that a parent will want to consider. Resistance may be related to developmental factors that involve both the child's expressive language skills and thinking skills. These factors are further discussed in the section on *struggling writers* because this is an important distinction. The source of the resistance determines what techniques should be used to help the child. We will make a distinction between the support techniques that can work for a parent who is concerned and informed, and the techniques that require expertise from appropriate learning specialists.

Timing is important in everything we do to support a child's growth and education. If the problem of resistance is allowed to continue without intervention, then writing and other academic areas may become a battleground. It is a battle that no one wins. A frequent by-product of the battle can be the development of anxiety. In a state of anxiety, a child may show behaviors that appear to have *the same characteristics as attention disorders or other learning disabilities, including memory issues or difficulties with expressive language.*

Section 4

Reaching the Resistant or Reluctant Reader

The ability to read fluently is of enormous importance in today's literate world. Print is everywhere, on posters, on electronic devices, and of course, in instructional materials. We cannot overstate the importance of early success in reading, as early success often sets the stage for further school achievement. Fortunately, there are many paths to success in reading. Some children just pick up reading as easily as they learn to skip. They cannot remember not knowing how to read. Some pay close attention in school and learn everything the teacher teaches. Some learn from a grandmother, a doting auntie, or from an older brother or sister. Some, we know, learn to read from connecting to the print on screens, or from successfully finding their way around town by reading street signs. And some are exposed to reading in many of the ways described in books such as the recent *How to Raise a Reader* by Pamela Paul and Maria Russo (2019).

However, as many parents can testify, some do not catch on easily. Here are some perspectives that may provide guidance for when that happens.

Possible Causes of Initial Difficulties

Some children struggle with making the first connections between the letters and the sounds they represent. These children may have had early ear infections or other conditions that have clouded or distorted the sounds within the words. They may have other issues such as impaired vision or immature speech patterns. They may have inconsistent attention or short-term memory problems that make it difficult to stay with the task long enough *to reap the reward of meaning*.

Some, who may not have been exposed to story reading in their very early years, may not really understand the connection between those marks on the page and the "message" those marks represent. Some, with limited access to books and print, have been deprived of the chance to slowly turn the pages of a book and puzzle out the sense of it. And in some cases, there are children who may finally be able to make the sounds of the printed words, but for various reasons have failed to develop *adequate background knowledge and vocabulary*. When this happens, the words they "read" have little or no meaning for them to connect to. They lose the benefit of being able to say, "*Aha, I have been wondering about that. That's so amazing.*"

Children as early as kindergarten often define themselves by whether they can or cannot read. Thus, it is critical to prevent early failure messages in a child's mind, or, if the messages have already set in, to intervene rapidly enough to turn failure into success. The activities in Chapters 8 and 9 using the *Language Experience Approach* (*LEA*) provide examples of the many ways that parents can promote reading success, At-Home. Happily, *LEA* is not only an effective instructional approach, it is also a way for parents to engage young children and to record what they have to say about the world through their dictated stories.

Signs of Resistance in Reading

As we did with the resistant writer, we begin with the possible reasons that your child might have become resistant to reading. In the early stages of reading, the child is managing multiple aspects of a complex task, with a great many unknowns from the child's point of view. Some children simply get overwhelmed with the task, even when they are participating in a structured program at school. On the one hand, parents are not expected to be trained teachers of reading. On the other hand, however, parents play a valuable role as observers while their children engage in activities that are related to the dictated stories or other forms of reading materials. Your observations are valuable even if you have watched only your own children and not whole groups of learners at the early stages of reading.

The Importance of Meaning

We will look briefly at some of the behaviors a parent can watch for, starting with the big picture. Has your child figured out *what reading is for*? This may seem an odd question to the grown-up who just assumes that most everybody knows what reading is for. But even young children who are surrounded by books and reading at home may not completely comprehend the full significance of what those marks on the page represent. It's an idea that adults may take for granted, but it's an idea that must be learned by each and every new reader. As adults, we take for granted that those marks represent meaning because we have learned what to do when we see the signs that say "STOP, SLOW, or CAUTION." We have an overwhelming need to make sense of those written words because they represent *meaning*.

Teaching children to read has changed a great deal since the time when today's grandparents and parents learned to read. Decades ago, we defined "reading comprehension" as the ability to "get" the meaning on the page, as if we could somehow transfer meaning from the print to the mind. Today, thanks to the research in executive function, neuroscience, and the science of reading, we understand reading comprehension as a process of "making meaning," when readers bring the meaning that is already in their minds (background knowledge, critical thinking, and vocabulary) to the meaning suggested by the combinations of words on the page, *to **construct meaning** that can be remembered, processed, and discussed*. This is what Maryanne Wolf suggests when she argues that "reading changes the brain." This new frontier in the teaching of reading can add a great deal to our children's ability to learn from what they read, and from what they write. It also adds much to what parents can observe when their children react to the reading activities they encounter in schooling and At-Home.

Thus, you might watch for and listen for clues about where your child is in this process of discovering *the meaning-making component of reading*. There will be some words your child can be shown that convey immediate and powerful meaning, such as his name, or the words that represent concrete reality to him: *Mom, sandwich, dog,* or *bike.* Other words will be abstract, and the meaning may not become clear for a while, until they appear frequently in sentences: *is, might, after, have, some, often, other, more, here.* Activities with the Word Banks from the dictated stories will provide good clues for how well your child is catching on to these more abstract words and how they can be used.

When children have started to read words in longer portions of text, such as the sentences and paragraphs that they might encounter in an early reading book, or even in their dictated stories, you can watch for some important responses that indicate that they are linking to the meaning. These responses can occur whether the child is reading aloud or listening to you read the words. You can note whether they focus on the lines of print and seem to be making the eye movements of a reader who follows the words. They may stop when they don't understand something and look at you questioningly. They may make spontaneous comments or ask questions that relate to the topic. They may vocalize along with you and say the same words as on the page. They may even use a finger to run along the line of the print being read. These behaviors are all indicators that the child is being *guided by the meaning.*

For children who have not yet connected to the meaning of the words, the behaviors are very different. Their eyes may wander and frequently look away from the print. They may exhibit restlessness and seek to change the activity. Their comments will indicate that their minds are elsewhere. Your job as a parent is initially to be the observer. If the child has obviously lost interest, you may consider the option of making your own comments about the topic, such as noting that you *"liked the way the book tells you about how the baby manatees move or where they find their food."* You might ask the child some questions related to the topic, or depending on the situation, you might change the activity and return to it later. In all cases, try to keep *meaning* front and center through your responses.

Letters and Sounds

Another important step toward becoming a reader happens when your child begins instruction in phonics at school. This is the process of learning how letters represent, or stand for, sounds. For many young children, this is a giant leap because of the many components that are involved in the act of decoding a word. They must first be able to *see the word clearly* and distinguish its visual characteristics. Many of the lower-case letters are easily confused at first (think *'m'* and *'n,'* or *'e'* and *'o'*).

In addition to the letters, words are composed of separate sound elements. This idea is a highly abstract idea in the first place since children hear the sounds of words as a continuous flow when we speak. Learning the sounds-to-letters principles requires the child to isolate the sound components from each other within words and between words, even when they are perceived as a continuous long flow of sounds that we hear when we are listening to spoken language. The child must be able to not only see the words but to hear their individual sounds and separate them, one at a time. It is no wonder that this process can take up to three years or more for the beginning reader.

Being able to distinguish the separate sounds in a word is only a first step. It is made more complicated when many of those sounds are represented using multiple letters or combinations of letters. The vowel sounds are a good example of this. Let's begin with the sound we hear when the letter A *"says its name"* (also called the sound of *long a*). That sound can be represented by a variety of letter combinations, as shown in the following examples: *name, play, table, oasis, wait, weight, sleigh*, and so on. You will notice similar examples for the other vowels. In contrast, most of the consonant letters represent either a single sound, like 'n,' or 't,' or at most, two to three sounds, like 'c' or 'g.'

Moreover, the vowel letters present another challenge. The letter A, for example, represents multiple sounds, depending on the word in which it appears, and depending on which other letters it is combined with: *apron, calf, all, hard, lake, breath, fear, address, easy*, and *spaghetti*. That letter may even have *two different sounds* in the same word: *again, apart*.

When children actively begin the practice of decoding, depending on what they are learning from phonics instruction, you, the parent, can provide a good set of eyes to observe the process and how it seems to be going for your child. You can take note of the kinds of words your child is confident enough to tackle on her own, and the words she immediately looks to you for help with. If she is a confident decoder, can you spot any patterns that signal either confidence or difficulty with certain types of words or letter combinations?

Key Behaviors in Decoding

Once a child is able to do active decoding, there are other key behaviors to watch for:

♦ Does your new reader appear to have any identifiable strategies for how to figure out a new word? What behaviors have you spotted (or heard)?

♦ Is he a persistent new reader who makes multiple attempts until he settles on a word that seems to fit the overall meaning, showing a good understanding of the context?

◆ Does he make a "guess" based on whether it's a long word or a short word? When he makes a guess, does the guess sometimes produce a sound that is not a "real" word, or a word that does not fit with the overall sentence and topic?

◆ Does he sometimes seem overwhelmed by the sheer number of words that can be encountered on a page, even when some of them are "known words?" Does he seem to find it difficult to keep his attention consistent over longer sentences and long paragraphs, or is he more relaxed when the words are widely spaced and even separated with pictures? Does the size of the print (font) seem to make a difference?

◆ Does the process seem to result only in frustration, or can he recognize success when it happens, and can he repeat the successful strategy next time?

You can see that this job of observing your reader requires you to be a careful detective. Remember that the purpose here is not to train you to become a *reading specialist* who can diagnose learning issues. That job can be best left to the learning specialists or the trained teachers. However, your input, based on your observations of these important areas in reading development, can contribute greatly to the teacher's ability to assist your child at school or make a referral if a learning specialist might need to be involved. Your observations can also contribute to determining a cause, if there is one, if your child has become a reluctant or resistant reader.

Section 5

Support Strategies for Struggling Writers at Grades 1–6

In spite of our best efforts as parents and teachers, in spite of great desire on the part of the child, some children will find the path to writing difficult, at any one of several stages. This section is not meant to give advice to parents about *how to diagnose a specific child's difficulties* or to provide labels. Rather, it is meant to highlight some areas of difficulty that deserve attention and that will respond to appropriate intervention, especially if it is *early intervention.*

Determining the Challenges

A. Forming the Letters

An early and often most obvious difficulty is the formation of letters when a child begins using pencil and paper, or crayon and paper. This is a "fine motor" process that many children are slow to master, even as late as third or fourth grade. If this is the case, a student study team or learning specialist at school can help you find an occupational therapist who can provide treatment for handwriting delay.

B. Connecting the Sounds to the Letters (Spelling)

This difficulty may emerge when children are first introduced to the alphabet and the idea that we use *letters* to represent *sounds.* This is part of phonics instruction, which helps prepare the foundation for decoding new words and for spelling. For most children, the process does not need to be a mystery. It is a matter of how best to directly teach each child how spelling and decoding work. However, when it is a mystery to the child, there will be early signs from the way they respond to or fail to respond to instruction. Children with this difficulty typically can receive special attention from the classroom teacher or from a reading specialist or speech/language specialist. If this difficulty is occurring at the initial stages of writing instruction, your child may experience anxiety about the whole process of writing. Thus, early intervention is important and can be very effective.

C. Expressive Language

Children who have problems with expressive language may produce spoken sentences that seem to be a bit scrambled, or they may find it hard to come up with the right words to explain their ideas. In this area, classroom teachers are very vigilant and may make a referral to the speech/language specialist for timely intervention. Fortunately, language-based learning difficulties have received a great deal of research attention, and there are many resources available to help both professionals and parents in this area (see *Helping Your Child with Language-Based Learning Disabilities* by Daniel Franklin, 2018).

D. Anxiety

When children observe their kindergarten and first-grade class-mates catching on to writing more quickly, they may make a faulty assumption that there is "something wrong" with them. At this age, children do not yet understand that development proceeds at different paces and in different areas for different children. But because writing is so visible, children are highly aware of differences in capability and output, especially when examples of "good work" are displayed on the bulletin boards for all to see. If anxiety sets in, a child may become reluctant to try and therefore may lose valuable practice in writing.

For children in the early grades, regular teacher conferences can provide the right occasion for you as a parent to bring up any observations you have made regarding your At-Home experiences with writing. Teachers rely on you for good first-hand information about what you are seeing as your child tries to write. If you have tried out the activities suggested here in this book, it is especially important to bring your concerns to the teacher, so that your child does not fall behind in this skill.

E. Strategies for Writers in Upper Elementary and Middle School

The suggestions for writers at these levels will be more general in nature. As students begin instruction in the various content areas like English, science, and social studies, the kinds of writing that are expected become more specialized to meet the demands of the curriculum. There will be structures that are shared in common, such as the standard five-sentence paragraph, or the five-paragraph essay, which are expected structures for written expression, but the nature of the content will now match *the purpose of the writing*. Writing assignments from the English teacher may involve aspects of literary analysis, whereas in social studies, students may be assigned persuasive essays and science students may be writing descriptions of scientific processes.

Parent involvement at this level may now consist of your help with decoding the terms of the assignment itself rather than familiarity with the types of writing required for any specific assignments, which is still the teacher's responsibility. You may have to change the timing of dinner to allow for more prep time, or you may be called upon for a late-night session of proofreading before the turn-in deadline. In most cases, the most helpful contributions you can make are your continued interest and encouragement through the struggle. You can cite the reminders of your shared history through early writing struggles and early writing victories, some of which you may still possess in the dated Family Response Journal or other saved souvenirs of the family writing journeys.

Section 6

Strategies for Struggling Readers at the Elementary (K–6) Levels

Readers at K–1 Level

♦ Emphasize meaning. Help your child understand that reading and writing are about sharing meaningful information and ideas. Do not assume your child already knows this, or that it is too obvious to mention.

♦ As children are introduced to the letters and sounds (phonics) in school, encourage them to share and use what they are learning. Encourage them to talk about and comment about new ideas they have learned.

♦ When your child gets stuck on a word that she or he can't sound out, say, *"Let's do it together."* Then model how to sound out the word by drawing out the pronunciation to emphasize each part of the word.

♦ A child who has persistent difficulty with sounding out words may be stuck with the idea that correct sounding out is the only goal. If you think this is the case, de-emphasize decoding for a while, by providing the word quickly for your child, to keep the flow of meaning.

♦ As children gain more confidence in using their decoding skills, do not let them get the idea that reading is just saying all the words out loud and saying them correctly. Have a conversation about the meaning of the message on the page. Do not leave the page too soon but stay with it and keep talking about it until the message has been thoroughly explored and discussed. Be especially watchful for any figurative language that needs to be explained.

♦ Encourage and recognize self-correcting when it occurs in either out loud or silent reading. When a child self-corrects an initial pronunciation, this is an excellent indicator that he or she was really paying attention to the meaning of that word in the sentence. When it happens, you say, *"Good checking!"*

♦ Focus on meaning through sharing and discussion: *"These words make me think about…" "This page makes me remember…"* In so doing, you may reduce anxiety, return the emphasis to meaning, and help your child continue to build vocabulary and concepts.

♦ Assure your child that reading might seem hard at the beginning, but with practice, it will become rewarding enough that you can bravely go on to even harder reading materials.

Readers at Grades 2–3

♦ Continue to emphasize meaning by making comments related to the meaning: *"I think the children in this story are going to be surprised…" "I think the author wants us to think about…"*

♦ Practice sounding out new or longer words together, so that your child has your voice for support and modeling.

- ◆ Remember that the goal of sounding out words is to help children make a match between the word that is pronounced and a word in their speaking and listening vocabularies. It is very important to keep their vocabularies growing with lots of family discussion and labeling of new items and experiences.

- ◆ If your child continues to have difficulty with new words, make sure there are plenty of opportunities to practice in "comfortable" level books to promote confidence, smoothness, and fluency. Search for books that match or extend your child's interests.

- ◆ By second and third grade, shift the emphasis to *silent reading* when your child begins to show more confidence, even for the child who struggles with identifying words. This will diminish anxiety about performance or potential embarrassment over poor oral reading and will give your new reader the opportunity to puzzle over the meaning and reread if necessary.

- ◆ *Be sure that the "out loud" reading of a passage or page is preceded by silent reading*. This allows the child to get a sense of the meaning and to use the strategy of rereading if they should detect portions where the meaning is unclear to them. Many children have experienced the pressure and sometimes humiliation of having to read out loud before others, as in a classroom, and having their uncertainties or errors observed by all. And there are many parents (who you might know) who have had this same experience in the past!

- ◆ When silent reading is used, check on comprehension by asking your child to retell or comment on portions of what he or she read.

- ◆ Watch for indications that your child is rereading to check on meaning and give praise for self-correcting whenever it happens.

Challenges at Grades 4–6

At this level, children will encounter more complex reading materials in their academic work. As a result, they may experience difficulties in one or more of the following areas:

- Recognizing new words, which now tend to be longer and have more syllables.
- Understanding complex new ideas, using advanced thinking skills.
- Understanding complex written sentences and longer paragraphs.
- Encountering text that requires a high level of inference (for meaning that is not stated directly) or that contains the use of figurative language and expressions.
- Keeping in mind the information from an earlier part of the sentence or paragraph and linking that information to the rest of the sentence or paragraph.
- Storing large amounts of new information in memory and retrieving the information as it is needed.
- Building confidence in their ability to learn how to read as well as the other students they may observe in their classes.

Support Strategies for Readers in Upper Elementary and Middle School

If you suspect word recognition problems, especially with multisyllabic words, help your student see that long words are often based on a shorter root word and may contain prefixes or suffixes. Encourage your child to look at longer words in terms of the syllable units, rather than sounding out letter by letter. For example, look for the word *magic* in *magician*, *depend* in *independent*, *regular* in *irregularity*, and so on. Encourage the use of these words in writing. There are many well-designed vocabulary books at this level that focus on the use of Latin-based root words and derivations (also known as *morphology*) as a means of enhancing both vocabulary development and comprehension. These series often promote a life-long love of words and their histories.

Children with comprehension problems often need additional explanation and discussion of complex ideas. Help them to see how these new ideas relate to something they may already know. This will take time. Encourage your child to record the new ideas in a written list or in short phrases.

Children who struggle to understand complicated language may need help breaking sentences down into smaller units. Parents may help by paraphrasing the idea in simpler language, and then having the child try paraphrasing "in your own words." Be prepared to do a lot of listening here. Let your child practice this, and resist putting your words in his mouth unless modeling is needed. Then say, *"I am going to model this for you,"* to identify the purpose of using "your" words as a model.

Children who have problems remembering larger amounts of information may benefit from simple concept maps or graphic organizers that show how the information is organized. Ask the child's teacher to show you some examples, such as "idea webs," "T charts," or "graphic organizers."

For children who lack confidence, focus on the positive. Give informative feedback. Let your child know that you believe she will learn to be a good reader, with time, practice, feedback, and support. Becoming a good reader does not happen overnight or even all at once but continues into adulthood. Practice and persistence have a good payoff. **The more you read, the better you get at it. And never forget: Reading makes you smarter. Finally, remember that children learn best when we engage their interests and build on their strengths.**

Section 7

When to Meet with the Teacher or the Learning Specialists

Persistent reading or writing problems require a team effort by parents, the classroom teacher, school personnel and other learning specialists, and the child. A child's progress through schooling is sometimes smooth and as expected, but problems may arise for even the most steady learner. In the case of school-related problems, the school has the responsibility to evaluate and monitor progress, supported by observational data that can be supplied by the parents. Remember that the most reliable solution to learning-related problems is *early intervention*. It has the best chance of success when it is available.

Parents who suspect school-related problems can familiarize themselves with whatever resources are available in their communities, starting with the school learning specialists. Literacy acquisition is a complex process that involves all aspects of language and cognition. If there are complex issues with any child, a set of specialists may need to be consulted, including speech/language specialists, educational therapists, clinical psychologists, and neuropsychologists. Pediatric psychiatrists can prescribe medication if it is needed for diagnosed attention-related issues. Parents are key members of the team. All parents need to be well-informed and all parents need to be well-supported in their efforts to help their children.

Being a parent in today's world is a big job, and there are many books and experts to tell you how to do it. You are your child's best advocate. You know more about your child than anyone else. When considering options for helping your child, you should always ask: *"Is this in my child's best interest?"*

Section 8

Questions Parents Should Ask about Packaged Instructional Programs

Parents today have access to a wide range of packaged instructional programs that are well-detailed and well-marketed through online sources. Some instructional programs are offered through local learning centers. Many are online, with the instruction given by means of a computer program or video. Educational consultants may be a source of information about such programs and whether they are appropriate for your child. It is important to be armed with a set of questions that may help you to better decide whether to invest time and other resources in such interventions.

The guidelines offered here are to help you work with a consultant regarding purchasing or enrolling in a programmatic system or method. The guidelines can also be used if you are examining the data yourself, online on a website.

◆ *Is my child expected to participate in the entire program from beginning to end? Are all parts of this program appropriate for my child even if the program is marketed as "individualized"?*

- *Do the targeted skills or strategies generalize well both to academic applications and extended applications such as real-life problem-solving?*
- *What are the resources, in terms of money and time, that might be better spent on other services or programs? Is precious instructional time being lost, or is it well spent?*
- *Does this program "guarantee" results?*
- *Is the instruction "program-centered" as opposed to "child-centered?"*
- *Is the program administered and/or delivered by "technicians" or by trained learning specialists?*
- *If the program is marketed as "research-based," is it possible to evaluate the validity of the "research"? Has the research been published in well-recognized journals or is it paid for by the company that markets or owns the program?*

Concluding Thoughts and Looking Forward

Parenting in a complex world is a complex challenge, particularly when you are committed to being involved in your child's acquisition of the literacy skills. There is much we do not know yet about the effects on learning and the brain from all the devices and screens that our children are exposed to, both at home and at school. There is also much we do not yet know about the effects of interrupted schooling or education that must take place in the home under unanticipated conditions, such as a pandemic. In the crucial areas of writing and reading, we do not know whether education for our children will continue to happen in mostly traditional ways, in ways that are emerging constantly in today's world, or in ways we cannot yet predict. Or all of the above.

There are valuable resources available from experts in the fields of neuroscience, executive function, attention and learning disorders, and reading and the brain. Some of the most current books have been written for educators and psychologists, and some are addressed to readers who are just really interested in these new and fascinating areas. Check out *Reader Come Home: The Reading Brain in a Digital World* by Maryanne Wolf for a profound and stimulating discussion of what we may reasonably anticipate from the digital world and how it might affect our children and their brains.

There's a Writer in Our House! is dedicated to the belief that the greatest gifts that parents can give right now are these: be engaged, be observant, and be informed. It is my hope, as an author, educator, and clinician (not to mention parent and grandparent), that this book will help you in this important task with your children and grandchildren. It is also my hope that as you make your own discoveries about literacy learning, through the use of these activities, you will be inspired to share what you have learned. Every child's learning journey is an important story. Your own story, and that of your own children, will inform and inspire another parent, in ways you cannot predict, but in ways that can make a lasting and important difference. Thank you for reading.

Bibliography

Cooper, J. David, Robinson, Michael D., Slansky, Jill A., and Kiger, Nancy D. *Literacy: Helping Students Construct Meaning*. 10th Edition. Australia, Brazil, Mexico, Singapore, UK and United States: Cengage Learning, 2018.

Franklin, Daniel. *Helping Your Child with Language-Based Learning Disabilities*. Oakland, CA: New Harbinger Publications, 2018.

Meltzer, Lynn, Ed. *Executive Function in Education: From Theory to Practice*. 2nd Edition. New York, London: The Guilford Press, 2018.

Paul, Pamela and Russo, Maria. (Editors, *The New York Times Book Review*). *How to Raise a Reader*. New York: Workman Publishing, 2019.

Wolf, Maryanne. *Reader Come Home: The Reading Brain in a Digital World*. New York: HarperCollins, 2018.

About the Author

Dr. Ann P. Kaganoff: *There's a Writer in Our House!*

Ann Parkinson Kaganoff, PhD, Board Certified Educational Therapist, has been active in the field of education for over six decades, at every level from pre-school to graduate school. Beginning as an elementary school classroom teacher, she was able to pursue her interest in helping children who struggled to learn how to read and write when she enrolled in the Reading Clinic Program at the Graduate School of Education, University of California, Santa Barbara. She served as a supervisor in the Clinic program while earning her MA and the California Reading Specialist Credential. She completed her doctorate in Reading and Language Development in 1981 at UCSB.

From 1985 to 1992, she taught the K–8 Reading Methods courses for the California Elementary Credential program in the UC Irvine School of Education. She was the founder and director of the UCI Reading and Neurolinguistic Clinic. Following her work at UCI, she gained an extensive background in staff development for public school teachers in the Orange County school system, specializing in the literacy skills at all levels from K–12.

In 1992, she was introduced to the practice of Educational Therapy and began a career as an Educational Therapist. She worked in private practice until she retired in 2021 to focus on her book for parents. Her clients have included children and adults with a wide range of learning issues and learning disabilities. In addition to being a Board Certified Educational Therapist, she is a Past President of the Association of Educational Therapists (AET). She has been a frequent presenter at conferences on topics related to literacy and the practice of educational therapy. She also serves as a mentor and trainer for new and veteran educational therapists. She is the author of *Best Practices in Educational Therapy* (Routledge 2019), a book dedicated to furthering the practice of educational therapy.

DOI: 10.4324/9781003452683-16

Because of the important role that parents play in all phases of children's education, Dr. Kaganoff believes that her experience as an educational therapist has contributed an important perspective that parents will welcome. Her goal as an author is to help parents become **Informed Guides** for their children in the development of literacy skills, based on her experience gained from teaching these skills to learners of all ages. She has developed ways to engage parents through specific learning activities that are designed for parents to do together with their children. The At-Home activities presented in *There's a Writer in Our House!* are designed to show parents how to tailor the activities to each child as a unique individual. It is widely recognized in today's books for parents that a child's active engagement is a key to learning in both writing and reading, and thus, all recommended strategies focus on a child's strengths, experiences, and interests.

This book provides useful background concepts for understanding a child's early cognitive and language development, in language that emphasizes and explains the specific benefits of writing and reading for overall child development. The activities presented here are meant to be customized and personalized, set within the framework of the familiar family environment, using the *At-Home Model*. Each activity focuses on not only the WHAT of the activity but also on the HOW and the WHY of each step along the way. Activities are supported with abundant prompts and with real-life examples of children's output. Each child's assets are recognized and expanded in creative ways. The chapters begin with *Easy Access Notes: What You Will Learn*, relayed in accessible language for busy parents. Markers of growth are provided to help document, track, and celebrate both the challenges and the achievements of the journey. Parents will benefit from having an ongoing window into their children's progress in both writing and reading, as well as an early window into any identified needs for intervention by specialists.

Dr. Kaganoff has learned from years of experience which activities are most likely to work for both the normally progressing learner and the struggling learner. She has found that often it is the child who struggles who teaches us the most when we must adapt to their needs. Most importantly, she has seen over and over again how children of all ages and at all levels of learning can benefit when they have the opportunity to confidently explore their ideas and develop their self-expression through writing and reading. She currently lives in Carpinteria, California, near to her two daughters, her succulent gardens, and the beach.